Justice in the West Bank?

The Israeli-Palestinian Conflict Goes to Court

Yonah Jeremy Bob

publishing house בית הוצאה לאור
JERUSALEM ◆ NEW YORK Est. 1981

Cover Photo: Yonah Jeremy Bob
Cover Design: Benjie Herskowitz
Typesetting: Optume Technologies

ISBN: 978-965-7023-16-7

1 3 5 7 9 8 6 4 2

Gefen Publishing House Ltd.
6 Hatzvi Street
Jerusalem 9438614, Israel
972-2-538-0247
orders@gefenpublishing.com

Gefen Books
140 Fieldcrest Ave.
Edison NJ, 08837
516-593-1234
orders@gefenpublishing.com

www.gefenpublishing.com

Printed in Israel

Library of Congress Cataloging-in-Publication Data

Names: Bob, Yonah Jeremy, author.
Title: Justice in the West Bank? : the Israeli-Palestinian conflict goes to court /
   Yonah Jeremy Bob.
Description: New Jersey ; Jerusalem : Gefen Publishing House, [2019]
Identifiers: LCCN 2018048364 | ISBN 978-965-7023-16-7
Subjects: LCSH: Criminal Justice, Administration of--West Bank. | Military
   courts--West Bank. | Palestinian Arabs--Legal status, laws, etc.--West
   Bank. | Israel--Politics and government.
Classification: LCC KMM546.8 .B63 2019 | DDC 349.5694/2--dc23 LC
   record available at https://lccn.loc.gov/2018048364

Contents

JUSTICE ELYAKIM RUBINSTEIN
DEPUTY PRESIDENT (Ret.)
THE SUPREME COURT
OF ISRAEL

القاضي إلياكيم روبينشتين
نائب الرئيسة (متقاعد)
المحكمة العليا
لدولة اسرائيل

השופט אליקים רובינשטיין
המשנה לנשיאה (בדימוס)
בית המשפט העליון
בישראל

Jeremy Bob, a lawyer-journalist, took interest in administrative detention as well as other subjects connected with the Military Courts in the territories. He has used the modern approach of writing on such matters, which is the "personal attitude" – that is, you look at the situation through the lenses of individuals. In this framework we have here a judge (the former president of the Military Court of Appeals), a former prosecutor, and a defense lawyer, each presenting the legal situation and the reality of their work in – naturally – a different light. This makes for very interesting and colorful reading, which brings you closer to the complexities of the areas involved and how the fight against terrorism is conducted within the law and its constraints and limits. While, having served as a reserve judge in the Military Courts many years ago, and of course as a justice in the Supreme Court until not long ago, I may not agree with some of the observations, there is much to be learned from them.

Israel and the Palestinians both find themselves entangled in a complex and sensitive situation which does not seem to be close to being solved. Meanwhile, with the hope for a peaceful solution one day, at not too long a distance, understanding the difficulties and the ways to cope with them is vital; the book significantly helps to attain the understanding.

רחוב שערי משפט, קריית דוד בן-גוריון , ירושלים 91950
شارع شعري مشباط، كريات دڤيد بن جوريون، القدس 91950
Shaarey Mishpat St.Kiryat David Ben-Gurion Jerusalem 91950, Israel
TEL: 02-6759778, מזכירות שופטים בדימוס 02-6759730 FAX: 02-6759654

Preface

It was an eye-opener for me like no other. Camp Ofer, an army base just slightly north of Jerusalem on Route 443 (which eventually takes you to Tel Aviv) that serves as the primary location of the Israeli army's West Bank Courts, was a proverbial Wild West or almost alternate universe where standard relationships between Israelis and Palestinians did not apply. The first time I, a recent immigrant to Israel from New Jersey, visited Camp Ofer, some fifteen minutes north of Jerusalem and almost right next to Ramallah, the Palestinian Authority's seat of government, I was bewildered and overwhelmed.

These courts, which ideally should be the symbol of democratic justice and unity, I would soon learn were at the fault line of the hundred-year-old Israeli-Palestinian conflict, symbolizing order and security for the Israeli side and occupation and oppression for the Palestinian side. The Israeli-Palestinian conflict is back in the headlines these days with the economic side of US president Donald Trump's peace plan rolled out in late June 2019.

A major point of global debate over the IDF West Bank Courts, also referred to as the Judea and Samaria Military Courts, came on January 18, 2016. Former US ambassador Dan Shapiro delivered a speech blasting the courts and related legal institutions, saying that "at times it seems Israel has two standards of adherence to the rule of law in the West Bank – one for Jews and one for Palestinians." Shapiro's attack set off a firestorm with Israeli prime minister Benjamin Netanyahu and other Israeli officials counterattacking – a debate that quickly found its way onto the *New York Times* editorial page on January 22, 2016. Top PLO official Saeb Erekat also commented on the issue on May 19, 2016.

Since then, the IDF West Bank Courts have broken into the news headlines on multiple continents in countries from the United States to China and points in between. Some stories were about the sentencing of Palestinian terrorists, some about hunger striking prisoners in administrative detention, and others debated the treatment of Palestinian minors suspected of crimes.

The courts grabbed special attention in the United States when Palestinian Muhammad Harub was sentenced to four life prison terms in March 2017 for three deaths and numerous attempted murders in the drive-by shooting of Massachusetts native Ezra Schwartz, who was spending a year abroad in Israel. Schwartz's family hosted a baseball tournament in his memory in Sharon, Massachusetts, on April 23, 2018, and is building a baseball field in his memory in Israel.

On March 21, 2018, the red-haired and photogenic sixteen-year-old Ahed Tamimi was sentenced to eight months in prison. The sentence was part of a plea deal in which she confessed to incitement, some of around ten incidents of disturbance, and trying to rough up IDF soldiers. In the main incident in question, a family member made a viral video of the diminutive Tamimi pushing and kicking two taller soldiers, who ignored her. The debate surrounding the case focused on whether she was later illegitimately arrested to address Israeli domestic political opinion or whether her actions represented real crimes and dangerous incitement, highlighting some of the ongoing controversies surrounding this judicial system.

The most recent case for a terrorist murder of an American that is currently being heard in the courts as of June 2019 is the ongoing case against seventeen-year-old Palestinian Khalil Yusef Ali Jabarin for the murder of Ari Fuld.

Fuld was born in New York and lived there until he moved to Israel at age twenty in 1994. On September 16, 2018, the well-known Israel advocate was stabbed to death in the upper back outside a Gush Etzion shopping center by Jabarin, of Yatta, south of Hebron. Jabarin was indicted in the Judea Military Court on October 22, 2018.

Where did these courts come from? The Israeli military courts in the West Bank (called in Hebrew Batei Mishpat ba'Ezor Yehudah v'Shomron) were established shortly after Israel took over the West Bank from Jordan in the 1967 war in order to maintain law and order until the fate of the territories Israel had captured was decided in international peace negotiations. As that has yet to happen, the West Bank Courts have continued to administer legal issues with the Palestinians, though they have evolved quite a bit.

The courts remain at the center of the Boycott, Divestment, and Sanctions (BDS) battle and even the battle over Israel's legitimacy as a Jewish state. But I knew very little about that in July 2011, and mainly my first visit to the courts left me physically disoriented.

I had spent most of my Israeli army service at the spiffier military headquarters in Tel Aviv – right across from the Azrieli Mall, one of Israel's beacons of modernity – with no danger in sight, some amenities, and ample technicians nearby to fix computer and other technological problems. In contrast, Ofer was a dump, with large areas randomly scattered with barbed wire, untended thorn bushes, and mud paths strewn with debris that you needed to walk through to get around.

The famous or infamous Ofer Prison was separated from the Israeli army's prosecutor's offices by a high wall, which meant it was not visible at all from the court offices. This made it feel as if the prison was in another universe. On the other hand, it felt literally next door. We ate all of our meals at the prison cafeteria on the other side of that wall with the prison guards. Overall, living and working daily right next to a prison with a reputation for housing some of the more dangerous characters around did not feel normal.

Later, when I learned more about the courts and the different kinds of prisoners, I had some contrary feelings of discomfort about some of the low-grade detainees being held there – a feeling harder to ignore when the prison is staring you in the face.

Mainly I had come to the courts because one of my commanders said that some other Anglos (English-speakers) who moved to Israel had transferred to the West Bank Prosecutor's Office, where there were lots of opportunities to work on my ability to write legal documents in Hebrew. He added that it was a chance to prosecute Palestinian terrorists and that it was only fifteen minutes south from my house, and I was in. But I really had no clue what I would be doing.

I had no idea that the courts in July 2011 mostly dealt with Palestinians who were illegally crossing into Israel to work or with light rock-throwing offenders. Incidentally, according to the IDF in February 2019, that is no longer true, with a solid majority of the cases now being related to more violent crimes. Regardless, I have no idea whether I would have taken a position as a prosecutor had I known that the vast majority of Palestinians being prosecuted back then were not terrorists. In retrospect, I went in relatively clueless about the courts.

But the story I am here to tell is not about me.

This is a story about a massively important and historic front of the Israeli-Palestinian conflict, the West Bank Courts, viewed through the lens of the stories of individual people – their fascinating personal stories, characters, and views of their experiences in this Wild West setting of human drama like no other.

In order to tell this story, I have chosen to focus on four main individuals who represent the spectrum of Israeli prosecutors, Israeli judges, and two different tracks of defense lawyers for Palestinians: Maurice Hirsch, who was West Bank chief prosecutor until February 2017 but was in office during most of the writing of this book; Aharon Mishnayot, chief justice of the courts from 2007 to 2013, who had just retired during the writing of this book; defense lawyer Merav Khoury; and defense lawyer Gaby Lasky together with her partner Nery Ramati.

Amidst all of the above confusion I describe, there was some bizarre magic on the base. It was a rare stage, a sort of gray zone, where Israelis and Palestinians, mostly lawyers, interacted every day, no matter what else was going on between the two peoples. Israelis and Palestinians could be in all-out war. But at the West Bank Courts, the lawyers from both sides always had work to do together. Some developed strong relationships from that work, some strong distaste, but work together they had to do either way.

This bizarre and human side has never been reported on before. It is a unique phenomenon and a story that is not just important, but compelling and fascinating. It is a story that will grab people who normally have no interest in the Israeli-Palestinian conflict.

This book is not the first about the West Bank Courts. But it is unique as the first written about the human story and the first by a journalist-lawyer who knows the courts from the inside and can unpack them in ways understandable to the general public. I would argue it will also be the first balanced book on the subject. Furthermore, other books have focused on the courts' history, not their current state.

For writing this book, I received unparalleled access from both the Israeli prosecution and judiciary and the Palestinian defense sides, including rarely granted extended on-record interviews and thousands of pages of documents from West Bank Court cases never before reported on.

This book will explore some of the most controversial issues of the Israeli-Palestinian conflict, but more importantly will try to tell that profoundly human and unusual story as Israeli and Palestinian lawyers both cooperate and crash into each other while occupying the gray zone.

Disclaimer

This book is not likely to earn me any friends. Parts of it will undoubtedly anger both the Israeli and the Palestinian sides of the debate. Getting top personalities on both sides to talk to me when I openly revealed I would be writing about both sides' views was no easy feat. While I emphasized to both sides that the book would be balanced, invariably I emphasized to the Palestinian side that this was a chance for them to get their message out to a wider audience from an author who cannot be attacked as anti-Israel, while emphasizing to the Israeli side that a balanced book on the subject in and of itself was an opportunity to confront head-on attempts to delegitimize Israel. Having told both sides that the book would cover both sides, I see no inconsistency in these dealings, and believe I was open to everyone about the direction of the book.

I do hope that despite the likely reality that both sides will dislike aspects of the book that do not buy into their narrative, at least both sides will feel they were treated fairly and honestly and that this book provides food for an improved debate over the future of the IDF West Bank Courts in a time when there is very little positive dialogue between the sides.

Some comments on terminology. Twenty-three years ago I was shocked when a teacher of mine at Columbia University convinced me based on philosopher Michel de Montaigne's *Essays* about how nearly impossible it was to reach objectivity. Neutrality on the Israeli-Palestinian conflict and the courts that deal with it is equally impossible. But that does not mean we should not try. I have tried to seek neutrality and fairness by a mix of terminology choices that have something for both sides. Though I mostly use "IDF West Bank Courts," because the West

Bank is more well known to the average global reader than Judea and Samaria, in dozens of instances I use "Judea Military Court" or "Samaria Military Court." Judea and Samaria are the Jewish biblical names for Jewish portions of the West Bank and reflect Israeli claims on those lands. While using varied terms is not consistent, this balance reflects both the names that the Palestinians use (West Bank) and those that many Israelis use (Judea and Samaria). I hope it does not confuse the reader too much.

Likewise, I mostly use the term "settler" to describe Jews living in the West Bank, as this is the most recognizable term globally, but I also sometimes use the phrase "Jewish residents living in Judea and Samaria." This is to reflect the perspective of many Israelis that these Jews are already now part of Israel, or certainly will be after a future potential peace agreement in which most estimate that 80 percent or more of Jewish settlers in the West Bank will be included within Israel's internationally recognized borders. Unlike the majority journalistic position globally which prefers "militant," I use the term "terrorist" frequently. For the record, factually speaking in terms of volume, in this book the term mostly applies to Palestinians who intentionally attack civilians or Israeli border police who are not threatening them (as opposed to Gazans fighting the IDF in 2014, whom I would call "combatants"). However, when I cover the few incidents in recent years of Jews prosecuted for terrorism, such as the 2015 Duma attack, I also use the term "terrorist." Once again, I hope the reader does not get too confused by my attempt at being even-handed.

A word on the four main characters. While two come from the Palestinian side, one of whom is an Israeli Arab and one a top Meretz activist, and two come from the Israeli side, none of them is Palestinian (Merav Khoury is a Christian Arab with Israeli citizenship, and I am using the term "Palestinian" to refer to West Bank Arabs living outside "Green Line" Israel, i.e., beyond the 1948 borders). I am well aware of the inherent problem with writing a book about a portion of the Israeli-Palestinian conflict and covering both sides without a main character being Palestinian. Nevertheless, I believe I made the right or unavoidable choice in this case.

First, I believe the two main Palestinian-side characters muscularly represent the Palestinian side of the story, possibly better than any other lawyer for Palestinians could. Both are major and charismatic figures. No argument that a Palestinian lawyer would make goes unmentioned. Further, even as the four main characters are not Palestinian, dozens of pages refer to a range of Palestinian lawyers in specific cases that the book discusses; I did include an extended interview with one top Palestinian lawyer and described the activities and views of two other top Palestinian lawyers I have interacted with.

The two main lawyers I picked (Khoury and Lasky) were also people I had some prior relationship with from my regular daily news coverage of the courts, which facilitated easier access and greater willingness to share more personal information (though you will note there is less personal information about Meretz activist Gaby Lasky – per her request). Last, picking the lawyers I chose to feature was dictated in part by trying to highlight cases that had unusual twists, including acquittals, and this made a very short list.

A word about these main characters after the main period covered by the book. Khoury, Lasky, and Ramati are performing similar work to what they did during the writing of the book. Mishnayot became a district court judge in the civilian courts and so has not altered his public persona in any way. Hirsch has become an activist lawyer for Palestinian Media Watch and other groups clearly on the Israeli Right. Readers can decide for themselves, but I would argue that during his time as West Bank chief prosecutor, he did not act on his personal ideology but can be viewed as having represented the system, even as many of his actions focused on security concerns that would have been supported by the Israeli Right.

Writing a book that focuses mostly on cases that went to trial, including a number of acquittals, is an anomaly because almost all cases in the courts are quickly dealt with by plea bargain deals with nothing "interesting" happening. If I did not discuss the plea bargain problem in detail, which I do, a legitimate criticism would be that the book misleads the reader into thinking most cases in the courts go to trial. However, I believe I have made it very clear that I selected cases in order to give the reader the most in-depth possible understanding of the courts and the players, not to underplay the dominant role of plea bargains in day-to-day court life. Also, these cases include the courts confirming Palestinian claims, at least in specific cases – something unique which does not come out of plea bargains.

Timing

My first discussions about this book took place in December 2012 with then IDF West Bank chief prosecutor Lt. Col. Robert Neufeld and with the IDF Spokesperson's Unit through the first half of 2013. The idea and focuses of the book evolved in unpredictable ways as I worked on getting access to IDF prosecutors and major defense lawyers and documentation from each side. By mid- to late 2014, I had performed initial interviews with a wide range of defense lawyers and received voluminous materials from both them and the IDF. In February 2015, I finally obtained extensive interviews with IDF West Bank chief prosecutor Lt. Col. Maurice Hirsch. In August 2015 and April 2016, I obtained extensive interviews and exchanges of information with former IDF West Bank Courts chief justice Col. Aharon Mishnayot.

I completed most of the book's serious writing in 2016. Around September 2016, I took on the new role of intelligence and terrorism analyst at the *Jerusalem Post* along with my role as legal analyst, which drew out my editing process. By the time the book is being published, more time has passed. In that light, I did my best to update various key issues through 2019 where relevant and possible.

Subsequent to my interview with him, Aharon Mishnayot was appointed a district court judge in the Israeli civilian courts in Beersheba, but I refer to him in the book as former chief justice, as that was his status throughout the time we were in contact and corresponded. Likewise, during my editing process, on January 31, 2017, Maurice Hirsch retired as West Bank chief prosecutor. I also refer to him as the current prosecutor throughout the book, as that was his status throughout the interviews and the book's writing, and his continued position influenced and bound his answers as well as reflected actual current policy.

Acknowledgments

Thank you to everyone who worked with me over six years, making this book possible. A special thank-you to the book's main characters: Maurice Hirsch, Gaby Lasky (together with her adjunct, Nery Ramati), Merav Khoury, and Aharon Mishnayot, who shared their time and gave of themselves. I also want to thank Maj. Gen. (res.) Danny Efroni and Brig. Gen. (res.) Moti Almoz, who approved my extended interview with Hirsch and special access to the courts, as well as Maj. (res.) Zohar Halevy – the real mover inside the IDF who got approvals. I want to thank the many other lawyers for Palestinians and human rights groups who worked with me.

My gratitude to former Israeli Supreme Court deputy chief justice and attorney general Elyakim Rubinstein, who generously contributed excellent clarifications to the "Israel's Argument in More Detail" section of chapter 11, on administrative detention, and provided other helpful information.

I want to thank the *Jerusalem Post* for consenting to my publishing the substance of some of my articles in this book, though the vast majority of the content here is being published for the first time. I want to thank the current and former *Jerusalem Post* Editors-in-Chief Yaakov Katz and Steve Linde for their critical support throughout this project. I also want to thank the many current and former *Jerusalem Post* editors, including David Brinn, Ilan Evyatar, Lawrence Rifkin, and Nechama Veeder, who edited early drafts of individual chapters and provided helpful guidance on a number of issues.

I also thank my mother, Joan Bob; my father, Harold Bob; and my wife's parents, Martin and Ruth Lockshin, for editing early drafts of individual chapters and making thoughtful suggestions throughout the process. Whatever is good in this book is an outgrowth of my parents raising me to be dedicated to values such as seeking truth, excellence, dialogue, and justice. I was blessed to marry into a family that also shares these values, and my in-laws are a constant source of support.

A special additional thank-you to my grandfather-in-law Professor Bernard Weisberger, who along with my father-in-law, Professor Martin Lockshin, spent extensive time with me on early drafts of the book as a whole, leading to vital large-scale edits.

Working with Ilan Greenfield and his talented staff at Gefen Publishing House has been an honor. Kezia Raffel Pride led the editing of this book with clarity and precision, tremendously enhancing it at content, structure, and style levels. Special thanks to the numerous staff members who assisted in the long checklist of issues that need to be handled to translate a text into an actual attractive book which people will want to read.

I would like to thank my wife Channa and our children Natan, Shahar, and Ayala. Channa is not only my life partner, but her critical observations and insights as well as her love and support throughout the process of writing and editing this book were invaluable.

Instrumental in allowing this project to come to fruition were lawyers Richard Heideman and Joseph Tipograph, who believed in and helped shepherd this project forward at a range of crucial points. David Silverstein and Miriam Shaviv also provided invaluable advice about a variety of aspects of book writing, marketing, and the process in general.

Finding support for a book is never easy, especially when it is already completed. I want to thank Yifa Segal and the International Legal Forum, who saw the value of this work as enhancing their mission and the values of a nuanced debate on Israeli-Palestinian issues. Special thanks also go to Noam and Aviva Lockshin, David Lowenfeld and Sally Mendelsohn, and Richard and Leora Linhart for believing in this project; they saw the value in searching for complex truths and balance and the other virtues this book represents. I would also like to thank the many other friends who showed their support.

Chapter 1

Introducing the Four Main Personalities

IDF West Bank Chief Prosecutor Maurice Hirsch

For the Palestinian Muhammad Sweti, an alleged terrorist, and Israeli army prosecutor Lt. Col. Maurice Hirsch, it was the closing of a personal circle.

"*Mah, ata od pa'am?*" (What, you again?), said the Palestinian-Arab alleged terrorist somewhat jokingly in Hebrew to the Israeli West Bank chief prosecutor, who himself was not a native Hebrew speaker.

Hirsch was born in South Africa, raised in England, and only immigrated to Israel at the age of twenty-three. Like a sizable group of British Jews, he had been interested in moving to Israel since he was a teenager, but he would never have imagined being the top prosecutor of – among others – Palestinian terrorists.

If he had pictured that much, he could never have foreseen an alleged Palestinian terrorist making an ironic joke to him in Hebrew, a foreign language for both of them, out of their national and interpersonal conflict.

Hirsch was a prosecutor's prosecutor. His job was to put Palestinians behind bars if he had evidence that they were common criminals, involved in "public disorder" or terrorism. Putting people like Sweti behind bars meant making Israeli society safe – and Hirsch thrived on the feeling that he was making Israelis more secure. So he was caught off guard that at least for one moment, he and Sweti, sworn enemies, were sharing a joke.

It was the summer of 2014, and despite years of reforms since 2008 by the Israeli army of the West Bank Courts' treatment of Palestinians, in particular minors, the courts were back at the center of an international controversy.

Order and security for Israel meant no terror attacks on Israelis, no rock throwing at Israeli soldiers, no protests that got "out of hand," and no Palestinians illegally crossing from Palestinian areas into Israel – even if the motivation was merely to work and make more money to pay the family bills.

Occupation and oppression for the Palestinian side meant that any attempt to assert themselves, their statehood, their sovereign right to self-determination, be it violent or nonviolent, would be crushed with force or with arrests and jail time to get them to keep quiet.

Obviously, the two sides did not agree on what was a legitimate protest, what was a protest that got out of hand, or a range of other issues in which Israelis sometimes imposed limits on Palestinian activities based on a combination of security and diplomatic considerations.

Looking into the heart and mind of an Israeli prosecutor such as Hirsch, in this case the one at the top of the pyramid, is one way to explore what it means to be a law enforcer over another nation and a protector of his own at the same time. It is a way to explore how people struggle with the moral dilemmas inherent in that job. What about the job makes them feel noble for defending Israelis' security and what makes them question their own actions?

How do they interact with Palestinians and their lawyers, whom they oppose and with whom they work and negotiate day in and day out? What kinds of relationships do they develop with the defense lawyers who are their opponents, but also the people with whom they spend most of their days?

But the story of Hirsch's and other Israeli dilemmas is easier to understand once their pre-dilemma story is understood. And jokes aside, Hirsch believed with all of his being that putting Sweti behind bars was his sacred duty.

Hirsch had first "met" Sweti in 2004 in his first case ever appearing as a junior IDF prosecutor in the West Bank Courts, where he was prosecuting him.

It was one of the few times that Hirsch, who had always had enormous self-confidence and a penchant for bold and daring moves, could admit that he had been terribly nervous. The nervousness had been exacerbated because

Hirsch was up against a living legend, Avigdor Feldman, already feared by prosecutors as one of the most brilliant and aggressive defense lawyers in Israel.

Defense lawyers and prosecutors are both part of the greater family of lawyers, but they are also mortal enemies in court. In civil cases in civilian courts, there is some greater understanding between opposing lawyers of the other side's dilemma. The same lawyer who is a plaintiff suing for damages today could represent a defendant being sued for damages tomorrow. Lawyers represent both plaintiffs and defendants at the same time in different cases. And so each side really has a sense of the emotional and legal challenges that the other is going through.

Not so in criminal cases, and almost never in criminal cases in a military court such as the West Bank Courts, which pit Israelis, as prosecutors and victims of crimes, against Palestinians, as defense lawyers and defendants being accused of crimes (though Palestinians would claim often they were still victims of Israeli occupation).

It is not that cut and dried, however.

All lawyers are somewhat cut from the same cloth, taught to think in similar ways based on a somewhat similar education.

Prosecutors and defense lawyers in the West Bank Courts mostly worked out plea bargains or deals in which each side moved toward a compromise between their initial positions of how much prison time the Palestinian defendant in question would serve for the alleged crime. The process of negotiating these deals and the desire of both sides to "get to yes" – to reach an agreement – encouraged a certain level of comradery that broke down some of the walls between them, even between Israelis and Palestinians.

There also were a very rare few former Israeli military prosecutors who eventually retired from the military and became defense lawyers for Palestinians. But they were exceedingly rare, had become rarer in recent years, and they were regarded by both sides in this battle as having crossed a battle line between Israelis and Palestinians. Israeli prosecutors in a sense might view such lawyers almost as traitors or special adversaries because they were helping the "other side," the Palestinian side, in the great legal battles that were an extension of the conflict between the Israelis and the Palestinians.

There were greater educational similarities between Israeli defense lawyers for Palestinians and Israeli prosecutors than with Palestinians defending Palestinians. They attended the same law schools and knew some of the same people. Palestinian and some Israeli Arab lawyers, in contrast, often attended law school in Jordan or Egypt, with some different educational and cultural approaches.

Yet ironically, the relations between Israeli Jews defending Palestinians and Israeli prosecutors were sometimes the most fraught and unstable. The Israeli Jews defending Palestinians were often emotionally angrier at Israeli prosecutors than Palestinian lawyers, who viewed Israeli prosecutors in some sense as their adversaries, but in another sense took it less personally – merely viewing them as doing their jobs as part of the other side in the greater conflict. Likewise, Israeli prosecutors viewed Palestinian lawyers defending Palestinians with some suspicion, but also as the natural course of things – which was not their reaction to Israeli Jews who "defected" to the other side.

Most lawyers for Palestinians now were either Palestinians or Israeli Arabs. It made sense in terms of the comfort that Palestinian defendants and their families had in dealing with a lawyer with a shared language and cultural perspective. But there was still a group of elite Israeli Jewish lawyers who took many of the hardest cases and were most likely to win (in a system where Palestinians almost never won), if you could afford them. Among those Israeli-Jewish lawyers, Feldman was among the best and the most feared by Israeli prosecutors.

When Feldman talked, the court fell silent, and even normally domineering judges, who would limit lawyers' speeches to a matter of minutes, were cowed by his booming voice, incisive analysis, and palpable certainty that he, Avigdor Feldman, would right what he viewed as the world's injustices. He would single-handedly bring the prosecution and the courts to heel. Even in the highest court in Israel, the Supreme Court, Feldman was known to thunder away at his opponents with a soaring voice and a dynamism that left prosecutors spellbound and made it difficult for them to get in a word.

Since at the time Hirsch was a junior prosecutor, still learning the ropes, he should have had an extended transitional period during which he accompanied and observed a more veteran prosecutor at work before he was thrown into a court case alone, let alone up against one of Israel's giants of the law.

Alas, that had not happened.

Hirsch was still extremely new to prosecuting and speechmaking in court, having spent his first few years in the IDF legal division as a legal advisor doing research and drafting legal advisory opinions – far from the in-your-face drama of a courtroom.

This was crucial. Many lawyers spend their careers in an office drafting contracts and other business-related documents. Even among lawyers who are litigators – the kind of lawyer who files and defends lawsuits in a court – very few actually appear in court. Most draft legal documents to file in the court, but do not necessarily make oral arguments there. So though he was an accredited lawyer, nothing had prepared Hirsch for this court hearing; many litigators after a brief taste of hearings in court run back to the office and ask to avoid the experience in the future.

Add in the fact that Hirsch was a new Israeli immigrant whose Hebrew was still far from perfect at the time, a point that could jeopardize his entire argument if he misspoke or misconjugated in a way that missed the nuance of what he wanted to say.

And this was a moment that Hirsch had worked for his entire career in the IDF legal division. In some ways, he had been building up to this moment even longer – since he was thirteen when he first visited Israel from England, first started to learn Hebrew, and first became dead set on making a life and ultimately a career and name for himself in Israel.

Hirsch wanted to see himself as one of those few lawyers who was at home in the high pressure and drama of the courtroom. This was his chance to shine, to show that he could be every bit as aggressive and persistent as any native-born Israeli prosecutor.

It was one of those moments when you can almost hear dramatic music building to a crescendo in the climax of your own personal movie.

Except it would not be that day. The imaginary music came crashing to a halt.

After all the bluster and buildup, this was a courtroom, after all, not an election debate on television or a popularity contest. A courtroom meant that even those far more boring and laconic than Feldman could win an argument or an appeal if they had legal precedent or some other technical legal interpretation on their side (even if it might make "normal" people's eyes glaze over).

Feldman had legal precedent for his appeal on behalf of Sweti that day, and that basically was all that mattered after years of buildup and all of Hirsch's hard preparation. Feldman won the appeal decisively, and Hirsch tasted defeat, a rare experience for IDF prosecutors. Most of the time, the IDF won hands down or the Palestinian defendants cut plea bargains without even putting up much of a fight. The debate about why that was so is explored in chapter 2.

In looking back on his rare defeat in his first round with Sweti as a junior prosecutor ten years earlier, Hirsch was not thinking about all of those arguments and counterarguments.

Despite Feldman's temporary win that day, Sweti was still eventually sentenced to fifteen years in prison. That was, at least until 2011, when Israel traded Sweti and 110 other Palestinian prisoners, many with "blood on their hands," for the release of the single Israeli soldier Gilad Schalit. The latter became a household name worldwide after he was kidnapped by Hamas while patrolling the Israeli-Gaza border on June 25, 2006.

The 2004 court fight and the 2011 release would have seemed to have ended any chance that Hirsch, the West Bank chief prosecutor and a resident of the religious-Jewish Alon Shvut West Bank settlement in the Gush Etzion block, and Sweti, who, redeemed from prison, went home to his Palestinian village, would meet again. Prosecutors and prisoners usually do not meet again once the prisoners have been judged and sent off to prison. They certainly do not usually meet when the prisoner is later released, pardoned, or exchanged.

And that was what was so striking about seeing Sweti once more.

After years of legal proceedings, wins and losses, being imprisoned and shockingly and dramatically released in a prisoner exchange deal that was watched and covered by the whole world, Sweti had been rearrested in June 2014.

With the kidnapping and murder of three Jewish teenagers, Naftali Fraenkel, Gilad Shaer, and Eyal Yifrach, Sweti and fifty-nine other Palestinians released in 2011 had been rearrested either for their alleged link to the murder, their suspected general support for terror groups such as Hamas, or their violation of certain more technical terms of their pardons.

Somehow in this surprising reunion, which was wrapped in national and personal tragedy, Sweti was coming close to cracking a joke or drawing attention to the irony that Hirsch would be fighting to put him back in jail after his release and after losing to Feldman in that first argument.

Feldman and one of his protégés, Merav Khoury, now a renowned lawyer in her own right, was back representing most of the rearrested Palestinians, trying to keep them out of prison – or from being sent back to serve the remainder of their pre-parole prison sentences.

But this time, Hirsch was no junior prosecutor. He no longer waffled when he spoke Hebrew. Hirsch was the chief. If he did not own these courtrooms as the judges did, they were his home and territory where he felt dominance. This time, Sweti never had a chance.

Defense Lawyer Merav Khoury

You've got to be kidding me, thought Merav Khoury.

Khoury, a defense lawyer like Avigdor Feldman and in fact one of his greatest protégés, could scarcely believe that Israel was about to "renege" on the Gilad Schalit deal.

Peering into the inner thoughts of a defense lawyer such as Khoury, in this case one of the leading defense lawyers who defended Palestinians in some of the most high-profile and internationally followed cases, is one way to explore what it means to defend your own nation from what you view as an occupying nation, while at the same time realizing that many individual clients are objectively guilty.

It is a rare chance to reveal how we as human beings handle the moral pitfalls inextricably linked to that job. What about the job makes defense lawyers feel noble for defending Palestinians from what they view as violations of their sovereignty and of their human rights? What makes them question their own actions?

How do they interact with Israeli military prosecutors whom they work with, negotiate with and work in opposition to day in and day out? What kinds of relationships do they develop with the prosecutors who oppose them, but are also the human beings with whom they spend most of their time?

One way to understand Khoury's story and other defense lawyers' dilemmas is to explore what is unique about her character and background: Khoury is a rare breed of defense lawyer for Palestinians, being a woman and Israeli Arab Christian.

The gap between Israeli prosecutors and the defense lawyers for Palestinians is obvious. Prosecutors are committed to putting Palestinians suspected of crimes behind bars. Defense lawyers are committed to acquitting those Palestinians and keeping them free.

However, Khoury is also in some senses separate from the club of defense lawyers for Palestinians. Over the years, quite a few women have entered the field of Israeli military prosecutors, which for a long time had been exclusively a man's job. This trend has occurred on the defense lawyer side also, but to a much lesser extent. So being a woman in a war between male lawyers over Palestinian defendants who were nearly all men made Khoury different.

Khoury's Christian background is another wildcard. Conventionally, most think of the Israeli-Palestinian conflict as a struggle between Jews and Muslims. And mostly that picture is true. But caught in the middle of this already ridiculously complicated conflict is also a group of Israeli Arab Christians such as Khoury, mostly living in northern Israel. Though these Christians are part of the Israeli Arab community and in most ways they stand with their Muslim Arab brethren on issues of conflict between Jews and Arabs, they have some different positions and attitudes, another point on a list of points that make Khoury unique.

Seriously respected by Hirsch, and even feared by some of the younger prosecutors under him, she appeared not only at the larger Judea Military Courts complex at Ofer, but also at the smaller location, the Samaria Military Courts complex at Salem in the North. Like many defense lawyers for Palestinians, she was ready to take a no-holds-barred approach to criticizing Israel and the West Bank Courts when she thought they were doing something unjust.

In her earlier years as a defense lawyer in the West Bank Courts, she had railed against the massive trend of pretrial and posttrial detentions of defendants. In civilian courts, typically only suspects of dangerous violent crimes are kept in police custody before and during their trials. Others are released on bail or under house arrest so as not to imprison them for a lengthy period before conviction – and in case they are acquitted.

Not so in the West Bank Courts, where a large percentage of Palestinians are held in police custody both before and after indictment, even for some nonviolent crimes, including in cases where they are later acquitted. Khoury's success rate in fighting those detentions had been almost zero, and eventually she realized she had been naive to think she could beat off pre- and posttrial detentions with any regularity because of the unique Israeli-Palestinian circumstances.

Beyond that, Khoury had distinguished herself as a trailblazer who could dismember the prosecution's evidence, then hand their cases back to them on a platter. She had distinguished herself as an Israeli Arab Christian in a world of Palestinian Muslim defense lawyers and clients, and as a female West Bank Courts lawyer, one of at most a handful in an overwhelmingly male world. If Arab-Palestinian women had broken taboos to become lawyers, being a lawyer on an army base representing security defendants accused of security crimes from Hamas and Fatah showed Khoury as a woman with nerves of steel.

Some of that was natural. She had been trained by one of the kings, Avigdor Feldman, to be fearless and demand rights and justice from all courts, civilian or West Bank – with no difference or exceptions.

Part of that perspective also made her an oddball in some of her more moderate views of the West Bank Courts. While most Palestinians' defense lawyers badmouthed the courts as occupation courts that were always more unfair than Israeli civilian courts, Khoury departed from the party line. She said that she had a better chance to win in the West Bank military courts, as long as she or any other defense lawyer came in to win and not just to cut a plea bargain. One reason was that she viewed the West Bank Court judges as very professional with good intentions, including those who lived in the settlements, such as former chief judge Aharon Mishnayot.

Khoury also is willing to say that she understands the IDF perspective of detaining some Palestinians until the end of their trials in cases that would not warrant detention if they were taking place within Israel. She is willing to admit that from the Israeli authorities' perspective, it could be too difficult or impossible to catch and bring to trial certain Palestinians if law enforcement had let them go after catching them the first time. As the IDF routinely explains, unlike in Israel, authorities do not necessarily know where defendants live. Further, the Palestinians have no incentive to present themselves in court, and the lack of legitimacy of the West Bank Courts in the eyes of the Palestinians militates toward not showing up to court hearings voluntarily.

Another reason she believed she had an even stronger chance of winning acquittals in the West Bank Courts than in civilian courts was less complimentary to Israel. According to Khoury, the Shin Bet (Israel Security Agency) – which deals with domestic security and terror issues, including interrogating Palestinians accused of security crimes – leaves more holes in their interrogations for defense lawyers to exploit in court than their police counterparts who handle interrogations in virtually all civilian court cases.

Khoury particularly notes the Shin Bet's failure to follow certain procedures and its weaker record keeping since, unlike the police, it believes it can operate entirely in the shadows without being questioned in court. Hence, the Shin Bet is always surprised when the rare defense lawyer hauls one of its agents out onto the witness stand.

Since most Palestinians' defense lawyers cut plea bargains without seriously challenging the prosecutions' evidence, often provided by the Shin Bet, the domestic security agency often does get a free pass.

Not when Khoury is running the show.

In one case she handled, the prosecution thought it had an unbeatable case against the defendant with seven witnesses to incriminate him. Khoury tore down the witnesses piece by piece, peeling them apart until it was apparent that none of them actually knew anything useful about the defendant.

And so Khoury is a critic of the West Bank Courts, but is viewed by some in the IDF as a more fair-minded and moderate critic. However, there was nothing middle of the road about her criticism of Israel rearresting releasees from the Schalit deal.

Besides understanding her character and background, the best way to comprehend Khoury's story and other defense lawyers' dilemmas is to understand them in the context of a heated and controversial case. The rearresting of the Schalit prisoner exchange releasees was one such landmark event.

The rearrests came in June 2014, around three years after the release.

There is wide disagreement about why the arrests were really made, but they certainly coincided with a follow-up to the killing of the three Jewish teenagers Naftali Fraenkel, Gilad Shaer, and Eyal Yifrach. The rearrests eventually wrapped into negotiations over a ceasefire to the 2014 Gaza War, catapulting them into the world's geopolitical consciousness and considerations.

Khoury decided to fight the move to annul the parole decision tooth and nail.

On July 14, 2014, defending Khadar Raadi, she told a three-judge panel led by Lt. Col. Judge Menaham Liberman that the Shin Bet and the prosecution were handicapping her by failing to disclose various portions of the evidence on national security grounds.

These kinds of controversial tactics were sometimes part of the special-track administrative detention proceedings. But they were not part of standard criminal proceedings, and Khoury was surprised to see the tactics in play where the stakes could be jail for life and not just temporary extended detention. She asked that Judge Liberman's panel, sitting as part of the Judea section of the IDF military court, carefully review the secret evidence for the purpose of recommending to the prosecution to disclose more material to Khoury to make her defense.

Then Khoury got very creative before the court, trying to turn the Israeli government's new weapon against it. At times pacing, gesticulating and raising her voice into a steady thunder of arguments, she blasted the government's case. She attempted creative analogies between two issues that seemed to have little in common other than they were major policy shifts, to try to shake up the proceedings and get the judges' attention.

And she was mad.

The issue really disturbed Khoury, who got animated when she discussed the dozens of Schalit releases who were rearrested, saying "I don't like fraud." That was how she referred to the rearrests. She said that Israel got Schalit back, fulfilling Hamas's end of the deal, and Israel had a duty to fulfill its end of the deal. Khoury said that when Israel released 110 Palestinian prisoners to the West Bank, many of them thought they had a fresh start, dropped their guard, and laid down roots for the first time, getting married and having kids.

Exhibiting some of her trademark sarcasm, this was where Khoury went into improvisation mode. She said that one moment Israel told the releasees, "Go get married and have children," then the next moment, it said, "Oops, sorry, we did not think that was a good idea." Summing up, she said, "That's just not fair."

All of this because Khadar Raadi received $10–12,000 from Hamas after his release. But Khoury noted that there was no evidence presented that he asked for or did anything to get the funds. She said the assumption was Hamas just wanted to be perceived as close to the released prisoners.

Khoury had won some shocking cases, including that of Jamal Haj, a pardoned and then rearrested senior Palestinian political leader, with some parallels to the cases of the Schalit releasees. But this time too many legal and political forces were arrayed against her. Taking money from Hamas for any reason was a crimson red flag for Israel. That meant that she, and her mentor Feldman, who shared some of the Schalit release defense cases with Khoury, would be trampled by the one-way train bringing the releasees back to jail for extensive or even life terms.

Defense Lawyers Gaby Lasky and Nery Ramati

Nery Ramati took a deep breath.

In some ways all of this was a mistake.

The case the court was about to hear was a flagship case for both the Israeli military prosecution and for Palestinian defense lawyers, and it should have been fully tried by famous human rights lawyer Gaby Lasky, his boss. But in a very short timeout from her role as human rights crusader, she had given birth to twins, and a good portion of the trial of this case ended up falling on him.

It was March 10, 2011. He was no rookie. He had been a lawyer representing Palestinians in the Israeli army's West Bank Courts for around two years, and before that had been connected to the legal proceedings in other ways. Still, he was about to cross-examine an important witness in a case with major implications that was already starting to make waves nationally in Israel and even internationally.

Digging into what makes individual leading defense lawyers such as Ramati or Lasky tick is one way to explore what it means to fight for the human rights of another nation against your own nation. Unlike Khoury, Ramati and Lasky were both Jewish Israelis, who "crossed sides" to defend Palestinians – though Lasky is fond of insisting that if you are a human rights defender, you must defend all kinds of human rights (she does take major human rights cases of Jews as well).

Also, whereas Khoury often represents some hardened Palestinian adult security prisoners, Lasky and Ramati represent mostly Palestinian minors accused of lighter crimes such as low-grade rock throwing (as opposed to rock-throwing that endangers lives).

What drives Jewish lawyers to defend Palestinians from what they view as their own country violating the Palestinians' rights? Does it matter to them whether their clients are objectively guilty? How do they interact with Israeli military prosecutors whom they come up against, but must also regularly cut deals with? What kinds of relationships do they develop with their adversaries, the prosecutors, who are their fellow citizens even as their Palestinian clients are foreigners?

Part of understanding Lasky and Ramati's stories and other defense lawyers' dilemmas is to understand them in a classic dramatic courtroom cross-examination.

Cross-examination has the potential for being the most dramatic gotcha moment in a court case. It is a competition of wills between a lawyer and a hostile witness when the lawyer tries to get the witness to say something that the witness does not want to say. It can grab victory and glory for the lawyer and break the back of the witness's case.

Like many lawyers who are talented public speakers, before Ramati made a major argument or questioned a witness, he always had a fire in his belly to jump up and start talking. In fact, Ramati hated that the prosecution almost always spoke first, even if there was a logic to presenting the allegations before the defense began trying to make holes in them. By the time he arrived at the courts in Ofer from Tel Aviv, a trip that usually took around forty-five minutes and could take over an hour in traffic, he always had had plenty of time to rehearse his arguments and wanted to blurt them out already.

As Ramati listened to the prosecutor's direct examination of the witness and waited his turn to speak, he lost himself in a moment of reflection, mentally traveling back in time several months. In some ways, he thought, his client's future and the fate of this landmark case could all come down to one video.

The first time Nery Ramati looked at a video of an interrogation of a Palestinian accused of crimes in the West Bank Courts was not in the case of Islam Ayoub, which he was arguing now. A few months before, Ramati had been the first one to start systematically watching videos of police interrogations. Since then, several minors had been freed from detention by the IDF's West Bank Courts on the basis of those videos.

Police interrogations were a major pillar of all criminal cases, whether in civilian or military courts. The police would question a suspect and try to get the suspect to confess or slip up on some detail of a fake narrative. Then a transcript of the interrogation was used to file an indictment against the suspect and could sometimes be produced to try to incriminate the suspect in court.

So that written record of the interrogation was key. As part of the interrogation and of the written record, there was also a requirement to inform suspects of certain basic rights, such as the right to remain silent and the right to a lawyer (called in the United States Miranda rights).

Many of the interrogations were now also videotaped.

Ramati had made a shocking discovery from the videotapes. Over and over again at the Binyamin and Hebron police stations, the written transcript that police were filing was contradicted by the video they were taking of the same interrogation. Ramati would go so far as to say the written record was "never" identical to the video record.

Not only that, but in case after case, he noted that detainees were not being informed of many of their standard rights during interrogations at those police stations even as the transcripts of the interrogations made it appear as if they had been appropriately cautioned. Once he noted the contradiction, he realized that it might be an untapped source for breaking open cases with massive holes and torpedoing prosecutions.

Until then, almost no one watched the videos of interrogations of Palestinians, and no one came to court on any kind of systematic basis with a computer to show the videos to the court. Hardly anyone had even thought about it. Ramati became known as the computer guy. And once other lawyers saw his success, others started reviewing the videos also and bringing them to court on computer to show the court. Today, already many lawyers come to court with computers and videos.

Especially with minors, who are more susceptible to suggestion and intimidation, it occurred to Ramati that the police might be lax about reminding them of their rights. Tactically, making the judge watch a video of a minor's rights being violated also would make it much harder emotionally for him to convict the minor of the allegations against him.

It was an instant breakthrough also in the case of Palestinian minor Islam Ayoub. He was accused of rock throwing, but was primarily meaningful to the IDF as a potential star witness against a Palestinian who was leading protests against the West Bank wall. In Ayoub's case, they found gold for a defense lawyer. Moshe Madyuni of the Binyamin police, located near Ramallah, who had interrogated Ayoub, had not only failed to tell Ayoub of his fundamental right to remain silent, which even the uneducated know from television and movies. He had three times substituted different instructions and statements in place of the standard right to remain silent formula they were supposed to read to Palestinians they interrogated.

Gaby Lasky, Ramati, and Limor Goldstein, the troika who made up Lasky's firm when she split from Smadar Ben Natan in 2009, had all watched the video together in the office. As the film unfolded, the three were buoyed (euphemistically, since Lasky, while able to be firm, can be a bit understated temperamentally) over this gold nugget, scarcely believing the police could make such an obvious and blatant error. Ramati imagined the pounding cross-examination against police interrogator Moshe Madyuni when he had the chance to get him in his crosshairs.

Even before viewing the Ayoub video, Ramati, Lasky and Goldstein were looking for how videos portrayed the police's other dealings with minors, which they believed had been problematic.

It had been somewhat natural for Ramati to pick up on the issues brought out from the video of the interrogation of Ayoub. Using videos of the interrogations as evidence to acquit Palestinians might have been new, but people had been using videos of protests and documentaries generally for years to try to help individual Palestinian defendants and the Palestinian cause. Ramati had been a producer, director, videographer, and writer at JCS, sometimes in that cause. He was thirty-one before he switched over to becoming a lawyer working with Lasky.

But it was not natural to expect Ramati would end up where he had ended up, in a career defending Palestinian clients from accusations by the Israeli army's prosecutor. When Ramati was asked about where he originally came from to have landed in his current role, he struck a playful, bashful, but also proud and unapologetic smile and would explain, "I was born here, in Israel, to a Zionist home in Ramat Gan. I knew Gaby since 2007, when I was working for JCS and also a law student, and I knew I wanted to work with her."

He would explain, "I knew what I wanted to do as a lawyer. Gaby and Smadar were in one office that worked on human rights in the way that I believe should be done – less in the Supreme Court and more in the field [meaning taking human rights cases to trial]. Because I knew Smadar even before, I met with them, and we decided that I would start working for them as a student and afterward I would be Gaby's law clerk."

Ramati continued, "Gaby believes in people, so when I became her law clerk [and she] was pregnant with the twins and just could not make it to Ofer, not emotionally and not physically...I was thrown into the cold waters of Ofer. Her faith in me and the way that she boosted my confidence not to give up and to continue turned me into a sincere admirer and follower." Back in the court room where Ramati was fighting to free Ayoub from prison, the dramatic cross-examination battle had at last arrived. This was the moment Ramati had been waiting for since he, Lasky, and Goldstein had spotted police interrogator Moshe Madyuni's violation of Ayoub's rights by failing to tell him of his right to remain silent.

The prosecutor finished. Ramati's round of questioning Madyuni on the issue went like this.

Ramati asked: "Who specifically warned the accused of his rights?"

Madyuni responded: "I think I warned him, I explained to him what he was suspected of and what his rights were." Madyuni went on to say that he had done a good job explaining Ayoub's rights to him.

Madyuni had already walked into the trap, but Ramati kept the charade of light questions going a little bit longer.

He followed up, but still with a light touch: What essentially were the rights that come out of the warning other than the right to an attorney?

Madyuni said: "Not incriminating yourself."

Innocently, Ramati asked: "What about the right to remain silent?"

Madyuni responded: "It's the same thing."

Ramati: "You said to him that 'you don't need to speak during the interrogation'?"

Madyuni answered: "I told him that he does not need to say anything."

Ramati: "Maybe you warned him twice."

Madyuni: "Maybe."

This was classic lawyering. Ramati already knew that in fact Madyuni had failed to tell Ayoub of his right to remain silent.

But why not let a witness start to hang himself so that he not only messed up in the past, but also messes up – or maybe even looks dishonest – in front of the court itself.

One thing that was not well understood by many non-lawyers was that lying or mixing up facts before the police or others in discussions or interrogations pretrial was nowhere near as important as what you said in court during the trial, which can potentially be ten times as powerful, convincing, and important.

So if Madyuni off the bat in court had immediately admitted he had messed up in not telling Ayoub of his rights, the judge might even have appreciated his honesty and integrity for admitting his error without a fight. Paradoxically, he could get points for being such an honest cop, for preemptively admitting error.

In contrast, if Madyuni doubled down and insisted in court that he had done everything right and denied violating Ayoub's rights, springing a video on him a few moments later that blatantly contradicted that story would mortally wound his credibility before the judge.

After destroying Madyuni's credibility, Ramati would win on other issues more easily because the judge might see Madyuni as a liar and be inclined to believe the Ramati-Ayoub narrative.

Ramati finally dropped the charade: "Two times you told him [about his right to remain silent]?"

Madyuni started to squirm a bit and equivocate: "Let's see the recording, and I will tell you exactly what happened."

So Madyuni had not yet admitted his error, a serious violation of Ayoub's rights and an error potentially fatal to the case, but was not unequivocally saying he was perfect.

Referring to the video was a convenient way to try to redirect pressure off of himself temporarily, play for time, and hopefully find some external evidentiary support. Had he known what the video would show, however, he would probably not have opened the further Pandora's Box trap that Ramati had laid for him.

The whole court watched the video, watched Madyuni fail to warn Ayoub of his right to remain silent and, just like that, Madyuni's last defense fell apart.

Ramati was no longer patient and pounced: "So you did not tell him even once that he had the right to remain silent?"

Madyuni tried to recalibrate his answer: "He [Ayoub] understood well, there was nothing intentional here, and it looks authentic that I explain to a suspect his rights and it seemed to me that he understood very well. We did not do anything intentional. What was said is what was said. I think that he understood that he had the right to remain silent."

Boom.

Ramati had blown Madyuni away.

First of all, Madyuni had abandoned his original story that he had properly warned Ayoub. Second, he was struggling to give explanations for his mess-up, but was having trouble staying consistent.

Did Madyuni forget to warn Ayoub of the right to remain silent because Ayoub already understood? Or was he not defending his mistake but trying to say it was unintentional?

It almost did not matter.

Madyuni and all of his testimony was now damaged goods and possibly even enough to throw out the entire case.

Former IDF West Bank Courts Chief Justice Aharon Mishnayot

This would be one of the decisions for which supporters, critics, and historians would know him – a lynchpin in his legacy.

A lesser man might have drowned in the intensity and momentousness of the moment.

But West Bank Court president Judge Col. Aharon Mishnayot was cut from a different kind of material. There was also no avoiding what the correct legal result was in the case before him, regardless of the overall moral paradox intertwined with his decision.

Mishnayot was a judge, but a judge in an alien position. Normal judges' sole preoccupation is justice for victims, offenders, and society. They are particularly concerned with the civil liberties of those accused of crimes – to ensure that they be given every possible benefit of the doubt before a conviction takes their liberty from them.

This was certainly one important part of Mishnayot's mission that distinguished him from Hirsch. From Mishnayot's perspective, an acquittal was a victory as much as a conviction. Not so for Hirsch.

But in other ways their missions converged far more than those of a typical judge and prosecutor. Mishnayot's other job was to maintain order in the West Bank on behalf of the Israeli army. Even some crimes relating to disturbing public order are not crimes within Green Line Israel.

How did Mishnayot handle that inherent conflict? How did he relate to Hirsch and his prosecutors, who wore the same uniform as him and had overlapping yet differing missions? How did he relate to Palestinian defendants and their lawyers, whom he was bound to keep in line, but for whom he was also the last line of defense of their rights?

A judge's relationships with all sides is more attenuated by the formal requirements of separation. But even judges develop a rapport with the lawyers who argue before them daily. What do those relationships look like?

One of the best ways to examine those questions is to see how Mishnayot responded to a high-profile case that most exposed the competing priorities and loyalties he faced as an Israeli military judge – the chief judge – over Palestinians in the West Bank.

It was August 27, 2012. The case of Jamal Haj, on which Aharon Mishnayot was about to rule, would lead to the release of a confessed murderer and would embarrass the government and the Shin Bet (Israel Security Agency) on a level likely not seen since the Israeli Supreme Court struck down the agency's torture interrogation tactics as unconstitutional in 1999.

This was the case that Khoury won and which she had hoped would help her win the later 2014 Schalit deal cases.

Haj was a member of the Palestinian parliament, but, until November 2006, was living outside the West Bank, since he was wanted by Israel for involvement in planning a major suicide bombing during the Second Intifada of 2000–2005.

In March 2002, as part of his involvement in the Al-Aqsa Martyrs Brigade, Haj helped plan the infamous suicide bombing of a Tel Aviv café on Allenby Street, murdering Rachel Cherbo and wounding others.

But in November 2006 and July 2007, Haj was included in an amnesty deal between the Shin Bet and the Palestinian Authority, along with a long list of other Fatah members who had been involved in violence during the Second Intifada.

Shin Bet head Yuval Diskin was personally involved.

The deals essentially said that Haj and the others would be removed from Israel's wanted list, would be given amnesty for prior crimes, and could return to the West Bank if they abstained from violence in the future. Shin Bet officials were hoping that with the Second Intifada over, some of the PA officials who had crossed the line into terror would convert back into moderates to keep the overall population moderate.

Mishnayot emphasized the extent to which Haj's return to the West Bank was open and coordinated with Israeli security officials. In reviewing the case, he noticed that after his amnesty, Haj passed through more than four checkpoints on his way back into the West Bank. Each checkpoint fully reviewed his paperwork and called in to senior officials to approve his entry.

Then on May 29, 2007, Haj was arrested, and the IDF prosecution threw the book at him with a nineteen-count indictment, listing every alleged crime he had ever committed, including prior ones for which he had amnesty.

While the IDF prosecution mobilized a range of arguments for justifying indicting Haj, seemingly breaking the amnesty they gave him, Mishnayot narrowed the case to two issues.

The fig leaf which Mishnayot quickly dismissed was that a condition of Haj's amnesty was that he not leave Shechem without prior approval of the security authorities. Mishnayot noted the scarcity of evidence that Haj had been indicted for leaving Shechem without prior approval of the authorities. The evidence included letters from the Shin Bet's legal adviser for the Samaria region and from "Benayah" (a fictitious name), head of the unit for thwarting terror in the

Shechem area. But the massive indictment had not been for leaving Shechem unauthorized, but for his past terror activities – for which he had amnesty.

So for Mishnayot, the IDF prosecution's only real argument was that Haj was a really bad guy and that Israel should not be held to its side of the agreement.

Mishnayot sounded off against the IDF prosecution and the Shin Bet for its conduct. With uncharacteristic directness, he rebuked them, saying, "The responsible authorities unjustifiably turned a blind eye to the agreement which was put together on the issue and unfortunately, it is hard to say that these authorities acted in good faith."

Wham.

Words like that coming from a religious Zionist yarmulke-wearing chief judge such as Mishnayot was like having the legal equivalent of a ton of bricks dropped on the IDF prosecution's head. Mishnayot was always firm that even as he and the IDF prosecution wore the same uniform, the judiciary was independent.

The then chief judge continued, "In my opinion, the severity of the deficiencies in the conduct of law enforcement officials with the very arresting of Haj, along with the problematic conduct of the prosecution which avoided providing" the full picture of the amnesty agreement to the trial court that handled Haj's case, "was enough to be a major harm to the overall sense of justice and fairness characterizing the proceedings."

Mishnayot tried to show sensitivity to the Cherbo family, saying he knew his acquittal of Haj would be hard for them, but that he hoped they would get "some small comfort" if Haj, after his release, stuck to his agreement and continued as a force for moderation among the Palestinians.

Even after the ink on Mishnayot's final appeals court ruling was dry, Hirsch would harbor powerful doubts about how justified it was and about the picture that Khoury and Feldman had painted for the judges, which he called "an alternative reality."

As far as Hirsch was concerned, Mishnayot had been hoodwinked, just as from Khoury's perspective, Mishnayot had been the only one who was honest and put the government's feet to the fire to comply with its promise.

Those kinds of rulings tormented Hirsch and the prosecution when critics of the IDF's West Bank Courts claimed judges and prosecutors were in league.

But that was Mishnayot's job, giving the "correct" legal ruling, even if that meant being the champion of fairness for a murderer, with a meek hope that the acquitted ex-murderer's freedom would lead him to moderation and "some small comfort."

Four Radically Different Individuals on One Bizarre Stage

How did Hirsch, Mishnayot, Khoury, and the Lasky and Ramati duo end up playing on the same field?

Hirsch and Mishnayot seemed to be the most closely related in their roles – in the same army and with almost identical uniforms.

But they had different masters, disagreed vehemently on rulings, and had completely different visions of the West Bank Courts.

The Haj ruling was a case in point.

When Hirsch talked about Mishnayot being taken into an alternate universe by Khoury, he said it with a passionate zeal.

Reflecting on the case years later, Hirsch would say, "I think there are until this day aspects of the trial at first instance which I cannot further expand upon, since I know exactly what the mistake made leading to that decision is. I can specifically pinpoint it and…undermine not a small amount of the decision that was handed down."

This was a classic move, a cat and mouse game many top Israeli army officers played with the press: sharing just enough to whet your appetite, but keeping their cards close to their chests and not revealing whether the secret was more mundane or as sensational and tantalizing as it sounded.

Asked if the reason for not revealing "the mistake" was national security, he replied almost impishly and with a wide smile, "Not for national security reasons. It's something which given the right situation…will be explained. Certain conceptions which were held were simply not relevant and were even misunderstood…that the defense specifically built in the court of first instance with tremendous, tremendous experience and creativity."

Then in a shocking moment of frankness for a man who has spent his career in a uniform in which he has had to toe the line, Hirsch declared, "I have – I cannot say anything else but to take my hat off to Avigdor Feldman and to

Merav Khoury. They managed to create an alternative reality and to convince the judges that that reality was true."

This was not a classic move. Top military officers never, ever criticized judges, and certainly not on record. Hirsch was explicitly saying that Mishnayot, the chief justice, had been swindled and bamboozled out of his experienced perspective in the Haj decision by crafty lawyering.

Then shifting back into the ever self-assured and indefatigable competitor that he was, and practically issuing a threat, Hirsch said, "Should the event arise, and should Jamal Haj return in any way to committing offenses…I know how to put my finger on the point which was problematic to the courts and how to explain that it isn't relevant."

This raw competitiveness, single-mindedness in the surety of the rectitude of his argument, and readiness to declare the military court's own chief justice not just incorrect, but fooled, was at the core of what made Hirsch a fearless prosecutor.

It was also part of what separated him from Mishnayot's equally confident but far more circumspect view of deciding what was true and what was gray. These men of the same uniform were operating on different planes even as they occupied the same space.

Hirsch and Lasky, who trained and mentored Ramati, also could have been thought to have a lot in common. Both were immigrants to Israel from foreign countries, both being drawn to the country as teenagers. Both again were spending vast amounts of their lives in the same space that was the West Bank Courts. Both were top-notch lawyers and dedicated to the purposes they believed in with every fiber of their being.

That was the end of the similarities. The two could not be more different in their views about the West Bank Courts and what purposes they were dedicating their lives to; in their interpersonal interactions, they could not come close to grasping each other.

If Hirsch's aliyah (moving to Israel) and experience of antisemitism in England helped explain his commitment to the army and Israeli security issues, Lasky's aliyah from Mexico –where "we never suffered antisemitism while we were there, so there was no trauma because of being Jewish that made us want to leave" – influenced her commitment as a human rights lawyer who would make representing Palestinians one of her signature marks.

Describing aliyah and its relation to the Holocaust, she said, "It wasn't the specifics, it was the idea of the state for the Jewish people. That was how I was brought up. And that it was very important after the Holocaust. I believe that after the Holocaust…or because of the Holocaust, Jews can get to two different conclusions regarding how the state should be. And…one of them is that we of all nations have to be different and not treat people as we were treated."

Lasky continued, with her eyes darkening and a noticeable determination coming over her face as she set her jaw, "And the other way is the opposite. In order that for what happened to us as a people, will never happen, we will have to live by the sword. These are two different conclusions that come up from the same starting point."

Then Lasky, the secular human rights lawyer, shows off her versatility and throws her audience a curve ball, quoting the Bible to criticize the Israeli occupation. "Actually, I believe as the Torah says that when you criticize someone, it is because you love them, because you want them to change for the better, and this is why I do what I do, because I believe that Israel has gone at some points in the wrong direction."

Not that Lasky is ignorant of terrorism. "I am aware that there is crime and terror and that people have to fight them. But still in a democracy there are things that you can do in order to fight crime and terrorism and there are things that you cannot do," says Lasky, her voice carrying the energy of someone slamming a hand on the table – if that were her style.

For emphasis, she concludes that point repeating herself as if pointing an imaginary finger at the state, "Because if you do them, you are one of them, you are one of them – that commits crimes."

Her message and slogan would be that "definitely the ends don't justify the means. Because it's not only life itself, it's free life, its moral life… If we want Israel to be a place where it is good to live, and if we want Israel to be a democratic country, where we can teach our children what is right and wrong, we have to give them an example."

So as Hirsch and Lasky are both committed to preserving Israeli democracy, they come into a grand conflagration over whether the greatest threat is terrorism and crime or the state and army's means for fighting that terror.

Khoury, a woman and a Christian Israeli Arab, came from the most different background of this group and in some ways was also radically different from the many Palestinian-Muslim male lawyers who defended Palestinians in the West Bank Courts.

But she was no less principled.

Some world-famous lawyers, such as Alan Dershowitz as well as Khoury's mentor, Avigdor Feldman, are adamant that they will take a case from any client, no matter how barbaric an act that client is accused of.

Part of the reason is a principled commitment to the adversarial system as the best way to ensure due process and boost our human instinct for fairness in courts.

These principles can act against the other human instinct to arbitrarily prosecute rivals or innocents whether they are guilty or not in order to win a political battle or answer the public's demand to solve a crime where the real perpetrator is still loose.

Khoury is different. She will and has refused cases of terrorists. Khoury refused to take the case of the murderers of the Fogel family in Itamar (discussed in chapter 10), though she was offered the case first. When she was a brand-new lawyer in the public defender's office, she was ordered to take on the defense of a grandfather who had sexually abused his grandson. She refused. Her boss told her she was not allowed to refuse, with an obvious implied threat about the impact refusing could have on her job. Khoury stuck to her guns.

And where she has taken on those accused of security crimes, it has often been to reduce prison time or demand the state honor a pardon (albeit not an outright acquittal) for someone she believes is trying to turn over a new leaf.

These were the scenarios playing out in the Haj case and in the dozens of Palestinians rearrested from the Schalit deal prisoner exchange.

Khoury did not talk about human rights with quite the same flair as Lasky, who also has had experience on the political stage, having almost made it into the Knesset multiple times with the Meretz Party, including in 2015 (in 2019 she was ninth on a Meretz list that won four Knesset seats).

But her very actions in taking on some of the most complex and high-profile cases bring into sharp contrast the cost of one nation judging another in court as well as the question of whether the West Bank Courts system is working fairly.

As a lawyer who makes her career defending Palestinians, she obviously has more exposure to and sympathy for one side.

Still, Hirsch respects her, and her critiques of the system cannot be ignored since she is even-handed enough to give the system credit in areas that most lawyers for Palestinians would not.

Then there is Mishnayot, who has some common views with prosecutors such as Hirsch and some with defense lawyers such as Lasky, Ramati, and Khoury. As a judge and not a lawyer, he was in some ways the most different.

Mishnayot fits the part for a judge – incredibly cerebral and natural at shielding his emotions from breaking through the surface. Getting Mishnayot to talk about his emotional relationship with his role as the chief justice of the West Bank Courts is no easy task. But he does highlight one moment when his otherwise invincible judicial veneer was broken.

"It happened to me once in the case with the killing of the Fogels," starts Mishnayot as he stares out into space returning back to a courtroom moment that it seems haunts him until this day.

On March 12, 2011, a sixteen-year-old Palestinian minor named Hakim Awad, along with his slightly older Palestinian cousin Amjad Awad, committed one of the most horrific murders ever perpetrated by Palestinians against Israelis.

Israelis called it the "Itamar Massacre" after the West Bank settlement where five members of the Fogel family were slaughtered at the hands of Hakim Awad and his cousin.

Remembering the case, Mishnayot said, "I had a child more or less the same age as one of the murderers there. That merely deepened my sorrow about the question: What have we come to? Where did things stand with my son? And where did things stand with the Palestinian boy? What does my son do? And what do they do?"

Drawing an extremely rare and long "Uhhhh" for several seconds for a man who seems to easily craft sentences in fine legal paragraph form, Mishnayot showed his trouble at reconciling his own questions.

He then continued, "This did not in any way impact the outcome [of his decision regarding the Fogel murderers]. It...it...it...it...brought me to a great sadness about where this unending conflict has brought us. And how important it is to do everything that can be done to somehow find a solution to this conflict. And when there is no solution, to somehow act correctly within the limits of the framework imposed by the conflict. As far as is possible."

Mishnayot actually finished his sentence throwing up his hands in frustration, again at a point where even very articulate words could not communicate the horrors presented by the conflict, almost all of which spill over into the West Bank Courts. In this way Mishnayot was trying to bring some nobility and humanity to the inhumanity that could so easily run through both the Israeli and the Palestinian sides.

Not that one can describe Mishnayot as the objective conscience of all the sides simply because he was a judge. As so many defense lawyers pointed out, any judge in the West Bank Courts system must accept its foundations and parameters– which in and of themselves take the Israeli side of the conflict being played out in the Ofer and Salem courts.

If anything, the existence of Mishnayot and the lack of existence of a corresponding Palestinian judge to compare him to only highlights the systemic issues in pursuing fairness and objectivity. Finding objectivity in its pure and philosophical construct may be impossible on such a disputed plane with so many entangled levels of complexity.

Still, during the years 2008 to present, extraordinary changes occurred in the West Bank Courts; many more changes that one side or the other wanted did not occur – heavily impacting the story of the decades-long saga which is the Israeli-Palestinian conflict.

The actions, interactions, and lives of these diverse individuals in the alternate universe that is the West Bank Courts tell a unique and spellbinding story of talented and committed and extremely human persons searching for their own truth.

It is a story of successes and failures to preserve security and democracy, all occurring at the same time. A story of people who, at the end of the day, are stuck occupying a gray zone together even when virtually all other dialogue and interaction between the sides has ground to a halt.

Chapter 2

The Wild West Bank Courts: Background

History of Major Changes to the Legal Framework, 1967–2016

In six days in June 1967, Israel overwhelmingly defeated Egypt, Syria, and Jordan's armed forces in a mix of preemptive strikes and responses to attacks and threatened attacks, in many ways rearranging the entire map of the Middle East. Israel's military victory led to control over the Golan Heights in the North, the Sinai Desert and Gaza Strip in the South, and over east Jerusalem, including the Old City and the Temple Mount. Crucially (for this story), by defeating Jordan's army, Israel took control over the Jordan River's West Bank area. The border between Israeli territory and Jordanian territory right before the 1967 war started is called the Green Line. Territories that Israel controls beyond the Green Line are those in dispute according to UN resolutions.

One radical change that has sometimes been less noticed was a new legal system. Israel now needed to administer the West Bank areas populated by Palestinians, which it suddenly controlled. To administer this new system, the IDF appointed a military commander of the West Bank.

The West Bank Legal System Immediately after the Six-Day War

In international law, the region of the West Bank, also called Judea and Samaria, is a special kind of territory subject to the law of what is known as "belligerent occupation." This legal term is neutral, is used by Israeli officials, and, at least in and of itself, has no connection to political accusations of "occupation" against Israel when critics try to compare Israel to an apartheid state. Instead, "belligerent occupation" is a technical term to describe a post-conflict change in who controls land.

Under the international law of belligerent occupation, when a foreign army establishes a military occupation of a territory, it can impose a series of laws that have been agreed upon in international treaties. This possibility was prepared for in advance, and on June 7, 1967, the first day the military government in the West Bank was in operation, even before the war had ended, three proclamations and several orders created the basic structure of the court system and established military courts in the districts of Jerusalem, Hebron, Jenin, West Nablus (based in Ramallah), and East Nablus (based in Jericho). The IDF's military commander of the West Bank implemented the Order Concerning Security Provisions (OCSP), the beginning of a code of laws governing the West Bank. It moved quickly to recognize the application of international law to the area.

One of the first pieces of legislation within the OCSP was Section 35, which expressly recognized that the Fourth Geneva Convention, a foundational document of international law on the subject of occupations, would take precedence over anything in the OCSP order that contradicted it. The courts continue, in theory at least, to view the Geneva Conventions as taking precedence over the OCSP.

The IDF's official legal website as of summer 2016 (officials have confirmed verbally that this has not changed) recognized international law, but subject to changes "for maintaining the safety and security of the area and its inhabitants." On one hand, Israel was saying that it tries to respect the requirement that the "occupying power" – here Israel and the IDF – keep the laws mostly the same and not change them to use against the population that it now controls. On the other hand, Israel said there were exceptions for (a) making the law function in a more modern way and (b) security purposes.

Making the law function in a more modern way generally means more rights and defenses for Palestinians. Security purposes generally mean fewer rights and defenses for Palestinians.

For these reasons, the laws applied in the West Bank include Ottoman law, British mandatory amendments, and Jordanian law, all of which were used prior to Israeli control. They also include IDF military orders, international law, and aspects of Israeli law, including Israeli administrative law.

The laws of belligerent occupation try to regulate the tension between the security needs of the occupying state and its duty to ensure the security and well-being of the foreign population whose territory it is occupying or whose territory is in dispute.

Most of the world views the laws of belligerent occupation as applying and also views Israel as an "occupier" of territory that should belong to a future Palestinian state. Israel contends that it is occupying disputed territory that Jordan illegally annexed in 1948 from no one. This means that it may belong to a future Palestinian state, but only as a result of peace negotiations that would make the territory's status no longer disputed.

The West Bank Legal System within International Law

Aspects of belligerent occupation law can be found in the 1907 Fourth Hague Convention, the 1949 Fourth Geneva Convention, and in the 1977 protocols annexed to the Geneva Conventions. This is considered a sub-area of the law of armed conflict, also known as the "laws of war" or "international humanitarian law." Advocates for interpreting the law to favor the Palestinians argue that the direction of these bodies of law has evolved toward increasing the importance of the occupying power's duty to the occupied foreign people.

The IDF says that the military commander operates a military justice system by virtue of articles 64 and 66 of the 1949 Fourth Geneva Conventions.

Article 64 dictates that the prior laws which applied must continue to apply, with the exceptions mentioned above: security on one hand and the best interests of the occupied people on the other hand.

Article 66 authorizes the establishment of military courts for bringing occupied persons to trial when necessary.

In practice, Israel says it voluntarily follows articles 64 and 66, even though it technically claims that it is not obligated to apply the convention to the territories, arguing they are disputed, with no prior legal sovereign. This legal tightrope walk in some ways is a matter of emphasis. When Israel departs from the convention because of a security situation, it wants to argue it was never obligated to comply. When Israel complies with the convention, it wants to get credit for its voluntary compliance. This is a major source of tension between Israel and its many global critics.

According to Israel's critics and most of the world, the Fourth Geneva Convention applies to the West Bank at all times. This means when Israel departs from it, it is a violator. When Israel follows it, it is merely doing what it must.

The Courts and the First Intifada

The First Intifada, which started in December 1987, was essentially a popular uprising by the Palestinians against Israeli rule. Though there were no battles between armies, the Palestinians not having a formal army, it was one of the periods where Israelis felt most insecure and endangered by Palestinians. While significant portions of the First Intifada were nonviolent or low-grade violence, such as non-dangerous rock throwing, an estimated 179 to 200 on the Israeli side were killed, and an estimated 3,100 were injured, including around 1,700 soldiers and 1,400 civilians.

In that sense, even as parts of the First Intifada were nonviolent, the violent aspects posed a major new security threat to Israel.

After the outbreak of the First Intifada, the number of courts expanded due to a massive increase in arrests and indictments. This era was one of the IDF West Bank Courts' most controversial from the Palestinian viewpoint because of these arrests and detentions, and because of an increasing number of claims that detainees were being tortured.

Statistics regarding how many Palestinians were arrested during the First Intifada vary and are notoriously politicized. Some define the Intifada as ending in 1991, others in 1993. The number of Palestinians who were arrested or who spent time in Israeli prisons has been estimated as high as 120,000 or as "low" as 57,000. ("Spent time in Israeli prison" may include Palestinians detained for questioning for a brief period and then released.)

An estimated 1,200 Palestinians were killed, with a much larger but even harder to estimate number injured. It is also unclear how many might be defined as innocent civilians versus civilians directly participating in the conflict on some level, but certainly a large number were noncombatant civilians.

Whether Israel or the Palestinians were more responsible for the violence and whether Israel overreacted or reacted properly are good questions to debate – but Israel certainly did need to respond to the concrete security situation.

However, as the Oslo Process kicked in in the mid-1990s and the area settled down for some years, arrests and detentions dropped to record lows, and most of the courthouses closed. From the 2005 IDF withdrawal from Gaza until 2019, when a new courthouse was added in Hebron, only two main courthouses existed, at Ofer and Salem, though the memories of those years still heavily impact both sides' views of the broader issues.

Important Innovations in the Courts

The IDF West Bank Courts do not operate in a void. In addition to the internal mechanisms for judicial review within the military system, almost from the beginning of the IDF administration in the West Bank, the Supreme Court of Israel extended its jurisdiction to allow appeals by Palestinians. This is true even though Palestinians are not citizens of Israel, the Supreme Court is outside the military system, and the possibility of appeal for Palestinians specifically to the Supreme Court is not required under international law (which requires only some kind of an appeal process).

Any Palestinian defendant who believes his rights were violated at any stage of the judicial process, or any NGO, can file a petition to the Supreme Court, which is much more accessible and hears many more cases than some other Supreme Courts (such as in the United States).

While there is a debate about how Israel's Supreme Court treats Palestinian issues, it is respected globally for its jurisprudence and independence. Its decisions have been cited by foreign courts, including the Supreme Court of Canada, the House of Lords in the United Kingdom, and the European Court of Justice.

The Supreme Court has also heard cases related to West Bank land disputes between Israelis and Palestinians and about the use of force by the IDF in conflict with the Palestinians. In 1999 the Supreme Court banned torture of Palestinian detainees, regardless of their actions.

The Supreme Court's authority to preside over these cases stems from the view that the security forces operating in the West Bank and Gaza Strip are public bodies, subject to the law.

Chief justice of the IDF West Bank Courts Aharon Mishnayot wrote in a 2014 article that the courts were heavily influenced by "direct absorption of norms from Israeli law into the security legislation; judicial absorption of principles that originate in Israeli law," and especially by "the close monitoring by the Supreme Court over IDF actions in the area in general, and the operation of the military courts in particular."[1]

Mishnayot notes that this attests to "a bridging of the gap" between the courts dealing with Palestinians and Israel's civilian courts.

But in addition to the availability of a Supreme Court appeals process, in 1989, a military appeals court was founded, signaling another major change to the legal system. Today, the IDF West Bank Appeals Court is also located at Ofer.

Recently, the Military Appeals Court has expanded the rights granted to defendants and detainees to be more similar to Israeli civilian law in the areas of arrests and detention. It has also increased its own independence and ability to intervene in the decisions of various IDF officials with authority over West Bank issues.

From 2004 to 2010, the process of selecting IDF West Bank Courts judges became more and more similar to the selection of civilian judges, including vetting by civilian legal experts from the Israel Bar Association.

Establishment of a Juvenile Court – The Most Significant Change

The most significant change since 2009 has been how the IDF's West Bank Courts deal with minors, with a flurry of rounds of reforms going through to strengthen minors' rights.

---

1 Aharon Mishnayot, "The Law and Jurisdiction in Judea and Samaria: Between the Current Situation and the Desirable Situation" [in Hebrew], October 2, 2014, available at https://ssrn.com/abstract=2504358.

On July 29, 2009, the IDF central commander for Judea and Samaria signed an amendment to the Judea and Samaria laws establishing a juvenile military court made up of judges who also sit on the IDF's regular Judea and Samaria Military Courts, but who have been given special training to handle cases involving minors.

Although the courtrooms and judges are the same as those for adult Palestinian defendants, in juvenile proceedings, only cases against Palestinians under the age of eighteen are heard. The 2009 reforms also included other special rules for Palestinian minor defendants, and another round of reforms took place in September 2011 and September 2014, when the defined legal age of a minor was shifted up from sixteen to eighteen. The reforms are detailed more in chapter 7.

March 2015 Reforms to Substantive Law

In March 2015, other substantial changes were made unrelated to minors. How military law regards mental states, as well as some of the penalties it uses, now resembles Israeli civilian law more closely.

One example is how the IDF West Bank Courts deal post-March 2015 with someone who intended to commit a serious crime and took almost all of the steps to get ready to commit that crime. Even if some of the steps themselves might constitute lesser crimes, the courts now deal more forgivingly with people who withdraw at the last second with their conscience kicking in.

A range of other major differences will be explored later.

Unique Aspects of the Criminal Justice Process

The IDF West Bank Courts' history, rules, and dynamics are unique. Yet, much of the "outer garb" of the criminal process, especially the functions of prosecutors and defense lawyers, is the same as in other criminal justice systems.

Security offenses handled by the courts range from violence and terror attacks to throwing stones or Molotov cocktails to lower level civil unrest. Other offenses include unlawful entry into Israel, property offenses such as theft, and even driving a car without a license.

In the West Bank, the army is part of the criminal proceedings; it performs many functions that are usually performed by the police. The Shin Bet (Israel Security Agency), an organization with similarities both to the United States' FBI and CIA, meanwhile handles interrogations in terror cases and in other cases of extreme violence.

Plea Bargains and Win Ratios

Plea bargains, in which a defendant cuts a deal admitting to some charges usually in exchange for other charges being dropped, are hotly debated. Prosecutors and courts love them, as they reduce caseloads and court costs and leave more time to try the more complex cases. Defense lawyers want whatever is the best result for their client, but sometimes view plea bargains as a blunt weapon used by prosecutors to push even innocent persons into confessing to crimes they did not commit.

The overwhelming majority of Palestinians cut plea bargains. The human rights organization B'Tselem reports that out of the 642 cases of Palestinian minors they reviewed between 2010 and 2015, 97 percent of cases were decided by plea bargain. Statistics for 2005 to 2010 are similar.

Plea bargains are also extremely common in Green Line Israel and in other countries. The same 2015 B'Tselem report says that from May 2010 to May 2011, defendants in Israeli civilian courts cut plea bargains in 76.5 percent of cases in magistrate's (lower) courts and in 85.7 percent of cases in (higher) district courts.

Critics say that plea bargains are more of a problem with the IDF's West Bank Courts. Because so many more Palestinians than Israelis are detained for extended periods, even the ones who might be innocent accept plea bargains just so they can get out of jail sooner. Defendants who admit guilt and are convicted sooner may end up being released earlier than those who fight a long trial. Even if a Palestinian wins a trial, he may, by the end, have spent more time in jail waiting to win than if he had just thrown in the towel and pleaded guilty at the start.

The IDF tends to respond that statistics comparing plea bargains and convictions with acquittal rates are not relevant without checking how many charges the prosecution dropped in the course of a plea bargain.

Even regarding the cases in B'Tselem's report, the IDF would note that in IDF West Bank Courts plea bargains, 40 percent of the original indictment charges were dropped. In other words, Palestinians achieved "partial acquittals" by using plea bargains in 40 percent of cases. B'Tselem would respond that these dropped charges were questionable in the first place, possibly inserted simply as negotiating chips, and that they lacked serious evidence to back them up.

In those few cases where there is no plea bargain, the classic part of a trial comes next with witnesses. The IDF wins most cases. Why that is exactly is a topic of heated debate. The IDF argues that it wins most cases for the same reason that prosecutions everywhere win most cases.

Most criminal law proceedings are stacked in favor of the prosecution, because the standard for bringing a case is so high that once prosecutors decide to file an indictment, they must already be convinced essentially beyond a reasonable doubt that they have a slam-dunk case. Any other attitude could lead to an embarrassing string of losses, leave actual criminals on the streets because of shoddy legal work, and set bad future precedents that could make it easier for other actual criminals to get off.

Nearly all of the prosecutors in the IDF West Bank prosecution are Jewish Israelis, with the very occasional Druze Israeli or Arab Israeli. Police prosecutors also tend to be Jewish Israelis, but their ranks may include slightly more Druze and Arab Israelis.

The vast majority of investigations of Palestinian minors in 2013, about 85 percent (560 out of 660), led to indictments. Only about 15 percent (100 out of 660) were closed. This could be a sign that the IDF prosecution carefully picked cases, only filing obvious winners, even if the police were ready to take risks on borderline cases. In cases that did go to trial, the prosecution's winning percentage was far more mixed, potentially showing that strong defense cases got a fair shake.

Critics of the IDF West Bank prosecution see it entirely differently. In their view only one word matters: occupation. The West Bank is in their view occupied territory, part of the spoils of Israel's victory in the 1967 war. The courts are an occupation court with "fake" military judges employed by the IDF "occupation" forces, who cannot possibly eliminate all of their biases toward their "enemy" the Palestinians, even if they tried. And even if they could eliminate their biases, the rules of the system are stacked against Palestinians, allowing proof into evidence that would not always be allowed in standard Israeli civilian courts or other democratic countries' courts.

Logistics

If a case leads to an indictment, it is filed in the Judea Military Court, located at the military base at Camp Ofer near Ramallah; in the Samaria Military Court, further north, near Salem; or in the new Hebron Court.

Smaller branches of these courts mostly deal with extending detentions, and are located within the Green Line in Israel. They are located near the Shin Bet interrogation facilities in the Russian Compound police station in Jerusalem and in the Shikma Prison in Ashkelon. The branches of the Samaria Court are located in the police station in Petah Tikva and in the Kishon detention facility in northern Israel.

Decisions by the two trial courts in Ofer and Salem can be appealed to the IDF West Bank Appeals Court in Ofer. Some decisions by that court can be appealed to the Israeli Supreme Court, even though that court mostly handles civilian cases.

The Israeli side claims that the Supreme Court's oversight and its occasional reversal of military court rulings are proof of a commitment to fairness and the rule of law. The Palestinian side disputes this, saying that Supreme Court oversight is simply window dressing to whitewash the system, since reversals are extremely rare.

Language Issues

One of the telltale signs that the West Bank Courts at Ofer are a universe unto themselves is the unique mix of sounds of Hebrew and Arabic – and of course, there is the constant presence of the nineteen-year-old baby-faced Israeli trans-lators, usually Druze.

Israeli civilian courts on occasion have translators. But the translation in those civilian courts could as likely be for Russian, Amharic, English, French, and Eritrean or Sudanese dialects as Arabic. Also, more Israeli Arabs speak Hebrew at a higher level and do not necessarily need translators. In any case, translators may not be rare in Israeli civilian courts, but they are definitely only present in a clear minority of cases.

In Ofer, nearly every case has a translator. In "regular" courts, the only voices you hear often are the lawyer and the witness the lawyer is questioning or cross-examining. The feel of cross-examinations is peppering questions moving forward like an unstoppable drumbeat, with pace and momentum generated by the lawyer leading the witness uninterrupted into a trap or a moment to be caught off-guard or to lose composure. Lawyer and witness: two voices.

In the West Bank Courts, there are always three voices: the lawyer, the witness, and the translator. The translator completely alters the pace and the feel of questioning and cross-examination. Every question and every answer is followed by a pause for the translation. Complex questions are nearly impossible to get through in one shot, as the long translation often loses the witness, forcing lawyers who want to be effective to break down their questions into far smaller pieces than in Israeli civilian courts.

Sometimes witnesses in civilian courts "play dumb" to try to frustrate a lawyer's pace and trap, but there are easy techniques to stop this. There really are no techniques to trap a witness who does not speak your language and really has no idea what you are asking.

Ramati is always very careful to get a senior translator, since your average translator, even after a months-long course, is still just very young, inexperienced, and not good enough at both Hebrew and Arabic. Ramati knows that especially when his Palestinian clients testify on their own behalf to try to claim their innocence and challenge the allegations of their guilt, the translator may be critical for the judge's overall sizing up of the witness's credibility.

Ramati himself had needed to pick up Arabic over the years on the fly at hearings at Ofer, during meetings with his clients and in relationships with the mostly Palestinian lawyers who represent Palestinian defendants at Ofer.

The Gilad Schalit Prisoners

Gilad Schalit was born on August 28, 1986. He was a fairly mild-mannered child and adolescent, joining the Israeli army after reaching the mandatory draft age of eighteen. A low-ranking corporal, he was not well known to anyone outside his small personal circle before the events that unfolded one dramatic summer.

Schalit was on a patrol on the Israeli side of the Gaza border on June 25, 2006. Suddenly, Hamas fighters ambushed his patrol from a hidden attack tunnel they had dug under the Gaza-Israel border, and they kidnapped him. It was a traumatic event for the people of Israel, who place an unusually strong emphasis on returning captive soldiers – even the bodies of dead soldiers. The vast majority of Israelis send their children to the army and think of the soldiers as "our children." Simply by virtue of being an IDF soldier, Schalit became the entire nation's son.

At the time of the kidnapping in 2006, there was enormous pressure on then Israeli prime minister Ehud Olmert to cut a deal with Hamas at nearly any price to return the kidnapped Schalit to Israel and his family.

Israel has a long history of trading a large number of prisoners for an adversary in exchange for one or a few Israelis or bodies of Israelis in return.

In prisoner exchange deals leading up to Schalit's capture and even after his capture, Israel released four hundred Palestinians and thirty Lebanese prisoners in 2004 in exchange for the return from Hezbollah of the bodies of three IDF soldiers and one Israeli civilian. There was a similar deal in 2008.

In March 2009, pressure continued on Israeli prime minister Benjamin Netanyahu (who replaced Olmert as prime minister), reaching its height in June 2010. That's when Schalit's family marched from northern Israel to Netanyahu's residence in Jerusalem in the center of the country, where they were joined by ten thousand supporters, in a heavily covered journey over nearly two weeks.

Finally, on October 11, 2011, Israel and Hamas announced that they had reached a deal, facilitated by German and Egyptian mediators. Israel freed a staggering 1,027 Palestinian prisoners in exchange for the release of Schalit. The actual prisoner exchange took place on October 18, 2011. Among the 1,027 released Palestinian prisoners were 110 Palestinians who were released to return to the West Bank. Controversially, many of the Palestinians who were released had "blood on their hands" relating to terror attacks against Israelis. In other words, they were not mere thieves.

When Schalit was released, despite the heavy and lopsided "price" in the prisoner exchange, it was considered by Israeli society to be one of Netanyahu's greatest victories. He made sure to greet Schalit at the Tel Nof Air Force base along with then defense minister Ehud Barak and then IDF chief of staff Lt. Gen. Benny Gantz in a nationally televised event followed by Israelis with bated breath.

By 2014, the political atmosphere surrounding the Schalit deal had already radically changed. Voices on the Israeli Right who had opposed the deal at the time (only around 20 percent of the country had opposed the deal) had gained the upper hand.

Some of those released in the deal had already returned to terrorism and committed high-profile terror attacks leading to a large amount of buyer's remorse from many in the Israeli public who had supported the deal originally.

One of the most notorious attacks occurred on the eve of the Jewish holiday of Passover on April 14, 2014: this was the drive-by killing of Israel Police Chief Superintendent Baruch Mizrahi, forty-seven, who was driving to his in-laws' home to celebrate the Jewish Passover Seder.

The failure of the July 2013–April 2014 Israeli-Palestinian peace negotiations sponsored by US Secretary of State John Kerry helped spark a spike in terror attacks, which along with the Mizrahi murder and other violent incidents shifted Israeli public opinion against future prisoner exchanges.

All of the above altered the Schalit deal from a Netanyahu political victory to a major blemish and vulnerability on his record, with his facing regular attacks from rival Israeli politicians on the Right trying to portray him as weak.

This was the security and political atmosphere present in the country on June 12, 2014, when three Jewish teenagers, Naftali Fraenkel, Gilad Shaer, and Eyal Yifrach, were kidnapped by Marwan Kawasme and Abu Aysha under the direction of Hamas mastermind Husam Kawasme.

In response to the kidnapping, Netanyahu took several aggressive steps both to find the three kidnapped teenagers and to send Hamas a message about the severity of the kidnapping. He ordered the initiation of Operation Brother's Keeper, including eleven days of the Israeli military and security forces arresting 350 Palestinians in the West Bank, including nearly all of Hamas's West Bank leadership.

A group of the Palestinians who were arrested were interrogated using aggressive enhanced interrogation measures that had not been used as much in recent years, in order to try to help locate the three Jewish teenagers.

Among the 350 arrested Palestinians were fifty-nine people who had been released in the 2011 Schalit deal. Israel said they were rearrested either for their alleged link to the murder, or as it appeared more likely over time, for their suspected general support for terror groups such as Hamas or their violation of certain more technical terms of their pardons.

Rearresting fifty-nine Palestinians prisoners who had been released during the 2011 Schalit exchange – in other words a mass rearrest operation of released prisoners even as they were not in the middle of anything violent – was not the kind of action Israel had taken after past prisoner releases. At most, Israel had on an individual basis killed or arrested a small number of individual terrorists in the middle of thwarting a terror operation after the released prisoners returned to violence.

However, the security and political ground had shifted as a result of the kidnapping of the teenagers, and regardless of the legal and moral issues with rearresting prisoners who had been released, the public was generally supportive.

On June 30, 2014, the bodies of the three Jewish teenagers were found. They had not been merely kidnapped, but also murdered. In the aftermath of all these events, Hamas and Islamic Jihad began launching what ended up being thousands of rockets at civilian centers in Israel, and from July 8 to August 26, Israel fought the 2014 Gaza War with Hamas forces.

Hamas insisted on all of the rearrested Palestinians being released before it would agree to a ceasefire and stop pummeling the Israeli home front with rockets. This catapulted the issue into the geopolitical consciousness of the world. Exhausted after fifty days from a war it did not plan and a length it was unready for, Hamas eventually quietly dropped the demand.

Next, the IDF formed a judicial commission to handle the irregular situation of considering all at once whether a group of fifty-nine Palestinians had violated their unique parole terms. The offenses the IDF presented as the basis for convicting those fifty-nine Palestinians were contact with the enemy and involvement in illegal fund transfers.

Marwan Kawasme and Abu Aysha, the kidnappers of the three boys, were eventually located and killed in a shoot-out with Israeli security forces on September 23, 2014. On August 5, 2014, Husam Kawasme, mastermind of the kidnapping, was arrested by Israeli security forces.

The following four major events are linked: (1) the release of Schalit and Palestinian prisoners, (2) the kidnapping and murder of the three Jewish teenagers, (3) the Israeli response of rearresting fifty-nine Palestinian prisoners whom it had released in the Schalit deal, including bringing them to the IDF West Bank Courts to try to return them to prison, and (4) the trial of Husam Kawasme in the IDF West Bank Courts for his hand in the murder of the three Jewish teenagers.

Following the development of these linkages is a recurring theme in understanding the story of the IDF West Bank Courts in recent years as well as the stories of our four main personalities.

Chapter 3

The Chief Prosecutor:
Maurice Hirsch

The Only Recorded Circumcision in Blumoff, South Africa

Maurice Hirsch was born in South Africa in a small village called Blumoff. His father was an engineer who moved from England to South Africa to work with Maurice's father's uncle on a farm. He met Hirsch's mother in South Africa.

Hirsch was born in 1973 and proudly said he was the only recorded circumcised Jew in Blumoff. Hirsch liked to say that being a Jew born in Blumoff earned him a name among South Africans. He told a story about meeting former Jewish Agency chairman and prominent South African Jewish community leader Mendel Kaplan years ago. "When I told him I was born in Blumoff, he said, 'Oh, you're the person I've heard about.'"

Shortly after his birth, his father finished working on the farm, and his family moved to Pretoria, where he lived until the age of eight. His mother worked for Nelson Mandela and anti-apartheid activist Saul Kramer, but later became a bookkeeper. During that period, his parents were arrested for illegal conduct and connections "with people of dark-colored skin." His family left South Africa in 1981, two weeks after being arrested and then released.

I had not asked Hirsch to tell about his early childhood or his family in South Africa. I had only asked him where and when he was born. The story about Blumoff was clearly part of Hirsch's self-narrative: he was proud to be a unique character with a unique past.

His parents' involvement with blacks fighting against apartheid in South Africa is even more interesting, since critics of Israel today try to equate Israel's control of the Palestinians in the West Bank with South Africa in the apartheid era. Hirsch commented that his mother never made that parallel, and for him it was also "never an equation to start with."

He explained, "What courts deal with and what I deal with does not in any way reflect on the idea of a small minority subjugating a tremendously large population based solely on the color of their skin."

Hirsch liked to add, "I truly believe a lot of Palestinians simply want to live their lives, raise their children like I do, make a living, and they could reasonably do that. It is only a small minority who go through the courts…and are involved in terrorism."

Once back in England, his family lived in Council Estates, in public housing. He attended Ilford Jewish Primary School. That was the first time he said he experienced antisemitism. When he was nine, local non-Jewish kids started a fight with him because he went to a Jewish school and wore a yarmulke, as required by the school. Although he currently wears a yarmulke and identifies as an Orthodox Jew, he said that at the time he was not Orthodox and did not wear a yarmulke all of the time. He merely wore it because it was a school requirement.

He said his family at the time was "traditional – we drove to an Orthodox shul [the Yiddish word for synagogue]," whereas Orthodox Jews do not drive on the Sabbath. He noted that his was the last bar mitzvah (coming of age for thirteen-year-old Jewish boys) celebrated at the synagogue, which eventually closed down and was converted into a mosque. By then, much of the Jewish population had moved to East London.

Hirsch said he left Ilford at age eleven, switching to a North London public high school, JFS, whose student population was entirely Jewish. He had to take the underground subway system to school every day.

Focused on Moving to Israel

At age thirteen, Hirsch applied for a program that "sent capable students to Israel for five months to Givat Washington outside Ashdod. I had the tremendous honor of going. At age thirteen, I fell in love with the country. I learned not a small amount of Hebrew at the time."

In high school he studied government, politics, economics, and French. At the end of high school, he came to Israel with Hanoar Hatzioni (Zionist Youth) for one year. The first five months of the program he spent in the then-developing town of Ashkelon teaching English in schools. That was when he really learned to speak Hebrew. Hirsch explained, "At the time there were no girls who spoke English." After some false starts with Israeli girls using poor Hebrew, he realized if he wanted to get to know any of the girls, he would have to improve.

Hirsch started out this story vaguely, revealing more about it after a variety of questions during which he started to play with his glasses again and eventually admitted in one of his favorite phrases, "without question," that improving his standing with Israeli girls was a big motivator for learning Hebrew.

Following that year, he went back to England and studied law at Bournemouth University. The program included two years of studies, working during the third year and further studies in the fourth year. A tremendous Thatcherite, Hirsch focused his legal studies on business law. He was influenced by a British TV program called *Capital City* about stock trading and business.

Eventually, Hirsch's parents got divorced. His father later married a non-Jewish woman and his mother married a Jewish man. Hirsch said he gets along well with both of his parents' spouses. Still, while some might move far away to avoid complex family issues, when Hirsch discussed his decision to move to Israel, he said that 80 percent of it was Zionism, 10 percent escaping the cold weather, and only 10 percent was "personal issues."

His parents themselves were "not necessarily Zionistic at all," though they were "always supportive of my making aliyah – they knew it was important to me."

Hirsch's third trip to Israel came in the summer between his first and second year of law school. He was at Kibbutz Givat Brenner for a few weeks until he "got thrown out of *ulpan* [Hebrew language class]," said Hirsch impishly. Asked what got him in trouble with "the law" in Hebrew class, he explained it was an answer he gave on a test. When asked, "Why did the teacher shout?" Hirsch's answer was "because she is a *mefageret* [moron]." He grinned ear to ear. "I was mischievous even back then."

Upon getting his diploma, Hirsch returned to Israel again on a Jerusalem fellowship run by the Orthodox outreach group Aish Hatorah: they offered a cheaper plane ticket and three weeks' lodging in a yeshiva in order to study traditional Jewish texts.

He worked during the day and found the Jewish studies classes at the yeshiva at night so interesting that he sometimes studied until around 3:00 a.m. He finished his degree in May 1996 and made aliyah in July1996 at the age of twenty-three and a half.

The Beginning of Hirsch's Army Career

Even though at age twenty-four, Hirsch was too old for compulsory service, he decided to join the IDF anyway. "I had no idea about what I was ready to be – all I wanted to do was jump out of airplanes!" he commented wryly.

But when he learned about the IDF legal division, he realized it might be an opportunity to use his legal skills. It was not an auspicious beginning. The deputy military advocate general (MAG) at the time, Yossi Telraz, wanted nothing to do with him. Telraz essentially told him, "Don't call us, we'll call you." Hirsch thought that might be it. His heart was not set on it, so he was not particularly bothered at the time.

At the end of basic training, Hirsch was sent to Bakum near Tel Aviv. Bakum is the main army base in Israel where new soldiers wait either to join their units or to meet with a human resources officer who decides which unit to send them to. The human resources officer told Hirsch he could not join the infantry since, at his "advanced" age, his obligatory army service was only another eleven months. Typical draftees who joined when they were eighteen or nineteen could join the infantry, since they still had almost three years left in their obligatory service.

The officer sent him to a second basic training, after which he returned to Bakum. He stayed there for ten days waiting for something to happen. Finally, he had a meeting with another human resources officer who told him he would serve as a regular administrative assistant office helper, filing and doing other busy work for officers.

Hirsch finally lost his patience, and his more audacious side came out in a way that determined his career for the next twenty years. He told the officer, "I won't be an office helper. I'm a lawyer, and I won't do that."

The officer said he could try to get Hirsch into the IDF legal division. He sent him to the intake division for special divisions. There he said he "met a sweet young girl who told me, 'You cannot go into the IDF legal division. For that, you need to be a lawyer, and the IDF legal division has to ask for you.'" With that, she tried to dismiss him: "Bye. We are going home now.'"

Hirsch became even more audacious. "I asked her for her name. Surprised, she asked me why. I told her I was going back to the recruiting office to tell them I would never come back because of her." Suddenly she looked very stressed, changed her tune, and gave him a form to sign on for Tzva Keva (the IDF's professional career service division), a longer commitment path, which could put him on an army career track if he excelled. Hirsch says he signed the form even though "I had no idea what Keva was!"

He signed on for three years with the IDF legal division and was sent to its offices. When he arrived, Deputy MAG Telraz saw and recognized him. Incredulously he demanded, "What are you doing here?" Hirsch played dumb, replying calmly and matter-of-factly, "The intake office sent me." Telraz was furious, storming out of his chair. According to Hirsch, the whole chair started to go with him, and it seemed that smoke was coming out of his ears.

Finally, Telraz grudgingly said, "All right, you're here, but forget about going to Keva. You won't be staying long." Telraz asked about his degree and credentials and then assigned him to the office of the Yoamash Ayosh (the Hebrew acronym for the IDF legal adviser for Judea and Samaria).

Again, Hirsch had no idea what "Yoamash Ayosh" meant or where he was being sent. He became the assistant to the IDF West Bank chief prosecutor, which at the time was part of the same unit as the legal adviser. In 2003, they became entirely separate units, with the prosecutor's offices currently located at Ofer and Salem and the legal adviser's unit near Beit El, on the opposite side of Ramallah from Ofer.

Hirsch's boss was Lt. Col. Avinoam Sharon. Sharon's original name was Paul, and, like Hirsch, he had moved to Israel from an English-speaking country, the United States. Hirsch calls Sharon "tremendously interesting," noting that he was not only a high-ranking IDF officer, but also a painter, builder, and opera singer.

Hirsch also served with other immigrants like himself, including Shlomo Politis, originally from Brazil, and Shaul Gordon, originally from the United States. As of April 2016, Gordon was chief legal adviser to the police.

After ten months in the legal division, Hirsch was brought before the committee responsible for cancelling Keva commitments, since Telraz had instructed that he not be accepted into the officer career track program. He said he was the last person to appear before the panel that day in a long line of lawyers who wanted to be released from further IDF service. It was 1998, and most budding lawyers in the program who could have made their careers with the army preferred to leave and cash in on the high-tech boom. The lieutenant colonels who ran the panel, expecting to hear the same from Hirsch, opened with the question "Why should you be released?"

This was Hirsch's second time surprising IDF officials.

"I want to stay," he told them. "I am a Zionist, and I enjoy the work." His commanders were present and backed him, saying he was contributing tremendously to the job.

Members of the panel told Hirsch, "You were the only positive person we heard, and you expressed the only semblance of Zionism." They overruled Deputy MAG Telraz on condition that Hirsch be sent to the special intense officers' course, which meant spending several months in the southern Israeli desert. He said, "Great, you're sending me to be an officer!"

He added, "I've stayed ever since."

Take-No-Prisoners Litigation

Meeting Maurice Hirsch, you are struck both by his overwhelming confidence and his unwavering belief that he is on the right side.

The story of his nervous early loss to legendary defense lawyer Avigdor Feldman shows that he was not always as confident as he is today. Yet other stories, like the ones about his experiences with antisemitism in England at a young age and about his independent adventures in Israel, show his early confidence and even audacity. This continued with his rugged individualistic approach to breaking into the IDF's officer corps and later his creative and savvy negotiating.

Hirsch's confidence is not only interpersonal – within his unit and with other senior IDF officers – but also in his take-no-prisoners style of aggressive and dramatic litigation.

He tells the story of Raed Sheikh, a Palestinian who was infamous in Israel during the Second Intifada for killing Israeli soldiers with his bare hands along with another Palestinian, Abdel Aziz Salha. Salha then rushed to a window to bathe in the praise from the crowd below of his and Sheikh's deed, as he brandished his bloodstained hands.

Hirsch describes the case against Sheikh as "rock solid." Conviction was a near certainty. But this was not enough for Hirsch. He tells how he beat down an argument from Sheikh's defense lawyer using "shtick" (Yiddish for a performance or bit).

The indictment said that Sheikh had killed an IDF soldier by beating him to death with a plastic tube. The defense lawyer rejected the theory as impractical, trying to show that it was untrue and Sheikh was innocent. Attacking the prosecution's evidence, he asked, "How can a plastic tube cause such damage?"

Hirsch started to grin again.

It just so happened that on that day, parts of the prosecution's prefab offices were being renovated. One of the prefabs was being fitted with a kitchen that included thick plastic tubing. He left the court room, cut off a piece of the thick tubing, and while no one was looking, slipped it under his desk in court. When the defense lawyer contended that plastic tubing was not strong enough to be used as a lethal weapon, Hirsch pulled out the tube and smacked it loudly on the table to show how strong and dangerous it could be.

He said he would have won the case anyway, but that his shtick had tremendous theatrical value. For Hirsch, a close win with some doubt was not enough. He sought to shoot down every argument his adversary could possibly muster. Incidentally, Hirsch also appeared earlier in his career as a prosecutor in a detention hearing for Salha.

Hirsch was not above being crafty if it could help win a case.

In a trial connected to the murderer of former minister Rehavam Ze'evi and one of the perpetrators connected to the assassination, the head of the Popular Front for the Liberation of Palestine, Hirsch argued with the defense lawyer over some new legal issues that Hirsch had not included in the indictment.

During the arguments, Hirsch lured the defense lawyer into raising some of the new issues that Hirsch himself wanted to get into, but could have been procedurally blocked from raising since he had not included them in the indictment. By getting the defense lawyer to bring them up, Hirsch later convinced the court that the lawyer had "opened the door" for him to legally add new issues into the case even though they were not in the indictment.

Such experiences have led Hirsch to his present-day role. He conducts friendly, almost chummy negotiations about potential plea bargains with the defense lawyers of accused Palestinians. Yet his approach to litigation seems warlike at times, with the goal of completely destroying his opponent's case.

But in the aftermath of the Gilad Schalit issue, Hirsch faced one of the greatest tests of his finely honed approach. Previously, in 2011, in a story that drew worldwide publicity, Hamas leaders had released the imprisoned Israeli soldier Gilad Schalit in exchange for 1,027 political prisoners. In June 2014, Hirsch launched a crusade to rearrest and revoke the pardons of fifty-nine of the Palestinians who had been released in 2011.

The Untold Story of Hirsch's National Security Law Decision

Hirsch was at a Sabbath bar mitzvah of close friends when he heard about the murders of Naftali Fraenkel, Gilad Shaer, and Eyal Yifrach.

Since Hirsch is an Orthodox Jew, he normally would refrain from using any electronic devices, including a telephone, on the Sabbath. However, the three teens had been kidnapped Thursday night, so he had arranged with one of his counterparts in one of the security agencies to call him on the Sabbath if there was an emergency, and he would know if they called that it was serious enough to be necessary to break the Sabbath prohibition on using telephones.

The two discussed arresting different people, setting the guidelines for administrative detention, which Hirsch decided about on the spot without the benefit of having gotten to hold meetings and consultations with a wider range of officials. Administrative detention is explained more in chapter 11, but briefly speaking, it includes an actual judicial proceeding but allows indefinitely detaining a suspect and does not follow standard criminal law rules or principles.

Hirsch noted with certainty that he had a firm legal strategy from the out-set. He divided his prosecutors into three different teams. One team worked on gathering information and documents. One team sat writing up requests to cancel the pardons. And one team spent a longer period of time coming up with all of the legal bases for "returning them" – Hirsch's preferred phrase for revoking the Palestinians' pardons. The third team also served as a "red team" for developing possible arguments against revoking the pardons along with how the IDF could legally respond to those defenses.

Hirsch takes "credit" for getting the Shin Bet and the Israeli government to go for canceling pardons as opposed to across-the-board administrative deten-tion. He explained that one of the individuals whom the Shin Bet asked for his approval to administratively detain had clearly breached the conditions of his release. "I then said to the security forces, this person cannot go to administra-tive detention. But we should approach the committee for canceling the condi-tional release in order to return him to prison."

Analyzing the circumstances of the discussion, he said, "Obviously the secu-rity forces hadn't thought of this option previously, or…they would naturally have brought this person with the recommendation to bring him before that same committee."

How did he make the recommendation to the Shin Bet?

Hirsch explained, "We have safe telephones in our use. A red phone…that is indeed actually red. I spoke to the security forces…on the telephone…and that is how the suggestion then traveled on."

Hirsch continued, "The next thing we hear on the subject was that the gov-ernment of Israel decides to rearrest those prisoners released in the Schalit deal who had breached their terms of release. Some sixty different prisoners were rearrested."

In Hirsch's analysis, the Palestinians were never "pardoned," they were merely conditionally released or given parole. Any violation of their conditional releases could lead to being "returned" to prison.

"Once we learned the basic legal requirements, the picture became much clearer, what our positions and arguments would be, how to tailor the arguments to align with precedents of the Israeli Supreme Court, and what the line of attack" against the requests to revoke the pardons would be, said Hirsch.

In his words, despite the controversy and the highly unique factual circumstances of essentially simultaneously rearresting fifty-nine Palestinians who had been released in a major prisoner exchange deal, "this was not a new subject. The law regarding release on parole was simple."

Hirsch noted important legal points that he tried and succeeded at winning to make a more favorable landscape, including framing the proceedings as administrative streamlined evidentiary hearings not affording a full criminal trial and allowing presenting certain classified evidence ex parte — meaning outside of the presence of the defense.

Hirsch revealed that the prosecution did not assume it would win as many of the cases as it did, in total sending fifty-two of the fifty-nine Palestinians back to serve out their sentences. Only seven Palestinians went free or were sent back for shortened sentences.

Asked how his staff reacted to the surge in their workload and the crisis situation, he said that everyone jumped in without a question, including prosecutors from the Salem base. That included his deputy for the West Bank prosecution, Inbar, who was a single mom but had family members helping her with childcare.

Hirsch said he made all key decisions fast and without consultation with his superiors, though eventually his decisions were brought before his top boss, the MAG Maj. Gen. Danny Efroni, who reviewed them. Explaining why he did not seek preapproval of his momentous national security legal policy decisions, he notes, "I have been dealing with these issues for fifteen years. I know them inside out. I don't need any further approvals."

At the end of the day, Hirsch would point out that out of hundreds of administrative detentions he approved, only four were cancelled.

Asked if he sought advice on tough policy judgment calls from his predecessor Lt. Col. Robert Neufeld, he said no, and added that Neufeld used to call him when Neufeld was West Bank chief prosecutor, because of Hirsch's prior experience in the unit.

Asked about differences between himself and Neufeld, he explained that "Robert is a product of Yahak [the legal adviser side of the MAG], where everything needs to be carefully written up as a formal memorandum. I'm more of a doer, not a writer. I'm happier as a prosecutor. I enjoy making decisions quickly."

The story of the rearrested Palestinian prisoners brings us to one of our first major crossovers between our main four personalities as Hirsch and defense lawyer for Palestinians Merav Khoury went up against each other in a clash of titans.

Chapter 4

The Defense Lawyer for Security Detainees: Merav Khoury

There is a myth that Israel is made up of only Jewish Israelis and Muslim Arab Israelis. In truth, as of December 2018 there were an estimated 175,000 Israeli Arab Christians out of the nearly total 1.9 million Israeli Arab population, within the total nearly nine million citizens in Israel. Though still a minority of the Israeli Arab population, the Christian sector is generally better educated, more integrated socioeconomically, and disproportionately located in the north of the country. Nazareth, where Merav Khoury lives and works, is unlike any other city in Israel. About 30 percent of Nazareth's seventy-six thousand residents are Christian Israeli Arabs like Khoury, with certain areas of the city being overwhelmingly Christian.

Christmas was in the air everywhere on a drive up into the hills toward Nazareth one December morning in 2014, winding through the curvy roads into Khoury's neighborhood. Pictures of Santa Claus and other Christmas decorations proclaimed the Christian-Arab identity and upbringing that distinguish Khoury's view of Israeli society and the courts from that of most Muslim Arabs. Although how this played out was certainly far more complex than could be packed into one sentence, in short, she was far less intimidated and far more comfortable mixing it up with authorities as someone who has inside understanding of how the system works.

From the outside, Khoury's office was certainly not what you would expect from one of the country's top defense lawyers. This pattern repeated itself with other defense lawyers for Palestinians: they might be doing well enough, but they are not getting hugely rich.

Walking up an alleyway alongside a moderately upscale-looking small shopping center led to another small alleyway with an unmarked entrance; up some stairs, past a small courtyard with a slightly out of place life-sized dwarf statue, was her office.

But inside was another story. The interior was very modern, clean, and even had a bit of a shine to it. In a conference room off to the left, Khoury set a laid-back and almost comical tone with a large photo of the Sopranos – the mafia television stars. Asked about the photo, Khoury made clear in her response that while the décor reflected her own quirks and appreciations of popular culture, it also represented her audacity as well as readiness to stand out and be aggressive for her clients on a level that not all defense lawyers reach.

A top Israeli Justice Ministry prosecutorial official had a similar mafia-style poster on his wall, and while he wears a smile most of the time, he is also a lawyer not to be trifled with.

Audaciously Attacking the IDF Prosecution

As mentioned earlier, Merav Khoury stands out in her field as a woman, a married (to a man who works in high tech) mother of three (ages nine, six, and ten months as of summer 2016), and an Israeli Christian Arab. But most importantly she is unique as a defense lawyer who in high-profile security cases fearlessly attacks aspects of the IDF prosecution's cases untouched by other defense lawyers for Palestinians.

Getting a Palestinian defendant acquitted in court by overcoming Palestinians' confessions induced by the Shin Bet as well as overcoming incriminating statements from other Palestinians is extremely unusual. Almost all defense lawyers for Palestinians who go to trial try to get confessions thrown out as coerced and to dismiss incriminating statements by other Palestinians as bad blood between the witnesses and the defendant. But almost none of them succeed as Khoury did.

In her first acquittal in a security case, she succeeded in disqualifying what had been presented by both the Shin Bet and IDF prosecution as a confession by the defendant as well as statements by fellow Palestinians incriminating the defendant.

Khoury did the same in a 2013 case in which a defendant had been sitting in jail for around eighteen months pending a judgment in his trial, which appeared to be an open and shut case because of a confession and incriminating statements. She did not merely get the confession and incriminating statements tossed. She essentially got the IDF prosecution to withdraw the indictment and immediately release the defendant without finishing the trial.

In a different case concerning Ibrahim Abuhara, Khoury disqualified a Shin Bet declaration labeling a group as a terror group. Once again, this not only almost never happens in IDF West Bank Courts cases, the very idea of challenging the Shin Bet on whether a group is a terror group or not would not even occur to most defense lawyers. It was in fact so surprising that it caught the IDF prosecution completely off guard.

In the Jamal Haj case (detailed in chapter 6), Khoury proved that Israel had given amnesty to a former terrorist turned moderate Fatah lawmaker. When the IDF prosecution denied the existence of an amnesty agreement, she brought in top Palestinian Authority officials – including top security official and potential eventual future PA president Mohammed Dahlan – to testify about their personal meetings with the Israeli defense minister and the Israeli head of the Shin Bet to prove the agreement's existence.

Few defense lawyers would have the audacity to think of calling such witnesses, and even fewer would actually have the reputation and connections to produce them, including their agreeing to enter an Israeli army base and testify in Israeli "occupation" courts.

In the summer 2014 cases fighting over whether fifty-nine Palestinians released in the 2011 Schalit deal and then rearrested had violated their pardons, Khoury mostly struck out by her standards. But in one case she obtained an initial acquittal in the lower court hearing the cases. Further, in six other cases she convinced the court to toss almost all of the IDF prosecution's evidence so that the lower court viewed the alleged pardon violation as warranting only a few years of prison and not a return to serve a full life sentence.

This is only a short list of some of the standout security (and often alleged terror) cases Khoury has won in her storied career, in which she has challenged nearly every aspect of Shin Bet and IDF prosecution evidence, which are normally taken for granted.

One reason for her successes could be that Khoury is unusual for her relatively moderate – or at least pragmatic – views regarding the IDF West Bank Courts. Like other defense lawyers for Palestinians, she unquestionably views the courts as illegitimate and the ideal situation as them disappearing entirely. She also feels that aspects of the IDF West Bank Courts (detaining defendants for an extended period, administrative detention, and special committee hearings for revoking pardons) are stacked against and unfair to Palestinians.

However, she views the courts as places where, in a regular trial stage and context, she has a real chance to win, sometimes even a better chance than in Israeli civilian courts. In that context, she also had a working relationship with her fiercest adversary, Hirsch, which at times even allowed some level of personal relationship to arise from their regular interactions.

Multicultural Upbringing, Lawyer of the Class

Merav Khoury was born in 1978 in the mixed Jewish-Arab city of Haifa. Her childhood was a model of coexistence.

She was the only Israeli Arab on her block of Jewish Israelis. She explained that she became part of their crowd, including culturally participating in their Jewish holidays. Unusually for an Israeli Arab child, she helped them build sukkahs (temporary outdoor huts connected to the fall Jewish holiday of Sukkot) and celebrated the Jewish spring bonfire holiday of Lag ba'Omer and other Israeli holidays.

Khoury's father died when her mother was only twenty-eight, leaving the widow to raise Khoury and her sister alone. In another time and place, the consequences of her father dying at a young age might have been different. But in her neighborhood, it meant that her neighbors fully took in her family as their own.

She attended the Catholic School in Nazareth, a special school that is one of a short list in Israel administered by the Catholic Church. She was not only mischievous in school, but "you could have called me rebellious," she said.

"In my studies I did not especially stand out because I was always unimpressed with the whole idea of tests and scores," she said. However, when she got older and the *bagruyot* (the crucial high school finishing exams) came around, she threw herself into her studies and passed all the exams with high scores.

The school was "mixed," including Christian Arabs, Muslim Arabs, and a small number of Jews from mixed marriages of Jews to Arabs. Her best friends came from these mixed-marriage families. She added that in her neighborhood she often spent her free time with Jews her age. Also, she explained that at the time the differences and physical distance between Jews and Arabs in Haifa were "barely felt."

She said that she does not have any special hobbies, though like many, she loves to sleep. Describing sleeping intensely, she explains that "this is the only time that the brain rests, or if it does not rest, at least I feel that it is not having to work."

Regarding sports, she said that as someone who grew up in Haifa and who spent much of her free time at the beach "near the rolling waves, the sounds of the flowing water and the sea," she loved swimming and the water, which "are my most calming refuge."

Khoury admitted that she smokes "like a *katar* [locomotive], no less than Maurice Hirsch." She says she would love to finish with this harmful addiction. "But I still have not found the appropriate time to do this."

Despite being acknowledged by many as among the top lawyers who practice in the IDF West Bank Courts and snag many of the highest profile cases, she added, "I am also not so perfect. In addition to the bad habit of smoking, I can be very stubborn and very frequently I cannot refocus myself" until the last minute.

Elaborating on being the "lawyer of the class" at a young age, Khoury related how she once saved her entire class from losing their class trip after a few students had vandalized a youth hostel the class was staying at during the exciting trip of the year to Eilat.

The class was staying at a hostel at Kibbutz Eilot, the southernmost kibbutz in Israel, less than a kilometer north of Israel's most southern city and international resort town of Eilat. A few students from the class were accused by the school staff of breaking a wall made of plaster from one of the structures at the hostel. The school decided that as a punishment, the entire class would be sent back to the North, essentially ending the trip for everyone.

"I remember that I stood there and acted as the defense lawyer of the specific 'accused' relating to the incident, and I argued at length before the teachers against using collective punishment," Khoury recalled.

"In the end, I convinced the administration in the North, after a long telephone call I had with them, not to cancel the trip and that whoever was suspected of breaking the wall would have to pay for fixing the plaster wall."

This story is noteworthy for several reasons. First, it shows Khoury's audacity – which is somewhat clear even when meeting her in the relative quiet of her office but jumps out at you when you see her in her element in the IDF West Bank Courts, parading and gesturing before the military judges with a confidence that few defense lawyers possess.

Next, Khoury was mentally the consummate defense lawyer from the start in advocating for her "client's" innocence. Even retelling the story decades later as an adult, she carefully referred to the wall incident and her classmates as those "alleged" and "suspected" of breaking the wall.

Finally, it is fitting that she framed the issue to her school's administrative staff as one of "collective punishment," one of the key code words in the Israeli-Palestinian conflict and a broad background claim for mistreatment of Palestinians in the IDF West Bank Courts. Even at a young age, she was offended by the idea of individuals or groups paying a penalty for the actions or faults of others in light of a bigger game surrounding the events in question.

A Young Lawyer's First Win

Khoury went on to attend law school at Shaarei Mishpat Law School in Hod Hasharon just north of Tel Aviv and just south of the city of Kfar Saba.

After graduating, she started off at the Public Defender's Office.

Eventually, she joined the office of the legendary defense lawyer Avigdor Feldman, who trained and mentored her and with whom she still has a strong relationship even after she founded her own law office.

Khoury's first acquittal, around 2003, is a story in and of itself. She represented Mohsen Aatzi of Bara Village near Kafr Qassem in the center-northeast part of the country.

Aatzi was suspected of being a member of Hamas and of gathering information about which parts of the Tel Aviv railway tracks have security cameras and which do not. The allegations of his performing surveillance were part of a very real plot by a terror cell to place a bomb on the tracks near the Tel Aviv Azrieli Mall train station. The question was whether he was really part of the plot or had been lumped in carelessly or by accident. The court accepted Aatzi's narrative of his innocence as she presented it.

Aatzi was a tailor in Azzun village in the northern Palestinian West Bank area of Qalqilya, north of Bara Village, where he employed Palestinians. Almost the whole time, he denied all the allegations against him. The one exception was in a Shin Bet written summary of one of his interrogations in which he seemed to one time admit the allegations, though he did not return to the admission.

Normally that one admission would have been enough evidence for a conviction or would at least lead to a plea bargain. The court, after Khoury's skilled work, unusually held that the Shin Bet summary did not represent what Aatzi was trying to communicate to the interrogator. Further, the court ruled that Aatzi's conduct and his indirect denial during the interrogation undermined the idea that he had confessed.

In another highly unusual move, the court accepted Khoury's argument and dismissed the statements of Palestinian workers who had incriminated him as having had improper motivations for doing so relating to an interpersonal dispute. Lawyers constantly play the "interpersonal dispute" card – or else try to discredit accusations by Palestinians against other Palestinians as a bid to please their interrogators and "buy" their freedom from whatever charges might be hanging over them – and when they do, judges usually do not give them the time of day. Attempts to take back accusations tend to be viewed cynically and as the defense lawyers and defendants simply trying to invent and change facts to get an acquittal.

But even as Khoury, like all defense lawyers in the IDF West Bank Courts, does not have a great winning percentage, she convinced the judge of Aatzi's unique circumstances in that case.

Three Different Kinds of Khoury "Wins" in Security Cases

First Case: Invalidating False Confessions and Testimony

Three additional major cases expressed the different types of wins that Khoury had obtained, each with a different unusual line of attack on evidence presented by the IDF prosecution and the Shin Bet.

The first was a 2013 case in which, as in her first acquittal in 2003, she succeeded in getting the Palestinian defendant's confession and incriminating statements from other Palestinians thrown out. This case is worth revisiting even though her technique was similar to the 2003 case: the highly unusual interaction between Khoury and the IDF prosecutor reveals a shocking story within the courts and highlights unexpected aspects of the defense lawyer-prosecutor relationship.

The defendant had been sitting in jail for over a year pending a judgment in his trial, normally a sign of a slam dunk for the prosecution. And it probably would have stayed that way had the defendant and his family not transferred the case from the original lawyer to Khoury.

Khoury explained that her predecessor had agreed to the defendant being detained until the end of the trial without reading or even making copies of the evidence for himself. Eventually the family of the defendant called her to take over. The first thing she did was to gather, photocopy, and meticulously review all of the evidence.

Asked whether her reputation and the IDF prosecution's greater respect for her was what turned the case, she responded that "it is not a matter of influence, it is a matter of reading the evidence."

While viewing the evidence, she saw that there was a confession in the file stating specifics about the Palestinian defendant taking part in a shooting terror incident. This obviously did not help his case. But she continued to review the evidence and found the statements of other Palestinians who had supposedly incriminated her client as having conspired with them as part of the shooting attack.

Most lawyers would stop at this point, weighed down by the evidence, and leave the case sitting, as the original lawyer did, or cut a plea deal.

Khoury dug deeper.

She found that all of the Palestinians confirmed that they had been involved in the shooting, but not a single one of them mentioned her client as being involved. In fact, some of the Palestinian witnesses who supposedly had incriminated him along with themselves even explicitly stated that they did not know who he was.

According to the laws of evidence that apply in the Israeli civilian courts, the IDF's West Bank Courts and most Western democracies, a confession on its own cannot stand as the sole basis to obtain a conviction. An additional confirming piece of evidence, such as an incriminating statement from another witness, is needed to combine with a confession to obtain a conviction. This stems from the long pre-democracy history of non-democratic regimes torturing defendants to get confessions – not caring whether they were true or not – simply to quickly tie up cases.

Even in democracies, the incentive to get a confession, true or not, at all costs, has led to police in many countries violating the rights of defendants. But with a rule that says such a confession is not enough, the theory is that innocent defendants are saved from their falsely or improperly obtained confessions. Also, police are generally discouraged from seeking untrue confessions, as they know those confessions will not be enough for a conviction.

It became clear to Khoury that the "additional confirming evidence" did not exist in this case, as the supposedly incriminating statements did not actually incriminate her client, with some even explicitly suggesting he had not been involved.

With this legal ammunition in hand, Khoury went to visit the defendant in prison. She asked him why he had lied in the interrogation and confessed to participating in a shooting attack that he had not been involved in. He started to weep. He described his hard life in a small home with nine brothers, with a disabled father and a mother who worked as a cleaning lady.

Her client explained that he thought that if he confessed to something, he would be jailed, which would save money for his family, who would no longer have to support and feed him. Further, he expected that he would get a salary from the Palestinian Authority during the time he was jailed as part of its policy to take care of and celebrate the perseverance of Palestinian prisoners.

Khoury says she immediately called a supervising IDF prosecutor on the case and requested a meeting, in which she laid out before him the state of the evidence in the case as she had unraveled it. She also shared with him what the defendant had told her about giving a false confession and his reasons.

At first, the IDF prosecutor seemed to brush off her findings as pie in the sky or an invented sob story, which many Palestinian defense lawyers try to throw at them, but which they often find is not grounded in the evidence on file. *What do Palestinians have to lose lying to an occupation court to try to get their freedom?* the IDF prosecution usually thought. Still, the IDF prosecutor requested some time to review the case, since one of his junior prosecutors and not he himself had filed the indictment.

Then something very unusual happened.

After only a few days, he called back. Not only did he tell her that she was right, but relating to her as someone he had an ongoing relationship with, he admitted total embarrassment. He said that he did not understand how this case had ever even led to an indictment.

Next, he went further. Asking Khoury almost as a friend, he said he was in a pickle, because he had a person who had been sitting in jail for eighteen months without any justification. The public embarrassment both in court and otherwise could be immense. He asked her how he could get out of this situation without fully airing the dirty laundry with the judge and in public generally.

Khoury said her answer to him was clear: release him from jail immediately.

As things stood, the defendant did not even have another hearing scheduled for a few months and would have just continued to sit in prison waiting for a hearing to inform the court about the new evidence.

Speaking on a Wednesday, Khoury explained to the supervising IDF prosecutor that she was ready "to help" only if he agreed to move up the hearing to the soonest possible date, the upcoming Sunday (in Israel the workweek runs Sunday to Thursday).

She said her client would also agree to admit to a tiny minor offense (not to the serious shooting offense of which he was accused) to justify for the IDF that he had been in prison, on condition that there be no suspended sentence and no fine. This might leave the judge with some questions about why the IDF prosecution was suddenly pulling the bigger case against the defendant, but would not be nearly as bad as the judge learning that the defendant had been in prison for eighteen months for no reason.

As Khoury told it, her out-of-court agreement with the IDF prosecutor went through. The defendant came to court that Sunday having no idea why he was there and was stunned to get released on the same day.

Summing up her reputation and influence in dealing with the IDF prosecution, she said, "When the prosecutor knows that there is a defense lawyer in front of him who knows a thing or two about the law, he will do all he can to check things and to do damage control. But it is not a question of influence."

Second Case: Calling the Shin Bet on Not Doing Its Homework

Part of what makes Khoury unique is her willingness to challenge "facts" and "evidence" put forward by the IDF prosecution and the Shin Bet – even from the most "holy" and normally unquestioned sources.

One tactic she tried and succeeded with was attacking security assessments, which IDF prosecutors never needed to defend and were totally unprepared to explain. There were a range of expected defenses that most Palestinians' defense lawyers tried, and IDF prosecutors were trained rigorously to defend against these. But they tended to relate to specific facts in their case, not to disagreeing with basic Israeli security assumptions underlying a case.

In other words, defendants liked to proclaim their innocence to a crime by saying "I didn't do it" or "I'm not a member of an affiliate of Hamas." They never said "the group you say works with Hamas has nothing to do with Hamas" and tried to beat the Shin Bet and IDF prosecution in their area of expertise. This brash or audacious tactic was what she threw at the IDF prosecution with Ibrahim Abuhara on February 18, 2013, in an appeal hearing before Judge Lt. Col. Zvi Lekach with wild and sudden unexpected twists.

In the IDF West Bank lower court, Judge Menachem Liberman sentenced Abuhara to twenty-eight months in prison for being a member of and holding an officer role in an illegal organization. Khoury explained that Abuhara's lawyer at the lower court allowed the IDF prosecutor to submit newspaper articles into evidence to prove that the group he was accused of being a member of was an illegal group. This, despite that newspaper articles are generally not considered real evidence, as they are often based on second-hand reporting and do not need to observe legal standards for evidence. But if prosecutors submitted something as evidence and the defense did not object, it could make it in.

From the outset of this appeal, Khoury put the IDF prosecution on the defensive. She told Judge Lekach that the IDF, the Shin Bet, and the lower court all made the same mistake. They all leaned on a general accusation that Abuhara was a member of an organization whose name sounded an awful lot like the outlawed and sometimes violent Popular Front for the Liberation of Palestine.

Almost comically, Khoury explained to Lekach that there were at least six different groups with names sounding like the PFLP to untrained and undistinguishing Israeli ears, all of which were different and should not be lumped together. One was the Popular Front for the Liberation of Palestine, another the Democratic Popular Front for the Liberation of Palestine and another the Popular Front for the Liberation of Palestine General Command. Khoury said that Abuhara's group was not the infamous and well-known PFLP, but one of the lesser known smaller groups. Next she slipped in that though the particular group was declared illegal by the Shin Bet in 1987, the group has not been militarily active since, and the security agency had not updated its assessment of the group in twenty-seven years.

Now flustered, the IDF prosecutor started to throw out half-baked improvised arguments. He contended that the rule should be that once a group was declared illegal, it should remain that way until it proved it had changed. Next, he added almost as an afterthought that the presumption from a declaration from 1987 was "living – it is not all that long ago." Finally, he added that the group was still declared an illegal group within Green Line Israel and that this would tend to prove the group was still engaged in illegal activities.

But all of these arguments constituted a slender reed.

The general rule was that to declare a group illegal in order to convict and sentence a defendant, information on the group's activities needed to be updated and declared within the West Bank specifically. Green Line Israel was a different judicial zone, often in ways that Palestinians did not like, but in this case to Abuhara's advantage.

All three of these arguments fell apart quickly under scrutiny, leaving one real argument for the IDF prosecution to fall back on. "It cannot be," he said, "that the expert opinion of security authorities that a group is illegal applies in Israel and not in the West Bank." In that spirit, the IDF prosecutor then cited a string of cases of other defendants who were convicted based on a similar Shin Bet expert opinion.

At that moment, Khoury pulled the rug out from beneath what was left of the façade of the IDF prosecution's argument. "There is no expert from the Shin Bet coming to testify about the group's dangerousness.… What could be easier for the prosecution than to just refer to other indictments and convictions" in similar situations, though no Shin Bet expert had testified in those cases either.

This was the crux.

The IDF prosecution was saying that the Shin Bet is the eight-hundred-pound gorilla whom no one can question when it comes to security issues: No one had questioned the Shin Bet's characterization of this group in past cases, so why should it be questioned now? The prosecution was also effectively daring Judge Lekach to overlook or maybe even overturn a long line of legal precedents about defining illegal groups and terror groups.

Khoury was providing a simple and thoroughly disarming retort. If the Shin Bet or military intelligence thought the group was dangerous, why weren't they there in court to testify in the way that courts regularly run, based on physical witnesses and not stale pieces of paper that cannot be cross-examined?

She added that she had seen cases where the head of military intelligence himself showed up to testify. So what if lazy defense lawyers and courts in other cases had let the issue slide – they should not have done it there, and she was not going to do it here.

The sword was turned on its wielder: the argument of the security forces' expertise now showed up the deficiency of the prosecution's case. Rather than proving the group's dangerousness, the 1987 ruling that the IDF prosecutor had invoked merely exposed the fact that no security expert was showing up in court to give updated and informed testimony.

Suddenly there was no case at all: the Shin Bet had not kept up with the group, which might not be illegal, and even if it was, the security forces had cruised for years on past data and failed to do their homework to make the case.

Khoury had caught them in the act.

Now the IDF prosecutor finally made a rare admission – "I don't know why [an update from the Shin Bet on the group] has not happened." He immediately recovered to explain the rationale and spoke about the group's connection with martyrs. But it was too late.

To hammer the nail into the coffin for the case, Khoury popped in and said, "*Martyrs* refers to any man who did not die naturally – it's meaningless." Her point was that the IDF prosecutor's discussion about the group's involvement with martyrs based on equating "martyrs" with terrorists was just another example of lazy and unusable logic.

What happened in court at this point is being made public only now for the first time.

For a few key moments, what occurred disappears from the official transcript, though Khoury confirmed it. In a "sidebar," the judge calls the lawyers up to his bench and quietly speaks to them when there is something extra sensitive to say. Such conversations are meant to be off-transcript, and neither the translator nor anyone else in the courtroom can hear them anyway, since the conversations are essentially whispers.

Blandly, the transcript just says there is a break and that afterwards, seemingly out of nowhere, the IDF prosecutor reported to the court, "After advising with my commanders, we have decided to accept the defense's appeal of the sentence such that he will be freed today."

What happened between Khoury's head-on assault on the IDF prosecution – which seemed to be slowly withdrawing, but also still trying to hold its ground – and this total surrender? According to Khoury, what the transcript did not say was that Judge Lekach essentially upended Judge Liberman's ruling, turning to the IDF prosecution and offering two options. "Either you and I can consider the issue for about a week, at the end of which I will almost certainly acquit Abuhara, and my decision will have the effect of making this group no longer illegal. Or you can just let him go right now, and I will not issue a ruling about the group," Khoury said Judge Lekach told the IDF prosecutor.

There was a break. The prosecutor spoke with his supervising commander.

Abuhara was released that day in record time.

Third Case: Sending Schalit Deal Releasees Back to Jail

In some ways, the revoked pardons of Palestinians released in the Schalit prisoner exchange were Khoury's most impressive accomplishment, while in some ways they were a great failure – certainly the way she saw them. She felt that her efforts were a "highly disturbing failure" in the cases of fifty-nine Palestinians (most of whom she represented) who were released as part of the 2011 Schalit deal, but were then rearrested in June 2014 during Operation Brother's Keeper.

As mentioned in chapter 2, the massive operation leading to hundreds of arrests of Palestinians in the West Bank came following the horrifying kidnapping and murders of Jewish teenagers Naftali Fraenkel, Gilad Shaer, and Eyal Yifrach. Among the hundreds arrested were the rearrested fifty-nine Palestinians.

Out of dozens of releasees whose pardons were on the chopping block, Khoury in all narratives lost a vast majority of the cases. In one case in which I had been told by Hirsch that she had "won" an acquittal, Khoury said the case reached the Israeli Supreme Court on appeal from the IDF West Bank Appeals Court. She said that her appeal was rejected as well as her request for a broader panel of Supreme Court justices to hear the issue. Khoury said that the same result occurred with seven other Palestinian Schalit releasees who were rearrested.

Regarding the numerous Schalit-Palestinian cases she handled in the context of the IDF West Bank Special Pardon Commissions, she said she only succeeded in convincing the commissions in one case to allow the pardon to stand. In the other cases, the pardons were revoked and the Palestinians sent back to prison.

She also said that there were six additional cases in which she convinced the commissions that the evidence presented did not prove that the releasee had committed a crime. Rather, at most that he had violated a narrow technical issue within the pardon. As a result, in those six cases, the commissions did not send the releasees back to prison to fulfill their original life sentences. Instead, they sentenced them only to a few years of prison. But being sent back to prison for a few years was not the same as a straightforward release.

When I had been told that she had won seven cases, these six were probably what Hirsch was thinking of as six of the seven. In other words, Hirsch and many on the IDF side argue that the defense has won and the prosecution has at least somewhat lost, whenever some charges are dropped or the prosecution seeks a long jail sentence and only obtains a short one.

In contrast, Khoury viewed sending any of these men back to jail after they were promised they could start new lives as a major defeat. She had also been frustrated at the pace of the proceedings, since in her view all of the fifty-nine Palestinians had been wrongfully imprisoned since June 2014.

Prior to being released in the prisoner exchange, Hamza Abu Arkoub was convicted of firing on and murdering Shlomo and Mordechai Odesser as they drove in their truck on July 30, 2002. He was sentenced to over two life terms in prison and would go back to serving those terms if the court held he violated his pardon.

Prior to being released in the prisoner exchange, Ashraf Rawi was convicted of the murders of Behor Hajaj, his employer at Moshav Kfar Yavetz, in 1992, and Air Force St.-Sgt. Gitai Avisar in 1993. He was also sentenced to two life terms in prison and would go back to serving those terms if the court held he violated his pardon.

"My expectation anyway was that the commission would reject all of the requests [for cancelling the pardons] of the prosecution since the requests, at the end of the day, were based on intelligence evidence from which one could learn that the prisoners received 'compensation' funds from Hamas," said Khoury.

"A large number of the prisoners were imprisoned before the law passed which prohibits receiving funds from Gaza and before the Hamas-related association Al-Nur was declared an illegal organization. It is unclear if [the released prisoners] knew about the prohibition on the issue," Khoury added.

Moreover, "the state knew that this was the custom, and it was obligated to give a specific warning regarding this issue at the time of their release and not to 'place an obstacle before a blind person,'" Khoury said in an ironic reference to Jewish religious law.

In addition, she explained that "they did not use any of the funds that they received for terror purposes or for aiding terror. Rather, they used the funds to start a new life after many years behind bars. I claim that to the extent that none of the funds were used to perpetrate terror or to aid terror, there was no basis to view the receipt of funds, in the circumstances which were described, as a violation of the release conditions or as committing an offense that justified sending them back to serve their full sentences." She also said that the state's accusations lacked all specifics and in some instances made no sense, accusing releasees who were lifelong Islamic Jihad operatives of collaborating with Hamas – for whom they would never work.

Some of the defendants, such as Khadar Raadi, also pleaded with the court, even coming close to tears talking about opening new bakeries and businesses, marrying new spouses, and having new children. They exclaimed that they would never jeopardize their new lives after having spent so long in prison. Raadi also mentioned he held meetings with supervising security officers "Captain Rami" and "Captain Samir" whenever he was supposed to, that they always complimented him on observing the rules, and that none of them ever hinted he was in trouble.

It was highly unusual for the chief prosecutor himself to argue these hearings. Usually, junior prosecutors handled hearings under his instructions while he managed behind the scenes. But Hirsch personally argued many of the Schalit cases and went "all in" to win. As usual he hit back with intensity. Like Khoury, he felt that he was one of the rulers of the courtroom and had no fear.

He stated that her claims were misplaced and that they misjudged the special proceeding by trying to superimpose standard criminal law concepts. The head IDF prosecutor explained that, as a general matter, in criminal proceedings, defendants' defenses arise from their rights as individuals, including a presumption of innocence. In contrast, he noted, all of the Palestinians here had already been convicted of serious security crimes and sentenced to long prison terms. Hirsch said that these Palestinians did not have standard criminal defenses or rights, since they were only free as a result of a pardon, and that the only question before the court was whether they had violated their obligations to the state under their pardons.

In other words, Hirsch said that the rearrested Schalit releasees had fewer rights than regular defendants. They were not innocent until proven guilty. They had already been found guilty of grievous crimes. Out of grace and to achieve other national interests, Israel had freed them early, and they could only remain free if they were careful not to offend that grace by one iota. To Hirsch, Khoury's arguments that these prisoners should have the rights of normal defendants or be released because they had been told they would get to live new lives ignored the very conditional context in which their new lives had been granted to them.

Addressing Khoury's arguments about the releasees lacking any criminal intent in receiving funds related to Hamas, Hirsch pounced again. He said that accepting such funds knowing that the source was Hamas as well as earlier statements by releasees such as Khader Raadi at his initial trial showed that he and others had never changed their ways, had violated their pardons, and should be sent back to prison.

The three judges pounded Hirsch with questions about whether the state was unfairly punishing these Palestinians because of other interests relating to the state's anger at Hamas for orchestrating the kidnapping of the three boys in June 2014. The judges were especially concerned about alien motivations intervening in light of there being no smoking gun of actual military terror activity.

Hirsch responded that security in the West Bank had deteriorated, including the kidnapping. He added that a deterrent message needed to be sent to Hamas and that Israeli Supreme Court precedent allowed arresting persons for violating their pardons even years after the violation. The reason for the timing of the arrest was legally irrelevant.

In a fascinating defense, Hirsch was all but admitting that Khoury was right about the state's mixed motivations. He was essentially admitting, without saying so explicitly, that the state would probably not have rearrested the fifty-nine Palestinians if not for the killing of the three Jewish teenagers in June 2014.

And yet he was saying that even if that were true, it just did not matter. As long as the state had a technical basis to rearrest the releasees for violating aspects of their pardons, however minor, additional motivations the state had were just not relevant.

In a round of decisions on the Schalit cases in December 2014, the court did note Khoury's arguments, but it sentenced Muhammad Tzalach and Abd Taami to return to serve their full life sentences and Imad Mousa to return to serve his original prison sentence of twenty-four years and eight months.

Responding, it legally justified declining to allow Khoury to see the secret evidence. It wrote that Israeli legislation permitted the court and even parole boards in Israel to hear secret evidence without the defense present, provided that a paraphrase of the secret evidence was given to the defense. The court noted that the defense did receive a paraphrase as required.

Defense lawyers such as Khoury say that paraphrased evidence is just a way to whitewash the problematic procedure, as it does not really give them a chance to properly respond to the prosecution's allegations. The prosecution always responds that the defendants are not even really "defendants," they are convicted prisoners who were conditionally pardoned. They say this means secret evidence can be used against the defendants even if it could not be in a trial where they still held the presumption of being innocent until proven guilty.

In analyzing the secret evidence, the IDF prosecution found that despite Muhammad Tzalach's and Abd Taami's denials, they had illegal connections and intentions regarding funds that Hamas transferred to them or to relatives. The secret evidence regarding Imad Mousa, for example, contained no claims about terror funds. But despite Mousa's denials, the court again found that his meetings with terror group members were not merely for catching up with old friends, but had connections to terror purposes.

Basically, the court found the secret evidence compelling. Strangely, it seemed to sidestep the central issue of whether the arrests were unfair revenge for populist political reasons. It simply said that its authority was limited to judging whether the defendants had fulfilled or violated the conditions of their release.

The court did not believe it could look broadly at whether the state had acted in good faith. This is in contrast to the Haj case, where Khoury proved that Israel had given amnesty to a former terrorist turned moderate Fatah lawmaker, and ironically, the final ruling was exactly the opposite. Essentially the IDF West Bank Appeals Court ruled that Haj should be released specifically because the state had arrested him in bad faith.

Why did the Schalit amnesty cases come out so differently than the Haj amnesty case?

There are some obvious non-legal reasons that could impact the law. In the Haj case, one amnesty recipient was in play as part of a whim of the Shin Bet or an accident. Haj was also a Fatah activist, meaning part of the Palestinian faction that recognizes and is recognized by Israel and is officially committed to nonviolence, though the United States and Israel have butted heads with Fatah over incitement.

Also, in general Fatah-Israel relations at the time were still more hopeful about possibly returning to peace talks, and that was the basis of the general amnesty agreement.

Israel has generally viewed the 2011 Schalit deal it cut with Hamas as having been made under duress. Hamas was not offering peace. There was no coexistence on the table. Hamas had launched its operation on June 25, 2006, and kidnapped Schalit. Israel had been trying to get him back for years.

A "standard" prisoner exchange would be one for one. Hamas, like Hezbollah, was using Israel's commitment to return its soldiers as blackmail to get over a thousand Palestinian prisoners freed.

In contrast to the Schalit prisoner exchange, in June 2016, Israel cut a deal with Turkey in which it would pay around $20 million compensation to the families of the Turkish IHH Humanitarian Relief Foundation activists who were killed by the IDF in a conflict on the *Mavi Marmara* flotilla in May 2010. Israel viewed the IHH activists as terrorists or at least as combatants. It also argued its soldiers killed them in self-defense when they attacked IDF personnel who were trying to commandeer the ship to prevent it from breaking Israel's Gaza blockade. If so, why was Israel paying their families money? It was a humanitarian gesture as part of a deal with many elements, which also included normalization with Turkey in business, a return to exchanging ambassadors, and other measures.

Israel is not the first state to trade something extra to get normalization and pursue other national interests. But the Hamas deal had no elements of coexistence. It was merely a blatantly unfair blackmail-style prisoner exchange. Israel was committed to following the deal to the letter of the law, nothing more. Violating the spirit of the deal held no downside.

If violating the spirit of the amnesty agreement with Fatah hurt attempts at future coexistence, violating the spirit of a deal with Hamas perhaps just made it less likely that Hamas would try to kidnap Israeli soldiers and attempt the same blackmail move.

This context was also important from a moral perspective, as Israeli Supreme Court Justice Elyakim Rubinstein ruled on September 8, 2014, on a procedural appeal from decisions involving seven Palestinians whose Schalit pardons were revoked. Rubinstein wrote that the Palestinians' "freedom is a result of extortion of the State of Israel by a terror organization to bring about the release of the kidnapped soldier Gilad Schalit." Incidentally, in a decision on December 3, 2015, in a parallel case of Palestinians whose pardons from the Schalit exchange were revoked, Rubinstein criticized the pardon-revocation process.

While again supporting the revocation of the specific pardons in question, Rubinstein said that the IDF West Bank Courts judges should have had more discretion about what kinds of issues and questions of justice they could consider in the revocation cases.

He said that the current rule limiting the judges to looking at the narrow question of whether the pardons were technically violated, absent broader considerations of justice, might even disproportionately harm the prisoners' fundamental rights to freedom.

So if one of the factors in analyzing the Haj case was whether Israel was acting in good faith and within the spirit of the deal, with the Schalit cases of Palestinians whose pardons were revoked, the question was much more technical about whether Israel could claim it followed the letter of the law.

Since Israel could claim some violation of the pardon, however small, by all or most of the Palestinian releasees, it could also claim it had the right to revoke the pardons. This was despite Hamas's and Israel's more general understanding that it would only actively try to revoke pardons of those who returned to terror operations.

It was clear that, whatever additional terror activities might be alleged in "intelligence evidence" that was not admissible in a standard trial court, none of the fifty-nine rearrested Palestinians were being accused of a full return to terror in open court. This was demonstrated by the fact that Ziad Awawde, also released in the Schalit deal, was not part of the pardons committee process and had been separately and newly indicted in June 2014 for the terrorist murder of senior police intelligence official Baruch Mizrahi on Passover Eve 2014. Awawde shot and killed Mizrahi while he was driving with his family to visit other family members. In other words, anyone who had committed real new terror actions was getting separately indicted, not just a pardons revocation process.

There were also factual arguments about whether Haj had even committed any technical violation of his amnesty agreement. But in any event, the IDF West Bank Courts clearly cared far more about enforcing even the spirit of Haj's Fatah-negotiated agreement than it did with the Palestinians whose Hamas-negotiated Schalit-deal pardons were revoked.

The above cases, along with the Haj case, showed that a highly talented lawyer such as Khoury could win in rare cases in the IDF's West Bank Courts by daringly challenging the facts, witnesses, and presumptions of the Shin Bet and the IDF prosecution. But they also showed how far one needed to go to turn the courts against the IDF prosecution and revealed that wherever the merits of the law might lie (something difficult for the outside observer to know, since only the judges viewed the classified intelligence evidence), politics and unusual procedures could make it significantly harder to win even for a superstar like Khoury.

This is not to say that Khoury's narrative that the Schalit releasees' pardons should have been allowed to stand is the right one. However, there is no question that the forces pulling at security cases that Khoury handles go far beyond the forces that regular courts face.

Chapter 5

The Chief Justice:
Aharon Mishnayot

Early Years, Yeshiva, and the Lebanon War

We have heard the life stories of IDF Lt. Col. Maurice Hirsch and defense lawyer for Palestinians Merav Khoury. What about former West Bank Courts chief justice Aharon Mishnayot, who made the famous ruling to release Jamal Haj from custody in recognition of his Shin Bet–granted amnesty?

Mishnayot was born in the Israeli city of Lod in the center of the country, near Ben-Gurion Airport, in 1959. Early on, his parents moved to Petah Tikvah, close to the Mediterranean coast and the Tel Aviv corridor. Mishnayot grew up going to Modern Orthodox religious public schools where boys and girls learned separately, eventually attending the Oranit School, and in high school the Sha'alvim school from 1972 to 1976, near where the centrally located city of Modiin stands today.

In his early years, Mishnayot was not as mischievous as Hirsch. Pressed hard repeatedly to come up with something risky or ill-advised he did as a child or a teenager, the best he could muster was traveling without school permission from Sha'alvim to Jerusalem to buy falafel. His other "crime" that he could remember was leaving the Sha'alvim campus without school permission to view IDF maneuvers on Independence Day. In both cases Mishnayot was careful to cover his tracks and was not caught.

From 1976 to 1982, Mishnayot studied Jewish law at two leading yeshiva institutions for Jewish studies: first at Mercaz Harav Yeshiva and then at the Gush Etzion Yeshiva as part of the Hesder program combining Jewish studies with Israeli army service. Mishnayot says that he was highly influenced by his studies at Gush Etzion, including some influence on his thinking as a judge.

Speaking in August 2015 (while he was retired from the IDF and before his April 2016 appointment as a Beersheba District Court judge), he told me, "I will explain immediately. Whoever is familiar with the approach of Rabbi [Aharon] Lichtenstein [a major religious-Zionist rabbi], who passed away a few months ago, knows about the openness, the wide perspective to weigh a priori all of the factors…to analyze all of the possibilities, and from that to find the correct answer."

Continuing, he said that besides finding the correct answer, it was also important "to be aware of other possibilities. The ability to see all things from different perspectives is for sure a tool that I acquired, and I hope that I use it to this day. It is a tool that I worked on during my studies at Yeshivat Har Etzion…and it is definitely something that helped me as a judge, to understand both sides, and in the end to find a balance between them. But first the ability to properly understand both sides is definitely a path which I started on at the yeshiva."

Asked about the specific impact, and if the openness to two different sides he was referring to applied to disputes between Israelis and Palestinians, he said it did. "The liberal position to understand the other side, to be open to the other side, to be familiar with what distresses the other side…is what I do as a judge today. When a case comes before me, I know how to evaluate, I hope I know how, in order to better understand what the prosecution says, what the defense says, to see the issues in a broader picture."

Another chapter in Mishnayot's life was his service from 1979 to 1982 in the IDF's tank corps. Despite his later rise to the top of the IDF's judicial and legal establishment, his initial obligatory IDF service had no connection to the legal department. During his service, Mishnayot fought in the First Lebanon War in 1982, including in the June 10 battle of Sultan Yacoub in which Israel lost eight tanks and thirty soldiers, including his close friend Zachary Baumel, and which was generally viewed as the product of a major intelligence failure.[2]

---

2   The body of Zachary Baumel, missing in action for thirty-seven years, was located by Russian forces in Syria and returned to Israel, where he was at last laid to rest with full military honors in Mount Herzl Cemetery in Jerusalem on April 4, 2019.

With that clash with Syrian Arabs in his background, many might be concerned that it would be impossible for Mishnayot to avoid carrying this baggage into the courtroom and that it could express itself in bias against Palestinian Arabs. Yet Mishnayot said that his open wounds from the 1982 Lebanon War, unlike his time studying at Gush Etzion, "don't have any impact at all" on how he has ever conducted himself as a judge. "War is war, each side does what it needs to do," he asserts, essentially saying that he did not even hold a specific grudge against the Syrians he fought against, as a soldier's job on both sides is to fight.

Generally, Mishnayot expressed more sadness about the battle than anger. He added hopefully, "There shouldn't be more wars," and in his typical understated fashion, "Wars are not happy events."

Lawyer and Junior Judge

From 1982 to 1986, Mishnayot studied law at Hebrew University in Jerusalem. Discussing his experiences with Palestinians, he said he had few interactions with them until he was an adult, when he worked as a law clerk for Jerusalem District Court judge Zvi Tal on Salahadin Street in eastern Jerusalem in 1986. He would sometimes walk from the Lion's Gate of the Old City through eastern Jerusalem to his office on foot, and had routine, everyday contact with Palestinian vendors there. Although this generally felt normal, there was one incident in which he felt someone was following him, after which he stopped walking to work through east Jerusalem.

However, this was in 1986, before the First Intifada, which ran from 1987 to 1991. So even in that instance, Mishnayot said he was not worried about nationalist-motivated violence against him as a Jew as much as he was about the particular person who was following him having non-ideological criminal motivations to rob him (the eastern Jerusalem areas he had been walking through were less upscale neighborhoods with serious crime issues, similar to any urban area with lots of crime).

From 1987 to 1990, Mishnayot worked at the law firm of Holtzer and Schechter in Jerusalem while also studying for and obtaining a second and advanced degree in law from Hebrew University. He rejoined the IDF in 1990, this time as a lawyer. From 1990 to 1996, he served in the Office of the Legal Adviser for the West Bank, reaching the middle management rank of major.

This was the first time that he came into close contact with Palestinians over explosive political issues, such as Israeli-Palestinian disputes over land, and sat in a position of authority over them. During his years in the IDF West Bank Legal Adviser's Office, Mishnayot said he came into close contact with many Palestinians who were "poor and downtrodden." He commented that the land issues he dealt with really impacted the day-to-day lives of Palestinians. He was "involved in reviewing planning for hundreds of villages' layouts all over Judea and Samaria, with questions such as how much can they build [as well as] with dealing with illegal building by Palestinians."

Mishnayot said he would hear arguments by Palestinians whose structures had been designated as illegal before he would make decisions about demolitions and that he "tried to reduce the harm on both sides. To destroy someone's house is not *na'im* [pleasant] or a cause for happiness." On the other hand, he said that "we have laws, we need to maintain the laws. What can we do? There were also demolition orders against Jews, but they were mostly against Palestinians. Sometimes we annulled" the demolition orders as a result of arguments made by Palestinians at the hearings.

A continuous theme with Mishnayot and other IDF officials is a strong desire to shield themselves from criticism by saying they focus only on the objective law and do not deal with politics. Critics say that the law itself is political and many of its accepted interpretations are political, which could make ignoring that political influence and acting as if the law is objective a political decision in and of itself. On the other hand, there have been seemingly clear cases in which Bedouin groups were offered substantial investments in critical infrastructure, but refused due to what the Israeli side viewed as politics, not wanting to let Israel look good for helping them.

As an adult, Mishnayot lived in Maaleh Adumim, in a part of the West Bank just outside Jerusalem, eventually moving from Maaleh Adumim to Efrat in the Gush Etzion bloc of the West Bank in 1993. He has lived in Efrat ever since. Explaining his choice to live in Efrat, he noted education and social reasons as well as that he had studied Jewish law in Gush Etzion around twenty years earlier. He had also thought about the fact that Efrat is in the West Bank. He explained that he had intentionally decided to live in a place thought of as part of the larger and more central Jewishly populated West Bank blocs that would always remain part of Israel and not in a more controversial outpost surrounded mostly by Palestinian towns.

This answer may leave people who want to try to categorize Mishnayot as a West Bank settler scratching their heads. Such are the contradictions of this man, who lives in a West Bank area yet considers himself progressive on relating to Palestinians and says he selected the area consciously, avoiding what he would call a radical anti-Palestinian West Bank area.

From 1996 to 2007, Mishnayot moved on to IDF legal positions that had no connection to the IDF's West Bank legal units. He was promoted to the senior-management rank of lieutenant colonel and from 1996 to 1998 served as head of the IDF legal unit for receiving complaints from soldiers, dealing with administrative law, employment law, and some criminal law issues. In September 1998, Israeli president Ezer Weizman appointed him to his first position as an IDF trial court judge. Later, from 2000 to 2007, he was deputy president of the IDF Southern Command and Land Forces Court.

He returned to working in an IDF West Bank legal unit when he was appointed to the rank of colonel and to be the IDF West Bank Courts chief justice in 2007, serving in that role until 2013. Asked what caused him to return to a legal position in the West Bank, he explained, "I thought that it was a big challenge on a professional level, very complex – I didn't even realize how complex. And I thought after I dealt with soldiers' work issues for nine years, that to move to an issue that was a little bit different, more professionally challenging, and also the fact that I would stand at the top of the system, and that I could have an impact by representing the system – this was also a challenge that I wanted to try for myself to see if I could handle it."

Mishnayot did not have a lot to say when asked about hobbies, clearly being a workaholic. He did mention that he swims every day, though not at a particularly fast pace. He added he likes old-style Israeli music – "the kind you would hear around 4:00 p.m. on Israel Army Radio."

Although even the most serious courtrooms sometimes break the tension with some comical moments, Mishnayot could not describe many humorous anecdotes from his tenure in the court. He also, unusually for a West Bank

Courts judge, did not recall too many instances of disruption of court proceedings by the emotions of the moment.

Mishnayot did have security concerns one time outside of the courtroom. Some on the Israeli Right, including a story on the radio station Kol Yehudi, criticized him vehemently and were personally angry with him after he ordered Jamal Haj released, enforcing the amnesty agreement despite Haj's past terror activities.

Mishnayot explained that he received a telephone call from the IDF that they had intelligence that he was on a list of targeted persons. He was on the list for two or three weeks. During that time, sometimes security was stationed outside his home, a police officer called periodically, and other times a patrol came by his house. However, he said that there was no impact on his predominantly Orthodox Jewish neighborhood's treatment of him (though Orthodox Jews as a general stereotype lean right on political issues). He explained, "This area is a very open and liberal place."

Mishnayot as Judge over Palestinians

Asked about how he kept his various courtrooms calm, Mishnayot said that he tried to "express lots of respect toward the accused, to wait for their families to arrive even if they were late and to be tolerant…to let the families talk to their arrested family member – sometimes specifically instructing the Shin Bet to let a Palestinian detainee and his family and lawyers speak after the hearing" before the accused was brought back to detention.

Mishnayot really was serious about lawyers and families of the defendant attending even pretrial hearings over whether defendants would remain in police custody pending the trial. While it should seem obvious that lawyers and supporters would be present at the trial when witnesses are called, many times defendants' pretrial hearings about remaining under arrest on a temporary basis are not as well attended. It is sometimes especially hard for Palestinians to cross through all the necessary checkpoints to arrive at the IDF West Bank Courts.

In an extreme case during his term as chief justice, on December 30, 2009, Mishnayot freed several detainees pretrial because the IDF had blocked their lawyers and family members from attending a hearing on extending their detention (the lawyers and family members were blocked when the checkpoint next to the Ofer Courts was closed following an attempted terror attack). He noted that he also threatened the IDF West Bank legal adviser, the West Bank police legal adviser, and the IDF Central Command that he would start freeing more detainees if the incident repeated itself.

Does this show Mishnayot to be a strong liberal on Palestinian rights or just that he drew the line at basic fairness? Answering that question is not easy. There are not many comparable situations in the world where foreign lawyers must appear at the military court of another country, sometimes in the middle of conflict between the two peoples. The absence of such comparable situations could be used as proof of how problematic the "occupation" is in continuing for so long. Alternatively, it could show how much less liberal other countries in the middle of conflicts are that lack judicial systems and may carry out a harsher "victor's justice."

Mishnayot also said he prided himself on reducing or eliminating excessive security checks of Palestinian defense lawyers upon their arrival at the army bases where the courts are located. Palestinian lawyers disputed this to me and said excessive checks on them continue. Which side of the conflict you are on may inextricably influence your view of what is a standard and necessary or excessive security check.

Overall Mishnayot presents himself as someone who has remained consistent in his beliefs and approach to the Palestinians. However, he did express surprise at the level of complexity he confronted heading the IDF West Bank Courts. How he dealt with that surprise is one of the signs of both Mishnayot the reformer and Mishnayot, a man of the system.

Before his work as chief justice, he stated, "I did not really know how the court interacts with these issues...." He added, "Minors, for example. Our ability to impact and to change the situation, to improve the situation, is definitely something...the realization of the ability to struggle with new challenges and also from a human perspective, from all perspectives. For example, the almost daily struggle with human rights organizations and how to interact with them."

Mishnayot articulated another key to openness and good interactions with Palestinians: "I tried to always have a positive atmosphere in the room. I would ask more questions of the prosecution" to make them give more specific and substantive answers, while "pushing harder to understand" the arguments made by the Palestinians in their defense.

Mishnayot is a man who was raised in a religious Zionist background, fought Arabs and lost comrades in fighting them, oversaw demolitions of Palestinian homes declared illegal, and yet views himself as open and understanding of the other side, particularly in his key position as chief justice of the IDF's West Bank Courts.

Chapter 6

The Shin Bet under Pressure:
The Epic Haj Trial

There were many unusual things about the Jamal Haj revoked amnesty trial, which brought together Khoury, Mishnayot, and Hirsch in a slam dunk for Khoury. If the Abuhara case involved Khoury challenging a Shin Bet declaration about a group's status as an illegal group, in Haj, she challenged the IDF prosecution's narrative that an amnesty agreement did not exist – despite the fact that the Shin Bet had in fact signed it. Her win in the Haj case would also be the forerunner of her push to defend the pardons of those Palestinians released in the Schalit exchange and then rearrested for allegedly violating their pardons.

Haj, as mentioned in chapter 1, was arrested for a 2002 terror bombing. But this was only after a 2006–2007 amnesty deal that led him to come out of hiding and return to his hometown of Nablus.

There were many unusual things about the legal proceedings against Haj.

When he was arrested, it set off a firestorm between Israel and the PA, since he was on the amnesty list and had become a PA-allied legislator in Nablus. The Shin Bet and the IDF were asked to explain themselves, including to the IDF West Bank chief prosecutor, about the basis for Haj's arrest. I reveal later for the first time the content of a key document that gave the Shin Bet's explanation, but the climax of the trial was the testimony of Mohammed Dahlan, formerly the head of the Palestinian Authority's security services.

Palestinian Power Broker Mohammed Dahlan Testifies in IDF Court

Dahlan is one of the most controversial and powerful Palestinian figures alive. For years, he was Yasir Arafat and Mahmoud Abbas's strongman in dealing with internal PA security issues, Hamas, and with outside agencies such as the Shin Bet and the CIA. However, he lost significant standing after Hamas defeated his forces and took over Gaza from the PA in 2007.

At some point, he reportedly also was involved in behind-the-scenes efforts to take over the PA from Abbas, whom he viewed as weak and incompetent. Whether he really did try to replace Abbas or Abbas merely felt threatened by his high profile, in 2011, Abbas tried to push him out of power circles and even to have him arrested.

Dahlan fled to the United Arab Emirates in response. However, he apparently has stayed in the loop both on the Palestinian and international levels and is still on the short list for potentially replacing the aging Abbas (many expect Abbas to step down or possibly to become unable to continue in office due to his health problems). In any event, when the amnesty agreement was signed in November 2006 and when Dahlan testified, he was a giant figure among Israelis and Palestinians.

On July 18, 2010, with Khoury questioning him, Dahlan testified on behalf of Haj to help confirm the details of his agreement with Shin Bet director Yuval Diskin, which the two negotiated personally so that it had been signed off on at the highest levels. Diskin had also been authorized to conclude the agreement after negotiations between Dahlan and then defense minister Shaul Mofaz.

Dahlan's testimony was unprecedented. Top current or former PA officials did not testify in the IDF's West Bank Courts for a number of reasons. The fact that Khoury pulled this off spoke volumes about her creativity and audacity as well as the respect with which she was viewed in Palestinian circles.

It also revealed the extent to which the PA and Dahlan viewed Haj's arrest as a flagrant violation. He would not have set foot in the courts without both a high level of respect for the lawyer requesting his assistance and a deep commitment to Haj as having been mistreated in a way that dishonored the PA itself in the ongoing Israel-PA relations.

The opening of Khoury's questioning of Dahlan in court started as follows.

Khoury: Were you in touch with Yuval Diskin or others who worked with him after Jamal [Haj] was arrested?

Dahlan: Yes. Unfortunately, I had previously left my position, but despite this, I continued to be in touch with Yuval, and I spoke to him specifically about the issue of Jamal.

Khoury: What did you say?

Dahlan: I said to him, "Why did you arrest him? What do you have? What has happened that is new?"

Khoury: What did he say to you?

Dahlan: He said to me that the army accidentally found him and took him along with the others. I don't want to go into the details, but I was convinced that Yuval was right when he said they took him by accident. Why? I don't know. Maybe because I trusted him. But at the same time, he promised me that Jamal would not stay in prison, but he said that there were legal problems, which he did not want to get into. I want to note that if I were still in my position, Jamal would not have been in prison. Because I followed all of these stories, there were hundreds of incidents, and we solved all of them with understandings. There were mistakes on both sides.

One can picture the two titans, Diskin and Dahlan, two of the powers of Israel and the PA, talking through the issue of Haj's arrest.

Dahlan is bewildered. Diskin is embarrassed and apologetic.

But he is not entirely free to act, due apparently to internal differences of opinion within the Israeli security establishment, especially among lawyers. The disagreement centered around the question of what the amnesty agreement constituted and whether arresting Haj by accident should be used as a chance to put a man behind bars who was responsible for some horrible terror attacks.

Dahlan thinks they have fixed the issue. But at the same time, he is no longer head of PA security. In other words, the PA's face in the amnesty negotiations is at least half out of the picture and unable to press Diskin as he might have if he were holding more bargaining chips from ongoing joint work together.

Haj fell between these cracks.

And yet Dahlan showed up to testify in Haj's case. Why? In his testimony, also on July 18, 2010, he explained his reasons.

> Dahlan: I do not come to defend the accused, and if I needed to come just to defend the accused, I would not come. Sentence him to whatever you want. But I am responsible for the essential fact that he finds himself in prison, because I was part of the agreement, and Yuval Diskin was part of the agreement and Mofaz…at the head, he was part of the agreement. It is unnecessary to state the importance of setting things straight with the example of Jamal [Haj], because no one knows what will be in the future.
>
> Today there is quiet. Tomorrow things could be a mess. And I hope that the quiet will continue, but if there are examples of people like Jamal, it will cause people to lose faith between the two sides. Therefore, I came to address the problem personally at a certain point with [then prime minister Ariel] Sharon's office, through, at the time, his lawyer Dov Weissglass.
>
> I came to an agreement with him regarding a man whose name was Jihad Masimi, a resident of Nablus, who was wanted. He was a wanted person, and it was important that he be a partner with us for the same reason: that there be quiet and that the issue be wrapped up. And after I agreed with them about a pardon, they arrested him.
>
> Khoury: And what happened when they arrested him? What did you do?
>
> Dahlan: I explained the severity of the situation to the Israeli army. I stopped the joint security cooperation. And they released him when they were convinced, after three days. He was released, and they brought him back to his house…. You are judges and not politicians, and I want to tell you that the entire project [of the Israeli-Palestinian peace process] would not have succeeded [as security cooperation would have failed entirely if Jihad Masimi had not been released by Ariel Sharon via Dov Weissglass], and until today we are the victims of violent actions. And therefore, I hope that this will be taken into account, also for the credibility of the agreements and also for the sake of the future.

Dahlan's testimony continued. In one of the most bizarre circumstances of his agreeing to be a witness for Haj, the former head of all Palestinian security forces who regularly dealt with the likes of Diskin and Israeli defense ministers eventually also found himself under public cross-examination by an Israeli military prosecutor in the Israeli military court case.

At one point, the prosecutor asked, "If I tell you that all of the people you mentioned by name, including Diskin, were not authorized to give a pardon from being brought to trial, what do you have to say to that?" Dahlan was not an intimidated witness even on cross-examination.

Dahlan: Then who does have authority? You, for example? We are sitting with you as the State of Israel. The next time that Yuval [Diskin] comes and he says he wants to sit with me, I should tell him, "Get out." This is unacceptable. This is humiliating on a personal level for Yuval and for [Shaul] Mofaz and all those who sat with them. Why did I waste my time with them? We sat…regarding the issue of wanted persons for around two thousand hours. If the defense minister of Israel is not empowered, and the most important man in the country, Yuval Diskin, is not authorized, then who is authorized?

The top PA official also described the criteria and thoughts that went into defining who would be pardoned and removed from the wanted list:

Dahlan: The agreement was complex and hard for Israel from a legal perspective and for us from a practical perspective. In any case, I took the risk from the Palestinian side, and from the Israeli side Yuval Diskin took responsibility. A security staff was assembled from the Palestinian side and the Israeli side, and we agreed on certain principles.

First, the Israeli side provided its entire wanted list to the Palestinian side. Second, any man whose name was removed [from the list] would receive a pardon from the Israeli side. *That means that he would not be judged about the past, and would not be arrested and no court decision would be made about him retroactively.* [Emphasis added.]

The Israeli side requested from us to provide a commitment that none of them would participate in any action against Israel – and we agreed to this. And [the Israeli side requested] that they would not be armed.... I demanded that a weapon be able to be on their person while under regulation of the [Palestinian] Authority because in the agreements on Gaza and Jericho I reached an agreement with [former IDF chief of staff] Amnon [Lipkin] Shahak, in the year 1994, the same thing regarding Gaza, and the project was successful.

But there were two mistakes from the Israeli side. They killed four of my friends by mistake. They said it was by mistake and I believed them. And therefore, I did not want the same mistake to happen again in the West Bank, and the Israeli side agreed.

However, they requested that all of the wanted persons would be in Jericho, but we refused and we wanted everyone to return to their houses, and this is how they returned to living normal lives.

Another top PA intelligence official, one rung below Dahlan, who testified about the Haj amnesty, was Taufik Tarawi, head of al-Muhabarat, the Palestinian Secret Police. He stepped in to continue and implement a series of amnesty agreements that Dahlan and Diskin had already agreed to in broad principles.

On July 7, 2010, Tarawi testified.

Khoury: The promise you received – it was that Israeli security forces would not enter Nablus to arrest Jamal [Haj]?

Tarawi: No. They said to me that they would not arrest him at all. They said that they knew where he was, and that they would not arrest him. After they arrested him, I asked Roni [possibly referring to Roni Alsheikh, who later became Israel's police commissioner] by telephone: "Why did they arrest him after he promised?" He answered me that he arrested him by accident.

Haj himself also gave vivid testimony of the situation, including when police interrogated him while under arrest:

Police interrogator: What do you have to say with regard to the suspicions attributed to you?

Haj: Before I respond, I want to say that, from the start, I did not act, I did not act or do anything in any way connected to violence or resistance violence, including when I was a high-ranking officer. And currently I am a member of a legislative body elected by the Palestinian nation, and I consider myself obligated by the agreements that the PLO and the PA signed with the State of Israel.

That means not being involved in terror such as that which the interrogator claims.… Whoever is involved in violence and terror would not act to return an American student who was kidnapped in Nablus [as he did], and the Israelis and the Americans know about this.

And also earlier, in the year 2002, in that period it could not be that I acted to commit terror and violence, as the Shin Bet interrogator claims, when I was acting to prevent the citizen Bashir Hashash from perpetrating an attack, and sent him back to his family. And he was arrested by you.

Haj continued in his testimony, giving at least three other cases where he intervened positively for Israeli security against his own Palestinian brethren. In three cases, he prevented three other terror attacks with at least two of the Palestinians getting arrested because of his sharing information with Israeli security forces. There was also another case in which a Palestinian stole an Israeli security forces car loaded with weaponry, and Haj returned the car with all of its weaponry to the Shin Bet.

The IDF prosecution did not bring witnesses involved in the agreement, and those Shin Bet officials who testified were brought by Khoury to testify about the interrogation of Haj and what he told them about his amnesty.

On April 18, 2010, the Shin Bet agent referred to as "Amos" testified.

Judge: It has been hinted throughout the trial that the fact that he [Haj] was not arrested for a long time was because he was a member of Fatah, and so there was an agreement or there was some kind of understanding with the knowledge of the top echelon of decision makers in Israel. Do you know about this?

Amos: *I know in general that this issue arose regarding him* [Haj]. Personally, as an interrogator, I did not get deep into the issue because the job I was given was to interrogate him. I was not in the circle of decision makers. Why did they arrest him? When? Why now? It never came up for the staff, *in a general manner, that there was an issue like this.* [Emphasis added.]

Khoury brought a range of other witnesses, including other top PA officials who worked for Dahlan and Tarawi and with Israeli security officials, all supporting Haj's amnesty.

The IDF prosecution brought no one, certainly not Diskin, to contradict Dahlan, Tarawi, and other defense witnesses' narratives about the amnesty. At least at this stage, the IDF prosecution even continued to be vague about affirming that any such agreement existed, let alone agreeing to Haj's interpretation of it.

Despite all of the above, Haj's central argument was not accepted by the lower court. Still, in an unusual development, the court split, with one of the three judges on the trial court panel accepting his argument.

On July 27, 2011, the three-judge panel of the Samaria Courts rejected by a 2-1 decision Haj's argument that the case should be thrown out on the basis of his amnesty agreement.

Lt. Col. Dalia Kaufman and Lt. Col. Yair Zadok voted that the amnesty agreement was not an absolute defense against the indictment, with Lt. Col. Eyal Nun voting that it should have blocked the indictment.

Judges Kaufman and Zadok accepted Haj's general narrative that there had been an amnesty agreement, that the burden was on the IDF prosecution to prove any violations of the agreement by Haj (unlike in the more recent Schalit amnesty cases of Palestinians whose pardons were revoked after being released in the 2011 prisoner exchange where the court put the burden of proof on the Palestinians), and that the prosecution had failed to prove that he violated the agreement.

However, the judges in the majority accepted the IDF prosecutor's position that the commitment to Haj was not absolute and that because of that he had not lost any rights by being prosecuted. In light of Haj's high crimes, they essentially said that the state was within its rights to break the agreement.

Judge Nun disagreed. He said that Shin Bet director Yuval Diskin was the only one who had authority to withdraw Haj's amnesty, and that he would need to do so explicitly. Since Diskin never did, and at most the IDF prosecution had offered memoranda from lower level Shin Bet officers (discussed shortly below) as evidence that his amnesty was withdrawn, Nun said that the conditions did not exist for violating the agreement.

He also added that since Haj would not have been arrested if he had not returned to Nablus, under a promise of amnesty, breaking the agreement illegally took away his rights – "making his situation worse."

This legalistic dispute between the military judges was important because it forecasted a deep philosophical disagreement that would emerge on the case between the IDF West Bank prosecution and the IDF West Bank Courts chief justice. Those on the side of sending Haj back to prison said that just retribution for his sins was what was most important: as long as some technical ground could be raised to get out of the amnesty he was given, the prosecution and courts should do all they could do to make sure Haj went to prison. Those on the side of freeing Haj said that what was at stake here was more than justice for the small group of terror victims Haj had allegedly impacted, even as the allegations were as heinous as they come. The spirit of the amnesty, not just the letter of the law, had to be upheld. Otherwise, future agreements with the PA and future coexistence could be undermined.

All of the arguments in court were legal. But this was another case in which it was impossible to say that the political context did not come into play in a way that regular courts do not need to cope with.

On October 31, 2011, the Samaria Court sentenced Haj to thirty years in prison on a range of terror offenses for which he was convicted, though he was still acquitted on a range of other offenses. But IDF West Bank Courts chief justice Aharon Mishnayot did not let the thirty-year sentence stand on appeal.

While the above events in the case were highly unusual, there was one more highly unusual development in the case: the revelation of Document 47 – disclosed here for the first time.

Document 47 – The Claims against Haj

On August 24, 2008, the legal advisor for the Samaria unit sent a memorandum, referred to as Document 47, to the IDF deputy chief prosecutor for Samaria explaining that Haj had violated the terms of the PA-Shin Bet amnesty agreement on two grounds.

Shin Bet memoranda to the IDF prosecution are virtually never publicly revealed, but this memorandum became part of the public evidence of Haj's defense to free him from jail.

According to Document 47, Haj violated two conditions of his amnesty.

First, Haj left the city of Nablus without asking permission beforehand and without receiving permission as required.

Second, Haj "was arrested in a concealed living space in which wanted militants were staying during the same time and who were the target" of an operation to arrest illegal operatives.

In fact, the IDF soldiers were not looking for Haj, but when they found him with other illegal operatives, they arrested him along with the others, Document 47 explained. That was how Document 47 played pretrial.

Initially during Haj's trial, the IDF tried to claim that its incidental arrest of Haj when it found him in bad company was not covered by the amnesty agreement.

In other words, the IDF prosecution argued that Israel had committed not to actively seek Haj's arrest, but had not given him immunity from being arrested if he was spending time with terrorists and potentially coordinating with them.

However, by the end of Haj's trial and throughout the appeal proceedings, the IDF prosecution never again mentioned Haj's spending time with illegal operatives as a violation of the amnesty agreement.

IDF West Bank Courts chief justice Aharon Mishnayot, who heard the appeal, viewed the IDF's essentially dropping that argument from its case as an admission. In other words, if the IDF prosecution stopped saying that Israel was allowed to arrest and re-jail Haj, it was an admission that the argument had never held water in the first place.

The different views of Mishnayot and the IDF prosecution about Document 47 were not small arguments about esoteric legal procedure, but a philosophical chasm with major implications. For Mishnayot, this was an example of the IDF prosecution trying to apply the rules of evidence in a way that makes it much easier for them to convict Palestinians than for the Israeli civilian prosecution to convict Israeli defendants.

He wanted the opposite.

As far as Mishnayot was concerned, without an exceptional security reason to apply the rules differently in the IDF's West Bank Courts than those rules were applied in Israel, the default should always be to apply the rules exactly the same way as in Israel.

This issue, the unprecedented testimony of Dahlan, Tarawi, and others, and the Shin Bet and IDF prosecution's general attempt to avoid sticking to Haj's amnesty brought on the wrath of the normally even-keeled Mishnayot. He took the side of the dissenting Judge Nun from the lower court. The majority on the lower court had performed legal gymnastics to both recognize the power of Document 47 and Dahlan and Tarawi and others' testimony on Haj's case, while still finding a narrow technical legal basis to uphold Haj being sent back essentially to life in prison.

Mishnayot dropped what he saw as legalistic formalities and pretenses trying to cover-up the cold facts that Document 47, Dahlan, Tarawi, and others had laid bare. As far as he was concerned, the state had had buyer's remorse for the amnesty or decided to try to bend it when an opportunity presented itself to "accidentally" arrest Haj. Mishnayot blasted them for turning a blind eye to the amnesty deal and questioned whether they had acted in good faith.

Khoury, Hirsch, and Mishnayot Interacting on the Haj Case

Khoury viewed the Haj case as basically identical to the Schalit cases.

According to Khoury, the rearrests of fifty-nine Schalit deal releasees was motivated by revenge and arbitrary punishment against Hamas, which was behind the kidnapping and killing of the three Jewish teenagers.

The issue really disturbed Khoury, who became animated when she discussed the dozens of Schalit releasees who were rearrested, describing it as plain black-and-white fraud. She said that Israel got Schalit back, fulfilling Hamas's end of the deal, and Israel had an obligation to keep its part of the agreement.

Khoury explained that when Israel released 110 Palestinian prisoners to the West Bank, a large number of them assumed they had a fresh start. So those Palestinians "let their guard down" by investing in what they thought was a future outside of prison, and set down roots for the first time, starting legitimate businesses, getting married, and having kids.

She said it was impossible to justify ripping these men out of their new lives simply because they had received money from Hamas that was not used for any terror purpose, was given for past deeds for which they had been pardoned, and under circumstances in which they did not understand this could lead to their being rearrested.

No one would accept "a few thousand dollars" (amounts were in the neighborhood of ten to twenty thousand dollars) at risk of being sent back to jail for life, and Israel had not explained to them that this was a possibility. They simply understood they could not be involved in terror, and she said they had not been and that the state was not presenting evidence that they had been. (In counterpoint, Hirsch's argument in court – which won – was that the small amount was irrelevant, and as soon as they received funds from Hamas in any amount, they had violated their parole.)

Khoury believed that all the distinctions about the Haj deal being with Fatah and the Schalit deal being with Hamas were irrelevant to the law, and so they should be irrelevant in court. That was for the realm of politics only, an area she and the courts should not deal with. She viewed the Haj decision by Mishnayot on the appeals court as correcting a historic injustice by the Shin Bet and the IDF prosecution in which the lower court had made the wrong call.

She viewed the lower court's decision as unexplainable legal gymnastics in which the judges knew they were stuck with the facts she had proven and the absence of facts the IDF prosecution had brought to prove their side. Yet the lower court, even with Haj's Fatah deal, had allowed politics or emotion over Haj's alleged involvement in earlier terror attacks in 2002 to improperly influence its decision. The lower court in a sense had been fooled or pushed around by the IDF prosecution.

According to Khoury, Mishnayot and the appeals court were not fooled by these irrelevant factors, saw the legal issues clearly, and did the right thing – even if the courts did not do the right thing in most of the Schalit cases.

For Khoury, many of the problems with the courts in such cases could be explained by the more passive and creeping aspects of the occupation and the courts being forever – even if involuntarily – thrust into politics. Even as she respected the judges more than some and believed that in many cases she had a solid chance of winning in the IDF's West Bank Courts, sometimes even better than in Israeli civilian courts, she still believed the courts sometimes slid away from the proper and fair criminal process into unfair and stacked administrative and politicized proceedings.

In contrast, Hirsch described Mishnayot and the other IDF West Bank Courts judges as being taken into an alternate universe, courtesy of Khoury. He confidently said that he knew how the court misunderstood or was misled about some basic facts and that, given the full picture, the courts would have ruled his way and against Haj. However, Hirsch said he could not reveal what facts were missing and what the courts had misunderstood. Later, I learned that internal IDF prosecution policy disagreements may have hamstrung the prosecution – though it was unclear whether the case would have ended differently even absent that roadblock.

From the way that Hirsch even complimented the defense lawyers for "convincing" the judges, as he put it, it is clear that however vague he is being, he genuinely believes that his version of the Haj case is the correct one and would blow Mishnayot's decision out of the water. He even finished his comments on the issue with a not-so-veiled threat to Haj about the IDF prosecution's readiness to rearrest him in the future – if he were to get sloppy in a manner that would allow Hirsch to reveal his full hand.

This was part of how Hirsch viewed the courts. They were eminently fair to the Palestinians, sometimes too fair, especially in light of the crimes that many Palestinians were committing against Israel. Harsh sentences and even revoking amnesties, such as for Haj and the Schalit cases, were necessary to maintain security – one of his primary duties. Palestinians' rights and protections in the criminal process were so strong that talented lawyers like Khoury could convince judges wearing the same uniform he wore to acquit them where they were guilty, as in the Haj case.

He disagreed with many court decisions in which the court acquitted Palestinians who were indicted. Hirsch said the IDF only filed indictments after carefully reviewing a case, including weighing evidence that could acquit the defendants. Even after courts ruled against him, he rarely believed his original decision to indict had been wrong. His job was to send as many dangerous

Palestinians to jail for as long as possible to keep Israeli civilians safe. And he was annoyed, if not angered, when the courts freed dangerous people whose freedom could lead to the loss of life.

Mishnayot was an entirely different story on the Haj case. When shown a video of Hirsch's commenting about his and the other judges being hood-winked, he leaned forward in his chair and focused intently on the screen. He laughed at Hirsch's comments about taking his "hat off" to Khoury and Avigdor Feldman about the creativity of their lawyering in the Haj case. But the laughter quickly faded as Hirsch directed criticism at the judges. Mishnayot's expression shifted to skepticism, and his pride appeared offended as Hirsch said Khoury and Feldman were "convincing judges that that alternative reality was true."

As he viewed Hirsch's continuing critique, however, Mishnayot laughed, parrying the attack: this was a hot potato. The laugh was also that of an experienced hand after someone has taken a hard shot at his professional work. He leaned back in his chair, likely starting to contemplate his response.

Finally, the playing of the video of Hirsch's comments ended. With formidable concentration, Mishnayot did not wait long to respond. "The specified evidence in the decision explained in the decision what was the agreement, what was in the agreement, what were the circumstances in which Jamal Haj was arrested, and what were the understandings between the sides…regarding interpreting the understandings.… I think the decision speaks for itself," he said.

"And I was convinced of the facts beyond any doubt. But more than that, the path was open to the IDF prosecution to appeal to the Israeli Supreme Court against the IDF West Bank Appeals Court ruling. If they thought that there was such a great mistake [in the decision], it was open to them to go the Supreme Court!" he said in obvious rising frustration and determination.

When asked specifically to focus on Hirsch's "alternative reality" comments, Mishnayot at first deflected the attack, saying that Hirsch was talking about the lower level trial court, not his appeals court decision.

Pressed about the fact that even if Hirsch's comments were generally directed at the lower court, Mishnayot's panel had made the final decision on the issue, Mishnayot responded again without hesitation. "I don't think that we were convinced of an alternative reality. I think it was very real. We saw the evidence as it was. We were sure about this decision," he said.

Asked if he knew what Hirsch was referring to as a secret that would and could later reveal that Mishnayot and the other judges had been hoodwinked, he said, "No, no, no, I do not know anything about an alternative reality. I cannot understand it because the documents were written, the agreement existed, the circumstances were clear, the claims of the IDF prosecution were clear about the circumstances and about why they thought the situation was different and about why not everything was in the agreement.

"We ruled very emphatically about this at the end of the day. So I don't think that they fooled us into accepting an alternative reality. I do not, not, not accept this. I do not think that this was what happened. I do not accept this in light of the circumstances in that case. I don't think so," he stated.

Mishnayot then asked for a copy of his Haj decision to read over some key passages. He noted, "Only at the stage of appeal did the state finally admit that the amnesty agreement existed." He continued, "I quoted the entire Document 47 so that anyone who reads the decision would know what we were talking about. And I explained our interpretation of Document 47. I do not think that the defense lawyers fooled us into accepting an alternative reality."

This encapsulated some of the differences between Hirsch and Mishnayot. They wore the same uniform and both represented the interests of maintaining order vis-à-vis the Palestinians. In this role they were unified, in conflict with Khoury and the Palestinians, who were seeking freedom and acting in their view to oppose the occupation.

But wearing the same uniform did not make Hirsch and Mishnayot approach the issues from the same perspective.

Hirsch had a full picture of the Shin Bet, security establishment, and political establishment's information and views of a case before it got to court. Some of this he and his prosecutors chose to share with the judges, and some of it they chose not to. Usually some of what was left out was intelligence that they did not want leaking to the defense side and the Palestinians in general.

But in the Haj case, Hirsch said explicitly that the issue was not intelligence and national security. Rather, the legal tactics of what to reveal were influenced by some unconventional or personal political considerations. Why did the state not want to reveal or officially confirm the amnesty agreement for so long when it became obvious that a highly resourceful lawyer such as Khoury could prove its existence and substance? Whatever considerations there were, they were likely not considerations that exist in civilian courts but rather uniquely characterized the IDF's West Bank Courts.

In some cases, the Schalit pardon revocations being salient examples, the judges accepted the unique reasons provided by the IDF prosecution and reached rulings unique to the courts. In the Haj case, however, Mishnayot acted with almost a level of revulsion to the conduct of the IDF prosecution. He demanded that if it would not observe standard rules of procedure and evidence about what to reveal and when to reveal it, he would decide purely based on the standard evidence before him, and the IDF prosecution would pay the price.

The Haj ruling would lead to some surprised admiration for the IDF West Bank Courts' judges, especially Mishnayot, from Israel's standard critics. They would still claim that the lower court wrongfully ruled against Haj and that he was wrongfully imprisoned for an extended period until acquitted and released on appeal.

It was bemoaned and viewed as a traitorous ruling by some Israelis, as their view was that judges who were detached from the evils of reality had acquitted and released a high-level terrorist. They viewed the judges as being more committed to a paper agreement (which Haj had at least partially violated) than to justice for his victims from 2002.

The Schalit cases, sending almost all of the releasees back to prison for life or long prison terms, were praised by the same critics for correcting an injustice in which the fifty-nine Palestinian terrorists had been released in an embarrassing case of national blackmail by Hamas.

They were slammed by those, like Khoury, who admired the Haj ruling. They said the Schalit cases showed the judges caving to politics, to using secret evidence and to the government's need to satisfy populistic impulses for taking revenge on Hamas after the three Jewish teenagers were murdered in June 2014.

The above case was a true exhibit of the unique factors and political importance that encapsulates high-profile cases at the IDF's West Bank Courts.

Chapter 7

Reforms for Palestinian Minors

We cannot really fully understand the claims about the treatment of Palestinian minors made by one of our four key personalities, Gaby Lasky, until after we review some history about the development of reforms for Palestinian minors from 2009 to the present. A round of reforms started in 2008–2009, was added to in 2011, and has been continuously added to since to make the IDF West Bank law enforcement system slightly more friendly and fair to minors, or at least less oppressive. This is simultaneously perhaps the biggest story of the IDF's West Bank Courts and the least comprehensively covered. While it is sporadically addressed in the media by human rights reports and discussed at law conferences on the issue, rarely does any of the coverage truly "dig in" to try to understand the issue's complexities.

The debate goes back to the qualifying statement "from 2009 to the present." In truth, the roots of the change for minors started before 2009. Whether they started in December 2007 as a result of a human rights report by the pro-Palestinian Israeli NGO Yesh Din or whether by initiative of the IDF West Bank Courts themselves in 2008 is another aspect of the question.

December 2007 Yesh Din Report

Although there is a debate about what launched the reforms, some role was unquestionably played by Yesh Din's 2007 report *Backyard Proceedings*.

The report summary claims it provides a critical view of the military court system in the Occupied Palestinian Territories, which is "a cornerstone of Israeli rule in the West Bank" for the last forty years. Each year, says the report, thousands of Palestinian West Bank residents are tried in military courts in the West Bank, yet "the military judicial system in the Occupied Territories (OT) has acted under a veil of almost complete darkness until now."[3] Whether the courts' operations are public or not is yet another highly debated issue with the Israeli and Palestinian sides unable to agree on what "made public" even means.

Continuing, the report says, "Few studies and publications have examined its activities, and it is subject to very lax internal supervision...."[4] *Backyard Proceedings* "examines the degree to which [the military court] system upholds and implements the due process rights of Palestinian detainees and defendants."[5]

Further, "the report also evaluates authorities' compliance with the defendant's right to be informed of all charges laid against him or her, as well as the right to prepare an effective defense and the right to be presumed innocent until proven guilty."[6]

Within that broader goal, the report "examined...how minors are adjudicated in this system, as well as other matters."[7] Regarding the treatment of Palestinian minors, the report concluded,

> The IDF, as previously mentioned, refrained from erecting military courts in the OT [Occupied Territory] for the adjudication of minors, and the prosecutors and judges handling their cases undergo no training in the treatment of minors. As such, these minors are prosecuted and tried under conditions identical to those of adult defendants.... Minors are usually seated in the dock alongside adults, and their cases are heard before and after adults' cases, usually in public sessions.
>
> In accordance with Security Legislation, minors are tried as adults from the moment they turn 16 years old, even if the crime of which they are accused was committed before they had reached that age.

---

3   Yesh Din, *Backyard Proceedings: The Implementation of Due Process Rights in the Military Courts in the Occupied Territories*, December 2007, 11.

4   Ibid.

5   Ibid., 182.

6   Summary of report, https://www.yesh-din.org/en/backyard-proceedings/.

7   Ibid.

With the Israeli-Palestinian conflict in the background, the punishment of youths is determined without taking into consideration the possibility of rehabilitation – neither with regard to "security" offenses nor with regard to regular criminal offenses.

Recommendations

1. Security Legislation is to be amended…that a person is defined a minor until he is 18.…
2. [T]he determining date relating to the penalizing of minors shall be the time of committing the offense.…
3. The closing of courtroom doors during sessions in the matter of minors must be strictly observed.
4. Special juvenile courts are to be established, in which prosecutors and judges specially trained in juvenile matters and proceedings will serve.
5. Until the establishment of a juvenile court, absolute separation must exist between adults and minors in the military courtrooms.[8]

Since that 2007 report, there have been some other updated reports on the issue of minors. UNICEF, for example, has issued several reports and even had an unusually open dialogue with the IDF, which has been semi-effective. But none of them have fully explored all the key issues in depth in a way that goes to the heart of the courts' complex dilemmas. And none of them have come close to telling both the Palestinian/critics' side and the IDF's side.

This is partially because none of them got sufficient internal access from the key IDF decision makers, such as Mishnayot, to do so – although UNICEF has gotten better access than some other human rights groups. In fact, until 2013, Mishnayot was a sitting military judge and could not be interviewed, and as of April 2016, he became a sitting Israeli civilian district court judge and once again cannot be interviewed.

However, in between that period, Mishnayot, whom some on the IDF side view as a father of the reforms, spoke in full detail, reported here for the first time, about his view of the reforms for minors' developments.

---

8   Yesh Din, *Backyard Proceedings*, 162.

Mishnayot – "A Minor Is a Minor Is a Minor"

Who brought about the minors' reforms? Was it Mishnayot and the IDF on their own? Was it forced on them by public pressure from the Yesh Din 2007 report? Were the reforms successful or superficial?

As always there are two sides.

Mishnayot dated the story to his entering the head spot on the IDF's West Bank Courts in 2007.

"I entered my position in March 2007. Very quickly, I realized that there was a general problem with the issue of minors. Regarding the handling of minors, it was not acceptable to me that the handling of minors would be like the handling of adults – exactly the same thing. It did not seem reasonable to me.

"At a judicial conference that year, I met with the president of the juvenile courts in Israel, and I spoke to her about this, and I asked her if the juvenile courts in Israel also deal with Palestinians. And she said yes. I asked, 'How do you do it?' She said that they have special social workers for the Palestinian population and to deal with the parents, and that there were procedures, even with all of the difficulties.… [She added] that they live in a place where the access and connection to it [the social-worker program] were a bit more problematic than in Israel.

"I presented to her the concept that we wanted to try to import some of the norms from Israel into the area [West Bank] in order to create some kind of unique mechanism to deal with minors. And she was a partner to all of this process along with the chief judge of the IDF courts Maj. Gen. Shai Yaniv, who was my commander – according to the chain of command, not in terms of jurisdiction. We are independent in terms of jurisdiction, but at least regarding chain of command. And I got a green light from him to take action on the issue. And in this way, I met with her [the president of the juvenile courts] in her office in Tel Aviv, and we started to organize to make some kind of change regarding this issue.

"In this framework, the first thing we did was a pilot program in the Samaria Courts which was led by the president of the court at the time and those judges there. One judge who came from the civilian apparatus, Yariv Navon, who came from the Northern District Attorney's Office and knew how the courts acted in Israel, really helped to establish the new programs in the area."

The pilot program started in the middle of 2008.

"The pilot appeared to be only on an organizational level, but the significance was far more profound. We had decided to voluntarily separate cases with minors from cases with adults. At the detention stage, no mixed groups of minors and adults. Also, at the stage of bringing witnesses and evidence. It was an administrative decision without legislation. We got very positive feedback about this separation. It helped."

When Mishnayot was asked if Palestinians and their defense lawyers viewed the reforms as helpful and positive, he said he also got positive feedback from Palestinians and defense lawyers, while seeming more focused on positive feedback he got from the other judges: "The judges saw that minors, without being lumped in with adult groups, were more open to speaking and more open to sharing their problems. What led him [the minor] to do what he did? Sometimes [minors opened up] in closed-door sessions even without the parents. And you [the judge] can think more about rehabilitation processes for him, much more than when you spend your day dealing with punishment and his mouth is shut in front of other adults. That was the general idea, but we wanted more than that.

"We held a seminar [in mid-2008]. The central speaker was the president of juvenile courts in Israel. We also invited the Jerusalem public defender, Moshe Yehuda Cohen, who now is a judge, along with someone who worked on issues concerning minors with him, lawyer Nohi Politis, and the head social worker. It was a long and intensive day targeted at helping set up the legal infrastructure-platform of how to manage the issue of minors in the area.

"I thought that the techniques used by the Jerusalem public defender might also be appropriate, and that we could learn from them about how to manage Palestinian minors in the area, in Judea and Samaria. When we saw that the pilot program in the Samaria Courts was successful, and there were good results, we widened it to the Judea Courts and in all of the courts. And it was a very successful initiative. And we immediately treated all minors up to the age of eighteen as minors and separated them from grown-ups as was done in Israel – even though the law on the books still said that Palestinians were only minors up until age sixteen.

"[We] turned to the [IDF] prosecution to try to anchor this separation into the official law. Part of what helped this move forward was the 2007 Yesh Din report. Following the Yesh Din report, the Knesset Foreign Affairs Committee held a hearing on the issue. Former top Justice Ministry official Yehoshua Resnick appeared along with then deputy chief of the Judea and Samaria Military Courts Netanel Benishu [who became chief justice when Mishnayot stepped down in 2013]."

How Mishnayot raised this issue was typical of how the IDF and government officials relate to NGOs' impact on their policy decisions and reforms. They do not like to admit or do not believe the NGOs' actions drive their decisions. Mishnayot relates to Yesh Din's report as giving some side support to his own voluntary initiative, but does not believe the report was what started his own thought process on the issue – or as the NGOs argue, what compelled him to act on the issue.

Mishnayot went on to further describe a visit of Knesset parliament member Amira Dotan (the Kadima Party) and others to the courts following the Yesh Din report and the public outcry it created.

"There was a visit from the subcommittee for Judea and Samaria to Ofer. In their report, they praised the courts, but they criticized [the courts] on two issues: [treatment of] minors and [problems with] translation [from Hebrew to Arabic].... This brought about meetings in the IDF Military Advocate General's office and a process to passing section 109, which formally established the juvenile courts in the West Bank. But initially it was voluntary both regarding separation and regarding elevating the age of minors to eighteen.

"It was signed at the end of July 2009 and it went into effect in September 2009. We also held a public ceremony for the wider public to know about the change, with top Israeli officials, Palestinian lawyers, including top UNICEF officials for the area. And I hoped that there would be some new organized cooperation between the international officials and the Palestinian officials, so that we could advance it and do greater rehabilitation of the minors before us."

Mishnayot described the first wave of reforms for minors as including (1) separation of minors into juvenile courts and separate detention areas in prisons; (2) closed doors for minors' proceedings; (3) greater involvement of minors' parents, except where minors are against their parents being involved; and (4) having social workers involved for properly tailoring the sentences minors receive to their overall situations.

He went on to describe the second wave of reforms.

"At the same time, Israel's reform of section 14 – limiting night interrogations, other aspects of interrogating, and length of detaining of minors was signed in July 2009. We have no recess, and I thought we could use the same principles from section 14 reforms in the Judea and Samaria Courts. Night interrogations hurt the credibility of what the minor tells the interrogator whether Israeli or Palestinian.

"So then I wrote the Nishmi Abu Rahma decision, 'Katin hu katin hu katin' [a minor is a minor is a minor], which had a broader goal of emphasizing that there was no reason to have disparate legal principles applied to a minor in the area versus a minor in Israel.... Sometimes minors just tell interrogators what they think they want to hear [out of fear]. So in Abu Rahma, I said evidence from the prosecution was weaker because it was obtained in a night interrogation. So they need alternative detention, and not detention until the end of the trial, and this created the pipeline from which we absorbed the norms of Israel into the area. This was done without the Knesset."

Once again, Mishnayot underplayed the role of the 2007 Yesh Din report, focusing on the courts acting on their own even without Knesset legislation.

"I can't debate over credit for the process. If these things come together, what do I care? That is fine. The main thing is that the result is good. To go back and to try to map out who influenced who" is a waste of time, he suggested.

Asked if he would have had the idea to do the reforms for Palestinian minors even if there were no reports, he said, nodding with some certainty, "I think so. I think so." He adds: "I'm ready to move on. Their reports address many issues, by the way...some aren't in our control, some are based on data that is very anecdotal and problematic, therefore we need to view them critically, with all due respect to them. By the way, I had an ongoing dialogue with these organizations. They met with me and asked me for information about many cases and to attend many hearings...and I told them if there was an error in my apparatus,

I would be the first one who would want to know about it. Things that you see from there, you don't always see from here."

There is another major party that has impacted the reforms for minors. As mentioned in chapter 2, the Supreme Court of Israel wields a heavy influence over some trends in the IDF West Bank Courts.

One example is the Avraham Ben Chaim ruling on March 6, 2012, by Supreme Court justices Edna Arbel, Yoram Danziger, and semi-retired chief justice Dorit Beinisch, in which the court disqualified evidence that had been illegally collected.

A policeman asked a bystander to empty his pockets, which it turned out included an illegal knife, but did so without sufficient suspicion or cause and without explaining to the bystander that he could refuse to comply.

Hirsch said that this Supreme Court decision was later adapted by the West Bank Courts as well, which had a considerable impact on a wide range of IDF prosecution cases as well as how the police in the West Bank could operate.

Relating directly to the reforms for minors, the Supreme Court had a big impact following a series of petitions to it filed by the Association for Civil Rights in Israel and the Palestinian Authority's Prisoners Affairs Ministry in May 2010. These petitions led to the court heavily influencing the IDF to reduce the length of many of its detention periods for Palestinian minors.

The Supreme Court kept the petitions active for years in order to continue to influence the IDF to make additional reductions in detention periods.

As a result of the Supreme Court keeping the issue in play, on November 28, 2012, a number of detention periods for Palestinian minors were shortened. From that date, minors under the age of fourteen had to be brought before a judge within twenty-four hours of arrest, while minors under sixteen not involved in serious violence had to be brought before a judge within forty-eight hours of arrest.

That was not the end of the petitions. The Israeli Supreme Court petitions are a complex process. They do not always follow the classic understanding of making a decision for one side or another. Often they threaten the government that they will issue a ruling that will set unfavorable precedents unless it makes some improvements to an issue on its own. In that case, the government often takes the suggestion to make changes rather than get a new judicial ruling that would make the changes obligatory. This achieves the goal of those who filed the petition, but avoids setting a formal judicial precedent.

That is what happened here. The Supreme Court kept an implied threat hanging over the government for an extended period requiring intermittent reports on the progress of the reforms, and the government periodically filed these reports to make sure the Supreme Court would not issue a decision.

Maintaining the petitions as active likely led to additional reduced detention times, which the IDF and the Israeli government updated the Supreme Court about in October 2013 and December 2016.

Those are the two versions of how the reforms for minors came about (in one view because of pressure from the Yesh Din report, and in the other view, due to Mishnayot's reforms with the additional backing of the Supreme Court). But did the reforms work? To better understand that, we examine the differing perspectives of Mishnayot and lawyer for Palestinian minors Gaby Lasky.

Mishnayot and Lasky's Contrary Views

Mishnayot's perspective was that "there is no doubt that we are talking about a success. There is no doubt. I think that even the Palestinians would admit to this."

Elaborating, he stated, "The success manifests itself in a few ways: (1) the separation [of minors from adults in the courtroom] made it easier for minors to speak freely, without pressures in the courtroom, thus helping the judge to better understand what is going on with the minor. Even technically, the act of separation of minors caused the proceedings to move faster.

"The average time until a hearing is held for adults [compared to] minors – it was much faster [for minors] out of a desire to avoid an interim situation where someone is detained and has not been tried versus someone who has been tried and sentenced and can receive all of the attention which the court and the prisons give to sentenced prisoners as opposed to pre-sentenced detainees. So definitely the result proves itself," he concluded.

On the Israeli government side, which Mishnayot could at least partially represent, there was a premise that the IDF said it had radically altered and improved the status of Palestinian minors so that past criticism was outdated. "Now 'a minor is a minor is a minor' does reflect how the system works today."

Chapter 8 extensively covers Lasky as one of the leading defense lawyers for Palestinian minors. Her depth on the issue of Palestinian minors' treatment, including confronting the reforms as they play out on the ground, makes Lasky a significant source for responding to Mishnayot. I asked Lasky her view of what Mishnayot had said.

In a rare and brief spontaneous moment, Lasky smiled (or winced at the pain of what she viewed as a skewed presentation of reality). Then she returned to her more standard serious and determined look. "Yes, in 2009, the military juvenile court was erected [with special training and different rules], but it doesn't mean that the situation for Palestinians for remand hearings or in punishment or in many other things got better. The only thing that happened is that this court seems to have been created for PR reasons."

This was a regular accusation against the IDF when it implemented reforms: that they were skin deep and designed to relieve pressure and bad press without real change. The IDF in turn tended to emphasize cases where the changes made a real difference.

Lasky, her voice rising, continued: "Because what happens is that still, the same rules that applied to them before, regarding arrests and remands haven't changed because of the erection of the new court. Nothing has changed regarding that. Not only that, they are not being remanded in the military youth court, they are being remanded in the regular court where there is no different legal basis that favors minors…

"For example, we are trying, as in Israel, to present a social welfare assessment for each child who has been arrested in order to present the judge with other material to see if there is a possibility to release him on bail…. The military prosecution is completely against that, and they are fighting it with all of their power, although the court permits us to present those assessments," she added. There have been potential reform developments from Israel regarding the social welfare assessment issue. But despite a 2015 decision by current chief justice Netanel Benishu pressing for more social welfare assessments, as of February 2019, the earliest the state said it might make a systemic change was summer 2019, and even that is far from a hard deadline.

In March 2018, the human rights group B'Tselem put out a report which acknowledged that Israel had substantially shortened pre-indictment times for minors to appear before a court, but contended that this was insignificant since post-indictment detention went on much longer and had not been shortened. Hirsch, no longer in the IDF, responded in March 2018 that post-indictment maximum detention times had been shortened from two years to one year and that efforts were underway to shorten it even more.

Pressed for an example of a case in which the changes had made positive movement, Lasky said she could not think of one, even as she acknowledged that they exist.

This could be indicative of her not recently experiencing them or else of the mentality of many defense lawyers for Palestinians to be careful not to praise any positive Israeli move too much. They are concerned Israel will use the praise to rebut their basic critique that the IDF West Bank Courts, reforms and all, treat Palestinian minors in negative ways in which Israeli courts never would treat Jewish minors.

The difficulty of finding convergence between Lasky's and Mishnayot's views about the reforms for minors (let alone if we included here the views of Hirsch, who is even more positive about the Israeli side) shows how hard it is to dialogue between the sides when politics and security come strongly into the picture. If there is little convergence on minors, an issue on which in theory the sides begin from much more similar starting points than they do on issues such as terror, what hope is there to converge and to improve cooperation on other issues?

The Defense Lawyers for Minors: Gaby Lasky and Nery Ramati

Islam Ayoub Steps into the Israeli-Palestinian Conflict

The views of defense lawyer for Palestinians Gaby Lasky and her partner Nery Ramati are best viewed through the lens of a specific case. Because of its importance and drama, I will spend more time telling the story of the Islam Ayoub case and trial than most other cases in this book.

The first question in the Israeli-Palestinian conflict is always where to start. Who was in the land first and can make the first claim? Israel often points to extended biblical Jewish rule and connections to the land, while the Palestinians point to extended periods of Muslim rule during the Middle Ages and in eras before and after.

The same questions can be asked about when to start the story of Islam Ayoub's case. From Ayoub's perspective, the prequel to the story started with Israel building a West Bank barrier in 2002–2003. The idea of the West Bank barrier was to block Palestinian terror attacks during the Second Intifada, 2000–2005. While the barrier was popular in Israel and objectively reduced the volume of infiltration of terrorists into Israel from the Palestinian territories, it was almost universally condemned internationally.

Taking the Palestinians' side, most of the world said the wall was illegal under international law on two main grounds. The first was that its specific path cut off Palestinians from some of their lands and cordoned off Palestinian villages into disparate "cantons" or cut-off areas.

The second was that it was viewed as a land grab – an attempt to unilaterally set the borders of the future expected Israeli and Palestinian states, grabbing pieces of land that were "supposed to be" part of the future Palestinian state under the 2000 Camp David II Clinton Parameters (announced by former US president Bill Clinton). But the "supposed to be" was contingent on a global deal resolving all issues to the conflict. The legality of the barrier reached the International Court of Justice in The Hague, which on July 9, 2004, ruled it illegal. The Israeli High Court disputes this ruling.

From 2002, Palestinians living in villages near portions of the barrier started to protest or riot near the barrier to press Israel into taking it down. The protests in Nabi Saleh, a small town of over five hundred people east of Ramallah, started in 2009. That was the prequel for Ayoub.

From the Israeli perspective, the prequel of Ayoub's story was the terror emanating from the West Bank during the Second Intifada, necessitating building the West Bank Barrier. Ayoub's story, from the Israeli perspective, started in early January 2011 or a little before, when he allegedly started to participate in rock throwing at IDF forces.

Rock throwing is not seen as a heightened form of political protest by Israelis. There is a growing list of Israelis who have been seriously injured or killed from Palestinian rocks thrown at their vehicles. For example, only eight months after Ayoub was arrested, in September 2011, Asher and Yonatan Palmer were killed by rock throwing near the highly disputed West Bank area of Hebron.

Asher, twenty-four, and his infant son, Yonatan, were killed by a rock thrown by Waal al-Arjeh from a moving taxi driven by Ali Saadeh when the rock broke the windshield and led Asher to lose control of the car. According to the Judea Military Court which convicted Arjeh and Saadeh, the stone that was thrown was large and deadly, not a small pebble of protest. We go into far more detail about the tragic Palmer case in chapter 10, but suffice to say that the case boosts the argument on the Israeli side that rock throwing can kill and should be treated as a security crime, not simply as a benign if envelope-pushing act of protest.

Human rights groups always hit at Israel for mistreating rock-throwing Palestinians, especially minors. But here were Palestinian rock throwers who caused a murder, and it was harder to say rock throwing was nonviolent after this.

As more people have gotten hurt, even Israeli civilian court law has gotten stricter in dealing with Palestinian rock throwing, passing a minimum sentencing law of three years in prison for lower-grade dangerous rock throwing. The bill was widely popular, with support from the opposition as well.

Israeli officials claim that many rock throwers also have a tendency to become worse offenders, including throwing Molotov cocktails, or even attacking Jews with knives and guns. When Israelis across the board think of rock throwing, they think of it at least partially as a security issue.

Ayoub's Arrest and Interrogation

With both the lethal potential of rock throwing and the perceived aggression of building the West Bank Barrier as the two sides' underlying context, the real story for Ayoub started around 2:00 a.m. on January 23, 2011, when about two dozen Israeli soldiers surrounded his house in Nabi Saleh and pounded on the door.

Fourteen-year-old Islam Ayoub thought they had come for his older brother. He was extra surprised that they had come for him. The soldiers handcuffed him, blindfolded him, allegedly roughed him up, and whisked him off from his home on a journey that was destined to change his life.

Most of Nabi Saleh's five hundred residents belong to the same extended family. Ayoub himself mainly became interesting to the Israeli police and IDF prosecution because he represented a chance to get at Bassam Tamimi. Tamimi, forty-four, was Ayoub's next-door neighbor and leader of the village's movement of – depending on whom you ask – nonviolent protest or low-grade violent riots.

Ayoub was allegedly taken to an army base, where he said he was held sitting outside for an extended period in the cold. Eventually, around 9:00 a.m., he was brought to the Judea and Samaria central police station in Givat Ze'ev near Ramallah and the IDF Ofer base which is the main location for the IDF West Bank Courts and prison system.

There, he was questioned by multiple police officers. The main interrogator was Moshe Madyuni. Interrogators Arnon Yahav, deputy head of interrogations

Jalal Ouida, and Nihi Susian, who had a secret and unspecified role, also played a part in aspects of the interrogation.

Madyuni, a twenty-six-year veteran interrogator, who had not previously interrogated Palestinian minors or done continuing education about new reforms for interrogating minors, led the interrogation.

According to Limor Goldstein, who worked for Lasky in representing Islam, he first learned of Ayoub's arrest shortly after 8:00 a.m. and immediately began telephoning various authorities to determine where Ayoub was being taken for questioning. Goldstein explains that he tried calling the Binyamin station first at 8:23 a.m., but Ayoub had not been brought there yet.

Next, he called the Ofer Prison to confirm that he had not been brought to the Israel Prisons Service there. At 9:01, 9:03, 9:04, 9:06, 9:19, and 9:26, he repeatedly called different police stations and Ofer until at 9:49 a.m., he was called by Ouida, who told him that Ayoub had been brought to his station in Givat Ze'ev.

Yahav made a notation in internal police documents at 9:24 a.m. about having spoken to Goldstein and told him that Ayoub had not yet arrived. At that point, there are already strongly divergent narratives of what occurred.

Ouida explains that Goldstein said he was in Tel Aviv and would come to Givat Ze'ev, which was sixty to ninety minutes away, but would also need to flag down a taxi to get there. Goldstein explains that he was right next to a taxi when they spoke and jumped in immediately after they got off the telephone.

He expected that they would not start questioning Ayoub until he arrived, which turned out to be at 10:49 a.m. He called Ouida to let him know he had arrived and requested to enter the station and immediately meet with Ayoub.

Ouida explained to him that they had already started interrogating Ayoub, but that Goldstein could still meet with him. However, about ten minutes later, Ouida called him to tell him a special police order had been issued to block him from meeting with Ayoub until 2:30 p.m. so as not to derail the interrogation midstream and that he would need to wait until then. How and what led to the issuing of that order during those crucial ten minutes was a story that would only be revealed at a later special mini-trial almost two months later in March 2011 about whether a confession Ayoub gave was valid or coerced.

Ayoub's interrogations went from sometime before 10:00 a.m. until 12:35 p.m., with a lunch break until 1:23 p.m. It stopped again around 2:45 p.m. for him to have a brief meeting with Goldstein, and then continued again until 4:52 p.m.

In the police's narrative, they initially viewed Islam Ayoub as just another Palestinian minor rock thrower who would spend at most a few months in jail and might name a few other friends of his to catch for rock throwing.

I am reporting here for the first time the details of the police interrogation transcript. The initial questions merely focused on Ayoub's rock throwing. Interrogators asked him how many times he had thrown rocks at IDF forces and under what circumstances. He said about twenty-five to thirty times. He gave as an example the Memorial Day for Yasir Arafat on January 1, 2011, a few weeks before. He explained that on his way to a store, IDF forces appeared firing gas grenades, one of which hit him in his leg, causing him severe pain.

Later that day, he remembered throwing around six or seven rocks at the IDF forces, presumably out of revenge. Ayoub also started describing a few people from his village in their twenties who were involved in rock throwing, remarking he could identify them because he was also using a special camera while working with a reporter part of the time. He described how a sixteen-year-old, Halil Hassan al-Tamimi, came to his school with a megaphone at the end of the school day every Tuesday and Thursday and hit home the message that "anyone who does not throw rocks is not a man and is a donkey [coward]."

Ayoub also noted that prior to his current arrest, he had been caught by the IDF before and released with a mere stern warning not to throw rocks again. All of that was pretty standard fare for an interrogation. But as it wore on, the police found that Ayoub was an investigator's goldmine. He was the first Palestinian witness to not only name Bassam Tamimi and Naji Tamimi as the ringleaders of the Nabi Saleh protests and riots, but to also do so in impressive detail that could help them finally send the leaders to prison.

The police – and later prosecutors – said that Ayoub's attention to detail in describing the Tamimis' activities blew their minds. In the most revealing portion, Ayoub gave a long, scintillating behind-the-scenes description of how the Tamimis organized the youth in Nabi Saleh.

Ayoub named Bassam and Naji Tamimi as always starting with peaceful marches, but then in parallel:

> orchestrating the recruitment of the village youth and of adjacent villages, dividing them into a number of groups, with each group having a different role as part of the violent demonstrations in Nabi Saleh. Over the course of the week, they conducted training for the groups in the village's council building. The role of one of the groups was to obstruct the flow of movement through the village every Thursday night with large garbage cans…making it more difficult for vehicles to maneuver in the village. The role of another group was, every Friday, to draw the security forces into an ambush laid by two other groups [which threw rocks at security forces].

Ayoub explained that simultaneously, an additional group's role was to gather gas grenades which were thrown or fired but had not exploded, in order to transfer them to another group which would throw the unexploded gas grenades at security forces. An additional group's role was to obstruct the flow of movement in the village by means of stones and burning tires which obstructed the security forces' vehicles maneuverability – while another group would throw rocks using slingshots at IDF forces.

Naji Tamimi also was said to have organized and trained a group from the Deir Nizam village to throw rocks at Israeli vehicles on the road to Halamish, near Nabi Saleh.

"As an aspect of the training of the village youth before the weekly demonstration," Naji Tamimi ordered "the division into groups of stone throwers to confront IDF forces frontally, while another group was ordered to outflank IDF forces from behind and to surround them and throw rocks at them."

Ayoub also identified fifteen other Palestinians whom the police had suspected of involvement in disturbances or rock throwing. The police had virtually never gotten such an unexpected gem before.

At the end of the interrogation, the police asked Ayoub if he was sorry for throwing rocks. He said he was not. They asked why. Not trying to feign any love for his interrogators to whom he had opened up, he simply replied, "Because."

When asked to sign a transcript of his interrogation, Ayoub refused, saying he would not do so outside the presence of his lawyer – reflected in a notation at the bottom of the transcript where a detainee's signature is supposed to appear.

Following his interrogation, Ayoub's detention was extended multiple times with him remaining in prison for around two and a half months, although that result was not inevitable.

The Mini-Trial That Captured International Attention

On January 27, 2011, Islam Ayoub's pre-indictment detention was extended on a temporary basis for an additional period of days with the expectation that it would culminate with an indictment. On January 30, 2011, he was indicted in the Judea Military Court for rock throwing.

By February 14, 2011, Lasky and Ramati had filed a motion for a mini-trial to disqualify his confession to the police on January 23, 2011, arguing the police violated his rights to get it. A so-called mini-trial to disqualify confession gets its name from the fact that it is a judicial proceeding that looks a lot like a trial with witnesses, counter-witnesses, documents, and lawyerly objections, but is "mini" in the sense that it only resolves the issue of whether a confession was valid – not the ultimate question of innocence or guilt. After a mini-trial concludes, the regular trial proceeds, though often the result of the mini-trial also dictates who wins the regular trial.

The mini-trial started on March 10, 2011, with the testimony of lead interrogator Moshe Madyuni and interrogator Arnon Yahav. His case would be covered by news outlets as major as the *New York Times* and as far away as one of Australia's major television stations.

What followed with Madyuni would flesh out the hotly contested yet poorly covered debates over the IDF West Bank Courts' reforms for Palestinian minors. But for understanding what happened next with Madyuni and in the following days with interrogation commanders Jalal Ouida and Yitzhak Shilo, the important thing to know is that by the time of Islam Ayoub's mini-trial in 2011, kids were already supposed to be treated with kid gloves. Whether Ayoub was, whether minors were in general, and what kinds of exceptions might apply to treat them more roughly is laid bare in the mini-trial.

The other key piece leading into the mini-trial is the power of video. As referred to in chapter 1, Nery Ramati, Gaby Lasky's partner, had pioneered using videos of interrogations to poke holes in the IDF prosecution's cases. In fact, several minors had been freed from detention by the IDF's West Bank Courts in recent months after, according to Ramati, he became the first defense lawyer for Palestinians to systematically watch videos of police interrogations.

Ramati had made a mind-blowing discovery from the videotapes. He said the Givat Ze'ev, Binyamin, and Hebron police stations repeatedly seemed to doctor their written transcripts in ways that contradicted the video they were taking of the same interrogation. In case after case, he noted that detainees were not being informed of many of their standard rights during interrogations at those police stations, even as the transcripts of the interrogations made it appear as if they had been cautioned regarding all of their rights.

Madyuni of the Givat Ze'ev-Binyamin police, located near Ramallah, who had interrogated Ayoub, had not only failed to tell him of his fundamental right to remain silent, which even the uneducated know from television and movies is a right police need to inform detainees about. He had three times substituted different instructions and statements in place of the standard right to remain silent formula they were supposed to read to Palestinians.

When the prosecutor finished his direct questioning of Madyuni, Ramati had carefully laid his trap for violations of the new "kid-gloves" rules and Madyuni had jumped right into it. With Madyuni already damaged goods and possibly even enough to throw out the entire case, Lasky and Ramati now felt – atypically for defense lawyers for Palestinians – that they might be gaining the upper hand.

They hoped to show inappropriate and conspiratorial behavior by the police regarding blocking Ayoub's access to a lawyer and leaving out his right to remain silent in order to coerce him into a confession during his interrogation. (The police meanwhile had a principled narrative for when they did and did not grant Islam Ayoub access to consult with Goldstein.)

Of course, all of this would only be possible if then Israeli army West Bank chief prosecutor Lt. Col. Robert Neufeld didn't drop the case and wash his hands of a run-of-the-mill rock throwing case that could turn into a massive embarrassment and garner more international attention – always bad for the prosecution.

Why were the police so sloppy even though they knew they were being taped? Why didn't the IDF prosecutor drop the issue before turning over evidence to his firm and before filing the indictment? Ramati was not sure.

But maybe "they convinced themselves no one would actually check and ever see, maybe it was not deliberate, maybe they did not care," maybe they were not used to being taken to task if they "forgot" to explain to a minor all of his rights during an interrogation or fudged the explanation to get a confession. In other words, they were insufficiently careful because their commanders back then were dismissive of the right to remain silent and did not penalize officers if they messed up a case, Ramati has said.

"But maybe they did not have an exact idea about what they were doing. Maybe they just had a lot of enthusiasm," Ramati would add. "Maybe they were just not careful; there was also a clear plan to get Bassam Tamimi."

This was actually undoubtedly a key part of the story.

Tamimi (father of the now-famous red-haired Palestinian teenager Ahed Tamimi, who was arrested for kicking an Israeli soldier in the high-profile case in 2018) is considered internationally by many to be the Palestinian equivalent of Gandhi, committed to nonviolence. But Neufeld, his prosecutors, the police, and the IDF had a whole different view of Tamimi: to them he was a dangerous and clever fraud.

They alleged that Tamimi organized parallel operations of teenagers for protesting the West Bank wall near the Palestinian town of Nabi Saleh. One engaged in peaceful protesting, but one was violent, albeit using rocks, amateur-style ambushes, and some of the IDF's own gas grenades against it.

For a long time, law enforcement could not prove Tamimi had any connection to the alleged violence, as he generally kept his distance from where some of his youths got violent. Ayoub became a star witness worth going the distance for because he was the first to finger Tamimi and describe his full alleged mixing of violent with nonviolent operations.

Tamimi's Palestinian and global supporters have an entirely different story of Israel trying to twist the facts and force accusations from minors to tarnish Tamimi's nonviolent reputation. But however one views Tamimi, the police and the IDF clearly viewed him as a serious threat to maintaining order.

Ramati also thought about the fact that the video was sometimes imposed on police because many interrogators do not know how to write Arabic, even if they know how to interrogate in Arabic. The idea was that there needed to be a verifiable record of the interrogation either written down in Arabic in real time or by video.

But they still might not be fully mentally connecting to the consequences of being "on camera" during the interrogations they conducted and might just be "checking the box," as many policemen viewed bureaucracy. All of this could be especially true if they rarely watched or were asked by others about the videos.

Language issues aside, was Madyuni, as a member of the Israeli West Bank police, an arm of the IDF courts together with the IDF West Bank prosecution and the IDF West Bank judges, or part of a separate and distinct entity? Critics argue that they are all pieces of one indistinct apparatus whose purpose is to keep Palestinian protesting down and to maintain order. However, on the Israeli side, many see these three groups as completely distinct and having different traits.

The Israeli police have been blasted numerous times not only for failing to respect Palestinian rights in interrogations, but also Israeli Jewish minors' rights, especially Jewish minorities. In 2016, a number of Israeli courts also criticized the Israeli police for bullying right-wing Jews who wanted to visit the Temple Mount. Some on the Israeli side would say criticism of the Israeli police in interrogations should be viewed as across-the-board and not as a specific Palestinian issue. It would be unfair, some say, to attribute interrogation violations by the Israeli police to the completely separate entities of the IDF prosecution and judges. And when the IDF prosecution or judges close or dismiss a case because of problematic police conduct, the Israeli side would say they should be praised for showing introspection and standing up for justice for Palestinians.

Critics can respond that if the IDF prosecution and judges do not toss statements obtained improperly during interrogations, then they are endorsing that behavior. But even in civilian courts, Israeli law essentially provides that if prosecutors and judges deem statements to police to be true, they should not ignore them due to police violations. Rather, they should admonish police to act differently in the future, while still using the statements.

It should be said, moreover, that the police themselves have no easy task in seeking evidence from suspects who not only might have perpetrated crimes, but also ideologically may view lying to police as proper if they categorize them as a mere arm of the Israeli "occupation." None of this justifies police departures from procedures designed to defend Palestinian minors' rights, but nor should the debate over these issues be ignored as we get deeper into how the police, IDF prosecution, and IDF judges each viewed Ayoub's case.

At a hearing before Judge Eti Adar on March 16, 2011, Ramati sought Ayoub's release from detention now that an indictment had long ago been filed. Adar was one of the few female judges in the West Bank Courts and was not among the sizable minority of judges who were religious. She was generally considered balanced, at least to the extent one would view IDF judges as being capable of being balanced.

Law enforcement (in Israel and the West Bank as well as in other countries) sometimes holds defendants in police custody until filing an indictment to make sure there is no witness or evidence tampering. However, outside of the West Bank, this is rare with minors, especially without a clearly violent crime.

Ramati told Judge Adar:

> Your honor, in your hands lies the fate of the liberty of a fourteen-and-a-half-year-old boy accused of throwing stones that hurt no one.... We had found deficiencies with how the police obtained a confession from Islam early on, but now we have reported to the court that the police did the interrogation and got the confession by breaking the rules and violating Islam's rights in a far graver manner than we had realized at the start.

Ramati would win this short-term "victory." According to Ramati, Islam Ayoub was released from custody in late March or early April 2011. But his release did not eliminate his confession or the charges against him. His mini-trial continued on March 21, 2011.

March 21, 2011, Testimony of Jalal Ouida

The "knock-out" of police officer Moshe Madyuni by Ramati had been huge. What was more, it set up Lasky with ammunition to use on the other police officers involved in Ayoub's case. But now, with her new baby twins who had kept her from the earlier hearing old enough to leave in childcare, Lasky needed to capitalize on that ammunition.

Trials are like sporting events in some respects. If one side gets the momentum, it can throw the other side off its game and "run up" the legal score with the judge. But just as in sporting events, momentum is a fickle thing, and it can reverse directions in an instant. With that in mind, Lasky honed in on deputy police interrogations commander Jalal Ouida, deputy commander of interrogations for the Binyamin regional division of the Judea and Samaria police at the Givat Ze'ev station.

There had already been a break after a battle of words and wits in the opening salvo of cross-examination. Ouida was spirited and combative, no easy nut to crack. He was ready to take questions in any direction he wished to try to boost the prosecution's case and denigrate the defense's case. That made him one of the more dangerous kinds of unpredictable witnesses. First, Lasky would try to hit him for preventing Ayoub from meeting with Lasky's law associate, Goldstein.

She would also try to nail him on failing to give Ayoub the right to remain silent, have parents present, or have an expert juvenile interrogator who is fully updated on reforms, as well as conducting the interrogation at night and missing signs that Ayoub was under duress or at least too tired to make sense. Lasky established the circumstances of Ayoub arriving at the police station while Goldstein was on the way and then dived in.

> Lasky: You knew there was a lawyer on the way – how come you did not wait [to start the interrogation until after Goldstein met with Ayoub]?
>
> Ouida: The lawyer said to me that he would come from Tel Aviv in a cab or cabs, something like that. So there was a decision to start the interrogation because getting to the Judea and Samaria police station from Tel Aviv takes a long time. He didn't say to wait. If he had said he would arrive within twenty or thirty minutes, I would have waited for him.
>
> Lasky: Who gave the order not to wait?
>
> Ouida: One of the officers, I don't remember, maybe it was me, maybe it was the head commander or the other officer.
>
> Lasky: Thirty minutes you could have waited?

Ouida responded yes, but that Goldstein had been very general about when he would be able to arrive.

> Lasky: If he had said he would arrive within ninety minutes, would you have waited for him?
>
> Ouida: No. From my perspective, that is not a reasonable amount of time. In light of the particular circumstances of this case.

Lasky asked what were the case's particular circumstances which made him unable to wait ninety minutes for a lawyer to speak to his client, a minor, before his interrogation.

> Ouida: You are talking about a specific condition that didn't happen. Maybe if he had said to me within ninety minutes, maybe at the time I would have considered it. The lawyer said he was coming from Tel Aviv in a cab.

He also added that he also might have acted differently if Goldstein had demanded that they not start questioning him before he arrived.

> Lasky: When a lawyer tells you he is coming to the police station regarding his client who is a minor, doesn't it seem logical to you that he is coming to meet him before the interrogation?
>
> Ouida: No. I want to emphasize that he did not give a time, an hour. He did not say to me I am coming to meet with him and hold off the interrogation like other lawyers say.

Lasky asked him if he had led Goldstein to believe that he would get to meet with Ayoub upon his arrival.

> Ouida: I can't predict the future, I did not say anything like that to him, and it is not within my authority to tell him something like that.

He added that making such a promise was bad policy, as he might need to break it depending on developments in the case.

In some ways this battle had been a draw. Ouida had a principled position on when he would and would not wait for lawyers before starting an interrogation and he argued he had remained consistent with that policy.

He also was trying to take shots at Goldstein for possibly not making specific enough demands about waiting for him, in order to shift the onus to Goldstein slipping on his duties as the reason the interrogation started without Ayoub getting to consult with him.

On the other hand, Lasky had made Ouida sound somewhat petty, fighting about thirty minutes versus ninety minutes, a point that Ouida himself seemed to internalize when he slightly backed off his initial total opposition to waiting ninety minutes.

Ultimately, the police's failure to let Ayoub meet with Goldstein before the interrogation was a point the court would note as a police failure. But Ouida's counterpoints and later witnesses would reduce the power of that failure in the eyes of Judge Sharon Rivlin Achai, who would handle the mini-trial and the main trial (Judge Adar only handled Ayoub's pretrial detention hearings and some of his testimony as a non-defendant witness in a separate case).

The IDF prosecutor came into the questioning of Ouida looking to defang some of the hits that Lasky and Ramati had landed in cross-examining Madyuni. A classic tactic in such cases is the public relations strategy to preemptively confront and frame "bad news" with the best possible spin. So instead of waiting for Lasky to ask Ouida about the police and Madyuni's failing to tell Ayoub about his right to remain silent, the prosecutor jumped right into the issue on initial direct examination – before Lasky got her chance to cross-examine.

But Ouida did not give the prosecutor the answer he was hoping for. Ouida, like Madyuni, did not appear to know that the police had not told Ayoub about his right to remain silent. He sang the praises of Madyuni's experience after Madyuni himself was slam-dunked on the stand and unraveled completely in his own changing explanations of what happened.

Ouida's alternate narrative, that Madyuni might have changed the literal text for the benefit of Ayoub's own understanding, was belied by the three times Madyuni told Ayoub he "must tell the truth" instead of "you have the right to remain silent" or a less legalistic explanation of that right.

On the other hand, Ouida gave the answer he gave despite the fact that Madyuni had already testified eleven days earlier on March 10. His answer showed he had not coordinated with Madyuni after his testimony, which at least in this case disqualified some accusations by Israeli critics that police always artificially coordinated their testimonies to help convict suspects.

Lasky also questioned and battled with Ouida over the fact that Ayoub's parents were not present during his interrogation and that he was arrested at night and interrogated when he was exhausted. In her decision, Judge Rivlin Achai would take note of Ayoub being tired – so Lasky got points with the court on some level.

March 29, 2011, Yitzhak Shilo Testifies

On March 29, 2011, Yitzhak Shilo came to the stand. Shilo was mainly important since he was the top commander over the police unit and had approved Ouida's request to block Goldstein from meeting with Islam Ayoub, at least for a few hours, even once he had arrived at the station.

Under direct examination, he explained that Ouida had called him on the telephone while he was out of the office to tell him that Ayoub had confessed and was incriminating others as well. He said that once he understood from Ouida that they had a chance to milk Ayoub's testimony to rake in a collection of other offenders they were going after, he approved delaying Ayoub's meeting with Goldstein so as not to disrupt the flow.

In cross-examination, Lasky started by pressing Shilo about the fact that Ayoub's parents were not at the interrogation. Shilo fought back harder, with a more sophisticated answer, and sounded less lazy than Ouida had on the issue. He noted that "the dynamics in the territories are different from the dynamics in other places." Shilo explained that soldiers, not police, arrest Palestinians outside Green line Israel because of security issues with entering Palestinian-governed parts of the West Bank. Here, Shilo clarified some points sometimes ignored by Israel's critics, who pile on accusations once they find one violation.

The highlight of the questioning of Shilo was a battle of intellects and wills between Lasky and the prosecutor over whether she could get him to testify on the stand about the police's ulterior motivations behind the questioning of Ayoub. Lasky was wondering why the police zeroed in on Ayoub even before some other Nabi Saleh protesters. She asked Shilo, in light of the fact that a Palestinian whom they had already questioned had incriminated not only Ayoub, but many grownups in the protests, why they had arrested a fourteen-year-old minor such as Ayoub first and before the grownups.

The prosecutor jumped out of his seat, calling out, "I object, how is this relevant to the mini-trial of the interrogation?" It was not the toughest objection, but he did not like where she was going and thought it was beyond the pale of the issues before the court.

Judge Sharon Rivlin Achai ruled that Shilo would need to answer the question.

Shilo tried to play down the issue, saying they mostly just used the IDF's most-wanted list without much planning, but then added, "I qualify my answer that it does not apply to two specific individuals."

Lasky sensed she was on to something now. The police commander had started to speak in code and with vagaries of speech to give full answers while trying to avoid something.

Lasky: Can you please specify who? Since there is no classified evidence privilege…I request to be given the names of those two in order to clarify if there were efforts to arrest them before the minor was arrested.

This time the prosecutor gave a detailed and strenuous objection, but unusually, Judge Rivlin Achai again ruled in favor of Lasky, though she noted that Lasky could only ask this one last question along this line of questioning.

Lasky: Who were they?

Shilo: I do not remember their names.

Lasky: If it please the court, why did you decide that they would be last?

Shilo: We started to understand at the start of the investigation that there were central suspects who were motivating the minors to get involved in offenses, and we thought that maybe they were the ones behind all of these disturbances of the peace. Therefore, we decided to interrogate the others first, and afterwards them.

Even without an admission by Shilo of their names, this still confirmed Lasky's bigger theory that everything that was thrown at Ayoub was a desperate attempt by police to get at Bassam Tamimi and, secondarily, at Naji Tamimi.

It was not necessarily as big a home run as nailing Madyuni on failing to give Ayoub the right to remain silent, but it did seem to be a powerful way to tie all of the violations together before the court and to argue that they were not accidental, but purposeful violations.

May 16, 2011, Limor Goldstein, Ayoub's Lawyer, Testifies

With the IDF prosecution resting its case, Goldstein was the first witness for the defense. He explained the history of his interactions with Ouida and the police preventing him meeting with Ayoub. He described how exhausted Ayoub was and how crushed his spirit seemed to be when he saw him, including Ayoub immediately bursting into tears.

But these were points Lasky had already scored in cross-examining Ouida. The more important part was the prosecutor's counterattack when he finally cross-examined Goldstein.

First, the prosecutor got Goldstein to admit that he is not a psychologist and that his testimony about Ayoub's emotional state was based on his subjective and non-expert observations. The prosecutor wanted to establish that Goldstein's description of Ayoub as exhausted and crushed should not be accepted as decisive or above reproach.

Then the prosecutor put Goldstein in a very uncomfortable position.

Ayoub had told Goldstein during their meeting that he had violated the offense of rock throwing, but only thrown one rock. Yet in the police interrogation itself, he had told the police that he had thrown rocks around twenty-five or thirty times and described multiple incidents in detail.

The prosecutor addressed Goldstein:

Prosecutor: I want to understand, you said that he told you that he only threw one rock. Can you tell me please why you think he lied to you – in fact, later you saw the interrogation video and we know that on that same issue he was not accurate in what he said.

Goldstein: I can make some guesses. It is not something that I really know.

Prosecutor: Can you explain, according to your observations of his state of mind, why he lied to you?

The prosecutor repeated the phrase of Ayoub lying for the judge to keep hearing it, even though he had essentially already asked the question.

Goldstein: I cannot make conclusions.

Later, the prosecutor returned to the same issue, showing Goldstein video footage of Ayoub in a calm mood as he exits the interrogation to see Goldstein and calm again as he returns to the interrogation after meeting with Goldstein.

The prosecutor tried to get Goldstein to admit that this proved that he had misjudged Ayoub's state of mind or that Ayoub was fooling Goldstein to create a cover story of having been abused to explain to other Palestinians later why he incriminated so many people he knew. Goldstein did not take the bait and fended off the traps. But the prosecutor's points got through to Judge Rivlin Achai, as she made clear later in her decision.

Next, the prosecutor moved to hit Ayoub's credibility in general about having been under duress or abused and Goldstein's credibility in judging what happened to Ayoub.

> Prosecutor: You said that you wanted to take a declaration at that time from the accused when you saw him and heard him tell you that he was beaten. Did you file a complaint with the army regarding the beatings which the accused claimed he suffered?
>
> Goldstein: We did not file. We considered the matter and came to that conclusion because filing a complaint would be accompanied by another interrogation by the harsh authorities, and in light of the harm that the accused had already suffered from his arrest and interrogation.

The prosecutor did not let down and listed off everything that the defense complained about in its motion asking for a mini-trial to disqualify Ayoub's confession as having been under duress. Then he continued:

> Prosecutor: With all of these violations of his rights, how can it be that you did not decide to file a complaint?
>
> Goldstein: We thought, we really thought, that it would harm the accused, so we dropped it.

The prosecutor went for the jugular.

> Prosecutor: Maybe the reason you did not file these complaints with the police was connected to the fact that it would have been difficult to show a basis for the beatings and violence claimed by the accused?

Goldstein rejected this narrative again, but the prosecutor had effectively highlighted the point to the court.

July 4, 2011, Dr. Gasriella Testifies

One other major dramatic aspect of the trial were the two expert reports, though really only one of the reports came into play.

Lasky tried to submit a report from international law expert Dr. Manfred Novak on problems with the impact of the Israeli "occupation" on Palestinian minors. Novak's report also claimed problems with how the IDF West Bank system specifically treats Palestinian minors and how that perspective should lead to disqualification of Islam Ayoub's confession.

Judge Rivlin Achai accepted the IDF prosecution's claim that the report was too general and did not accept it as evidence, saying it did not relate specifically enough to Ayoub's case.

However, the court did accept into evidence the second report on the impact of certain kinds of arrests and interrogations on minors by Dr. Gasriella Carmon, a psychiatrist with thirty-six years of experience, and Carmon eventually testified in court.

In tailoring her arguments to Ayoub's case, Carmon reviewed transcripts of IDF West Bank courtroom testimony in three cases involving minors as well as the video of Ayoub's interrogation.

The prosecutor tried to use her lack of familiarity with the case and with the other cases beyond those materials as a sword to deny the relevance of her testimony and expert report. Judge Rivlin Achai would disappoint the prosecutor by accepting Carmon's report and her testimony. But the real battle, as the judge noted in her ruling, was how much legal weight she would give it compared to other incriminating evidence.

January 2012, The Mini-Trial Ruling

Judge Rivlin Achai was not indifferent to some of the gaping holes that Lasky and Ramati had torn into the IDF prosecution's case. One can sense from Judge Rivlin Achai's decision that she herself was torn between two conclusions. On one hand, she was very disturbed by the police's conduct in interrogating Islam Ayoub. On the other hand, she found that the video of Ayoub's interrogation clearly showed a minor who, however tired, was strongly in control and of sound mind when he confessed and incriminated others, such as Bassam Tamimi.

There is a sense in her decision, which zigzags between pluses and minuses of disqualifying the confession, that in a theoretical world, she might have just wanted to describe the problems on both sides without having to make a specific concrete ruling about it. But in the end she faced a concrete question and made a concrete decision, however grudgingly.

She said Islam Ayoub's rights were violated, but that his confession was still valid because under Israeli law a confession is valid even when the detainee's rights were violated as long as the judge determines that the confession was still genuine. Put differently, Judge Rivlin Achai essentially said: yes, the police treated Ayoub poorly, but even after that Ayoub was tough enough that he voluntarily gave a true confession.

She listed the main problems with the arrest process and the police's interrogation of Ayoub which could theoretically have led to disqualifying the confession as follows. Judge Rivlin Achai wrote that Ayoub was only fourteen and was questioned when he was exhausted. She noted that he had no grown-up, whether parents or a lawyer, to support him during the interrogation. He was not told explicitly verbally that he had a right to remain silent. Further, she was disturbed by the police preventing him from meeting with his lawyer through several hours of the interrogation.

She notes that the problems with Ayoub's interrogation were not merely IDF West Bank law issues. They were also Israeli constitutional law issues under the Basic Law of Human Dignity and Freedom and international law obligations that Israel had taken upon itself when it ratified the United Nations Convention on the Rights of the Child.

Judge Rivlin Achai said that it was these constitutional law and international law obligations which brought about the revolutionary Amendment 14 to the Israeli law for minors – the basis and inspiration of all of the IDF West Bank system's new reforms for Palestinian minors.

At the same time, Judge Rivlin Achai said that based on the video, she rejected the argument that the interrogation was used to pummel or intimidate Ayoub into a confession at all costs. She referred to some pressure on him, but said "he was not under such pressure that it would cause him to give a false confession."

Crucially, she said that her observation of Ayoub was that he felt fine, freely gave information, and even felt secure enough to make efforts to clarify the exact meaning of some of his descriptions. Supporting this narrative of Ayoub giving the confession freely, she noted that he had steadfastly refused to express regret for throwing rocks – not something you would expect from a detainee who overwhelmingly fears his interrogators so much as to falsely confess to them.

Moreover, Ayoub was told verbally of his right to a lawyer (it is unclear why she notes this when his lawyer was prevented from seeing him pre-interrogation), that anything he said could be used against him, and he was given the chance to read the full list of warnings, including the right to remain silent.

After reading the list, he even signed a statement that he had read the warnings, she wrote (though he did not sign at the end of the transcript of his testimony that he affirmed the accuracy of the transcript).

Judge Rivlin Achai also wrote almost apologetically that it was difficult for her to estimate how negatively he was impacted by the circumstances of the interrogation because Ayoub did not testify in court for her to evaluate him in person. Only with his testimony might she have been able to override her observation of the video and of Ayoub signing on his confession that he was given all the warnings. Only with his testimony could she have trumped her observations which supported validating the confession even in problematic circumstances.

Despite her overall ruling, she cited two decisions to show the growing sensitivity of the IDF West Bank Courts to the treatment of minors and to reforms on that front in Israel.

In criticizing the police, Judge Rivlin Achai wrote she viewed them as lacking a commitment to the spirit of the new reforms for minors in those cases and the foundational principle of "a minor is a minor is a minor" proclaimed by former chief justice Aharon Mishnayot. This refers to the basic understanding that minors should be treated and viewed differently from grown-ups even when involved in crime and regardless of whether Israeli or Palestinian.

She said even as she understood that there were unique circumstances in the West Bank which mean that Palestinian parents will not always be able to get to Israeli police stations, every effort should be made to make it happen.

Judge Rivlin Achai laid into Ouida on the issue, saying, "My views are not like the views of investigator Ouida that the presence of parents from the area [in interrogations] is something which essentially does not exist." She said she had seen many cases with parents videotaped inside the interrogation or where at least the minor got to consult with the parents before the interrogation.

Next, she said that even as the police had discretion to start an interrogation without the minor consulting with parents, that discretion must be reasonable and fair. In contrast, Judge Rivlin Achai said, the police in Ayoub's case did not make a real effort. But she ultimately gave the police a pass as having acted merely problematically, but not illegally, since questioning Ayoub was part of a bigger, more complex investigation to catch Bassam Tamimi and others.

Strangely, Judge Rivlin Achai suggested one reason it was not illegal to start the interrogation without the lawyer was that Ayoub was probably tired from being up all night as part of the middle-of-the-night arrest. In that way, she justified one violation or irregularity because of the impact of another irregularity. Another view could have been that they could have let Ayoub sleep until the lawyer arrived. Judge Rivlin Achai wrote:

> There is not much in most of the defense's claims that the interrogation was draconian and that it eliminated the accused's ability to understand what he was saying. I already detailed that the impression I got from the recorded video of the interrogation was that the accused felt fine, provided information totally voluntarily and even pressed to ensure that his words were understood and clarified. The accused had his right to consult with a lawyer explained to him, it was explained to him that anything that was said to him could be used against him in court, and he was given the opportunity to read the full text of the warning (which included the right to remain silent), upon which he signed.

At the same time, Judge Rivlin Achai showed an independent and critical streak again when she wrote that the fact that the police told Ayoub he had a right to a lawyer did not mitigate the problematic issues, since Ayoub was so young that, without meeting his lawyer, he probably did not understand the powers and rights that gave him. She wrote:

> None of this should suggest that the accused's interrogation was free from failures. We are talking about a fourteen-year-old accused who was questioned while he was tired, without the presence of an adult to speak on his behalf, a right which was not told to him expressly, and he was prevented from meeting with his lawyer in the early hours of his interrogation.

But the bottom line, according to the judge, was that the violations were minimal enough and Ayoub was tough enough that the confession was valid. Ironically, the video of Ayoub looking mostly calm, despite revealing police violations that could undermine his confession, was the trump card for validating it.

Ayoub was convicted in 2013 and Bassam Tamimi was later also convicted. The final result, despite criticism from Judge Rivlin Achai, was a home run for the IDF prosecution.

Lasky's View on Ayoub's Case

Lasky summarized the titanic struggle over the Islam Ayoub case as follows:

> Lasky: Islam Ayoub was a minor. He was fourteen years old when he was arrested in a night arrest. He was taken from his bed in the middle of the night. He was handcuffed and blindfolded and taken to a location unknown to either his parents or anyone else.
>
> Early in the morning the next day, although he was not allowed to sleep or given any food to eat, he was taken to a police station for questioning. His lawyer was not allowed to be present at the interrogation.... At different times, four different policemen or others were in the interrogation room together with Islam.

He was falling asleep and crying…in the end, Islam was indicted because of a confession that was taken from him after he went through all of this ordeal – although he was only fourteen years old.

Regarding his right to remain silent. Although the policeman who interrogated him said that they told him his rights, when we were able to get video evidence of his interrogation, [it was clear that] he was never told that he has a right to remain silent.

Actually, the opposite: instead of being told that he has the right to remain silent, he was told that he has to speak. And he was told this not once, not twice, but three times during his interrogation.

So all of his rights were blatantly infringed during interrogation and arrest. Although we brought the issue to the military juvenile court to annul his confession because of all of the infringements of his rights, the court decided that his confession was acceptable and should not be annulled. And he was found guilty of throwing stones. And now [in June 2015] we are in the midst of the appeal of his case.

Questioned about whether Judge Rivlin Achai was being brave writing in the court decision to send a reprimand to the police, Lasky demurred. "The only way that the court can really be brave is if there are real consequences for the police. If the court had annulled Ayoub's confession, it would be sending a message to the police: although it is important to get confessions, you only can give me confessions that were obtained legally," she said.

With a rising voice and sense of righteousness, she made clear how she wished Judge Rivlin Achai had ruled: "This kind of confession was not legal, and it will not pass in my court – in this juvenile military court, it will not pass. So you better start working as you should, according to law, and not only bringing me confessions for the fact that you are bringing confessions."

She continued, "The most important thing is access to justice during interrogation and during detention. And if those things are not being preserved by the police and the army, specifically regarding minors, then the court shouldn't accept those confessions."

Delving deeper into the topic of consequences for police when they violate detainee rights, especially minors' rights, Lasky was asked if she knew of policemen being fired in any of the rarer cases where the court reprimanded police. She answered, "Not that I know of, but I can tell you that this is not special to the occupied territories. Over in Israel, I can show you cases where we have evidence that police have beaten people who are arrested. And they have not really been reprimanded or fired."

It seems clear that the court showed independence and a readiness to criticize the police on behalf of a Palestinian minor. It would seem inaccurate to tar the court with the police's actions in this case. The central question then regarding the court's acceptance of the confession is whether it would have done the same with a Jewish minor. Whether we think it would have or not again probably reflects how we approach the global political context.

After all that criticism and with all the problems with the police's conduct in the case, a fundamental question remains: Did Islam Ayoub give a false story about himself and Bassam Tamimi to please the police following heavy pressure? Or was the judge correct that the story Ayoub gave the police was still true despite their having violated his rights?

Lasky's full response to this question comes at the end of the book as she paints a picture of how the Islam Ayoub case works into her worldview in broad strokes. Foreshadowing Lasky's answer, it is important to note that she rests her view on attacking the use of Islam's confession not just on the basis of coercion, but also on the grounds of the "fruit of the poisonous tree." That legal concept essentially means sometimes it is better if society disqualifies a confession even if true, if it was obtained improperly. Ultimately, Lasky's view of whether Ayoub's confession was true – and whether that question is the main issue or secondary – works into her views about the lessons of the Holocaust and what kind of free and democratic Jewish state she wants Israel to be.

Chapter 9

An American Terror Victim: Ezra Schwartz

In running through the many illegal border crossings and rock-throwing incidents that come through the IDF West Bank Courts, it becomes almost easy to forget that the courts do not exist merely to maintain order.

Massachusetts native Ezra Schwartz makes it harder to forget. Schwartz was murdered by Palestinian Muhammad Harub in a drive-by shooting in 2015 during Schwartz's year abroad in Israel after graduating high school. Two others, forty-nine-year-old Jewish educator Yaakov Don and forty-year-old Palestinian from Hebron Shadi Arafa, were also killed.

When Ezra's mother, Ruth, first got notice that something bad had happened with Ezra, she was doing a physical therapy home visit. "I was at a visit when my husband called. I didn't answer because I was busy. He texted: 'It's an emergency.' I called back…. I had two little twenty-month-old babies (twins) sitting in front of me with their brand new au pair. My husband told me Ezra was attacked. I didn't understand what he meant. He was yelling and crying. He repeated that Ezra was shot, and it was bad. I frantically but calmly excused myself. My mind was racing. I was nervous and scared but hoping he would be OK. I got to the car. I called my sister in Israel and told her to go find Ezra."

She said she felt "scared, helpless, disbelief, responsible! I sent him to Israel…. I was worried that our family would be broken forever, and that this was just the start of our tragedies. I couldn't imagine life without Ezra."

She described her initial interactions with the military justice system, including a first meeting with Hirsch. "I met with Maurice Hirsch at my friend's house in Alon Shvut in April 2016. He was very sincere and compassionate. He answered my questions very frankly. He reiterated that the court proceedings can be very difficult, as the terrorist does not show remorse, and the family is proud. The prosecutor I spoke to the most over the year was very nice and always kept me up to date on the hearings."

Ruth and Ari, Ezra's father, debated attending the sentencing hearings for Ari's killer in March 2017. Recounting their decision that she would attend, but Ari would not, she said, "Everybody deals with grief and loss differently. My husband and I both want very much to focus on celebrating Ezra's life. He does not want to talk about the attack or to focus on Ezra's death. He also does not want to talk about the killer, use his name, or discuss too much about the proceedings in the court. (I did share with him my experience there, and he wanted to know, but since then we haven't talked about it.) It's too emotional and painful. We talk about Ezra all the time, we look at pictures and watch videos, and we share stories. We read letters: happy, sad, funny, emotional letters and memories from his friends all the time. But going to the sentencing was not something he wanted to do. He would have come if I had needed him, but I was OK going myself (with my support people). I didn't feel that it was a choice for me. I felt that I had to go and be there for Ezra. I am his mother! I needed to share Ezra with the judges. They needed to hear about the special person Ezra was, not just what was in the media. I didn't go to court to look at the terrorist. He was there, and that was strange and horrible and really disturbing, unbelievable, and very emotional. While I was in the court, I did not focus on all those feelings, though, because I was determined to be strong and talk about Ezra proudly. I did also have a lot of support. Coming home was very hard, depressing. Nothing had changed. My son was still dead!"

Describing the difficulty of attending Harub's sentencing at the IDF West Bank Courts at Ofer Prison in March 2017, Ruth said, "I went to the sentencing only, no other hearings. Maurice [Hirsch] recommended that the first time we spoke.... The US Department of Justice paid for me to go with two support people. Heather Cartwright came with us from the DOJ. We had an interpreter and another person from the DOJ stationed in Israel came with us to court.

"My sister that lives in New Jersey and my rabbi came with me from America as my support people. My other sister and brother-in-law and two of my nephews and a few other family members who live in Israel came with me. Several close friends that live in Israel came as well. In addition, two of Ezra's friends from yeshiva that were in the van that day [he was killed] came each with a parent from America, and the *rosh yeshiva* [yeshiva dean] and his son came as well. I believe we had around thirty people. The prosecutors [three prosecutors were present, including the prosecutor who relayed updates to her dating back to 2016] were very touched by everyone being there. They said this never happens.

"I was briefed before about what to expect at the Ofer Prison. It was a makeshift courtroom in barracks-type buildings. The prosecutors and the judges were in uniforms. When I spoke they looked at me. They were respectful.

"The only guards I remember seeing were in the court standing in the middle. There were three judges. I had no contact with the terrorist or his lawyer. The terrorist sat on the right side of the courtroom in a square-shaped, gated-off section, with two guards facing him and sort of protecting us from him or him from us – I don't know.

"I saw the killer. I did not make eye contact. I remember that he was heavy, and I was thinking, 'He's been in jail for sixteen months – why isn't he thinner?' I remember my sister noticing that he had new sneakers. I tried not to look at him, but I did, and he was looking toward us. He did not have remorse. He looked pleased with himself. He smiled.

"He had three or four people there for him. His parents were there. They came in after us through a back door of the court and left before us. They were kept away from us. They sat in the back right corner, and we were all along the left side, right behind the prosecutors. We had five or six rows of six seats all along the left side. There were four guards by the two sides of the court, and we had all been asked to be silent in court. There were one or two outbursts – nothing crazy.

"The terrorist's family had asked to be moved forward near their son. But they were not allowed. My friend mostly translated for me; the interpreter [for Hebrew to English] was not very good, and what she did interpret she seemed to do for the Americans from the DOJ…. I spoke and one of Ezra's friends spoke….

"I think Ezra's friend spoke about Ezra and being in the van on a normal day and losing Ezra, but that the terrorist didn't accomplish his goal. We are only stronger and more united. I spoke about Ezra.… I just felt I needed to be there for Ezra. I'm his mom. I needed to be there to tell his story and to make sure the person who killed him was punished."

Continuing her description of her visit to the courts, Ruth said, "As we were leaving the prison, the prosecutor came to me and took his pin off his uniform and gave it to me and told me he admired my courage and will always remember Ezra. He also shared the below text with me later."

> This war pin is from "Tzuk Eitan" (the 2014 Gaza War). For me, it symbolizes the strength of the Jewish people, the power to stay strong and united despite everything. It's a reminder for us not to break down even when it's hard, but to stay strong, for ourselves and our families. Although Ezra is not with us in body, his soul is always with us, and we all should spread his legacy all over the world.

Ruth added that the prosecutor appeared at a ceremony memorializing Ezra in November 2017 even though the legal proceedings were over by then.

Harub was sentenced to prison for multiple life sentences by the Judea Military Court in March 2017, ending the legal proceedings. But the Schwartz family has made sure that people do not forget Ezra's story. The Ezra Schwartz Memorial Baseball Tournament took place April 19–22, 2018, with the goal of honoring his memory and keeping his legacy alive. A spokeswoman for the tournament said that throughout his life, Ezra was a passionate sports fan and player, who took a particular interest in baseball. He played locally through the Sharon Little League as a kid and went on to play for his Maimonides High School baseball team as a teenager.

Baseball also bonded Ezra with his older sister and three younger brothers, all of whom have played for years at the Sharon and Maimonides baseball fields.

The tournament boasted Jewish high school teams from Maimonides in Boston, Flatbush in Brooklyn, Frisch in New Jersey, and Yeshiva University High School of Los Angeles.

A statement from the family noted, "Ezra's death didn't only affect his family and those who knew him, but touched the hearts of thousands of Jewish

Americans across the country who have traveled to Israel themselves, or who plan to send their children abroad to Israel to study."

They added, "He has become somewhat of a symbol to many who could imagine Ezra as being a part of their own communities.... That so many schools…feel it's important to send their students…to participate in this tournament…is a testament to Ezra's character and showcases the healing power of coming together as a community in times of tragedy and sadness."

In addition to the tournament, Ezra's parents, in partnership with the Jewish National Fund and the Israel Association of Baseball, are currently building a baseball field in Raanana, north of Tel Aviv, in memory of Ezra.

A fund-raising campaign has already taken in over $350,000 for the field, and the family expects the field to be completed, but noted in April 2018 that permits and other processes may draw out finishing the field for some time.

Furthermore, Ari is an avid runner and recently completed a rim-to-rim run through the Grand Canyon in memory and honor of Ezra.

Asked about the varied programs in Ezra's memory, his mother said, "I guess there is a feeling that every different thing we do is meaningful to different aspects of Ezra's personality and for different people he cared about."

Ezra's mother related another haunting and wrenching memory, but one which showed her family's commitment to Israel. "Two days before Ezra was killed, someone asked me how I could send my kids to Israel. The State of Israel is very important to us. After all the history of persecution, the Jews need a place – we need our own home. So you just trust…. We still go back," she said.

Still there are also happy memories. The family shared a story from Ezra's girlfriend which they said embodied his commitment to his team and his genuine sweetness.

She describes going to Ezra's baseball game one chilly Sunday afternoon when she was having trouble keeping warm. After a difficult inning in the field, Ezra came and sat on the bench looking frustrated, but he turned, they locked eyes, and he winked at her quickly.

After the game he apologized about how bad a game it was and that he had forgotten to tell her to bring a blanket to keep warm. She told him that the highlight of the game for her was when he turned around and winked, even though he was frustrated and busy with the game.

Ezra's mom said, "Every day as I drive into the cemetery to visit my son, I have about two minutes of happiness as my car approaches the place where he is buried. My mind tricks me. Every time, I expect to see Ezra waiting there, with his big smile and his arms open wide, running toward me with his legs practically dancing with excitement."

Chapter 10

Terror Trials

Israel and the IDF have faced a wealth of terror emanating from a variety of West Bank Palestinian terror organizations, with Ezra Schwartz being just one of many victims. The terror organizations as well as lone wolf attackers view themselves as acting against the occupation, responding to a death of a Palestinian they knew or acting after social media incitement. Many terrorists "martyr" themselves or are killed by Israeli security forces in the act. Many others are arrested and enter the IDF West Bank Courts system, either undergoing criminal trials or being placed in administrative detention. This chapter examines some of the most wrenching criminal terrorist trial stories.

It is impossible to fully explore the spectrum of terror attacks and terrorists who come through the courts. But five cases from recent years encapsulate some of the recent major trends.

The trials of terrorists Hakim Awad and Husam Kawasme for, respectively, the 2011 Itamar massacre and the 2014 kidnapping and murder of three Jewish teens portray the terrorists at their most violent and brutal levels. The lawyers for the Palestinian defendants and the defendants themselves frame their actions within the greater context of the conflict, while IDF West Bank chief prosecutor Maurice Hirsch frames their actions in terms of their horrific ideology and the challenge of terrorism.

Next, the rock-throwing murders of Asher and Yonatan Palmer by Walid al-Arjeh and Ali Saada show the difficulty of drawing a line between obvious violent terrorism and lower-grade violence or protest that migrates into terrorism.

The Palmer case also illustrates a new trend in fighting against the economics of terrorism. This is a trend also framed by the Rasmia Baluna case (the grandma who raised money for Hamas) in which Hirsch helped set a new precedent for raising fines against Hamas's bundlers (fundraisers) – even if those bundlers have no specific connection to violence.

Last, a brief discussion of an assassination plot against then foreign minister and now defense minister Avigdor Liberman shows that the courts deal with both random acts of terror and premeditated campaigns aimed at Israeli officials at the highest levels.

Amjad Awad – The Itamar Massacre

At the same time that former IDF West Bank Courts chief justice Aharon Mishnayot in 2011 was implementing reforms for Palestinian minors in the IDF West Bank Courts, one of the worst West Bank crimes ever was perpetrated by a Palestinian minor. That a minor perpetrated such a heinous series of murders sent a signal that sometimes liberal considerations of how to treat minors must be tempered by the reality.

On March 12, 2011, a sixteen-year-old Palestinian minor named Hakim Awad, along with his slightly older cousin, Amjad Awad, perpetrated one of the most grisly, brutal, and literally hands-on series of murders ever committed by Palestinians against Israelis. It became known in Israel as the Itamar massacre, after the West Bank settlement in which five members of the Fogel family were slaughtered at the hands of Hakim Awad and his cousin.

The murdered Fogels were the father, Ehud "Udi," thirty-six; the mother, Ruti, thirty-five; and children Yoav, eleven; Elad, four; and Hadas, two months old. Three other children survived. The oldest, Tamar, twelve, was out of the house at the time of the attack, while the other two, Roi and Yishai, slept through the entire attack and were not noticed by the attackers.

Leading up to the massacre, there had been reduced strain between Israelis and Palestinians in the broader sense. However, specifically between Itamar and the nearby Palestinian village of Awarta, both located in the northern West Bank about five kilometers southeast of Nablus, there had been a spike in tensions. Palestinians accused Itamar residents of chopping down their trees and burning their cars in the weeks before. Slightly more than a week before the attack, ten Palestinians and one Jewish settler were reportedly injured in a clash involving live fire.

Despite the tensions beforehand, the murders of the young children and the horrific pictures published afterwards caused shock both nationally and globally. Condemnation was widespread (though not universal) even among many on the Palestinian side.

After initially denying their actions, Hakim Awad and his cousin confessed to the murders on August 2, 2011, in open court leading to their convictions.

On September 13, 2011, marking almost exactly ten years from the heinous September 11, 2001, mass terror attacks on the United States, the court heard arguments about what Awad's sentence should be.

Speaking for the IDF prosecution, former chief prosecutor and predecessor to Hirsch Lt. Col. Robert Neufeld gave an unusual personal address to the court. Typically, the chief prosecutor stays in the office and sends his team of prosecutors to the courtroom. The chief prosecutor shows up in court personally only for cases of the highest importance. Neufeld told the court:

> As can be gathered from the indictment, we are discussing that the three children were murdered as they fought for their lives, the point at which they realized what was happening with the accused and his partner from the window…one held one of the boys and the second stabbed him….
> It is hard to make comparisons to a situation like this where the accused is in a struggle with four-year-old and eleven-year-old boys, children… who awoke hearing noises and their sins with regard to the actions of the accused were that they woke up, since anyone who continued sleeping was spared. Also, Hadas, two months old, was murdered, and why was she murdered? Because she cried, and that was her sin. A baby only days old, completely innocent, who was murdered because of her crying. She was murdered, and unfortunately, she was stabbed with a knife in her head. This murder is a murder which cannot be described in words…. The sin of the Fogel family it seems was that they left their door open as they were waiting for their daughter Tamar, twelve, to return home.

Neufeld continued that the murder was especially grisly because "there was no question of distance to distinguish it from another case where a bomb was set off and the accused does not know who the victims are. Rather, here it was done with the hands of the accused."

Next, Neufeld specifically addressed the question of whether Awad should get leniency since he is a minor. He said, "in this case it would be fitting for this claim to not even arise. I believe that this is a cynical claim. When a minor along with another takes the life of children, this is an outrageous claim."

Then Neufeld made a particularly interesting move. He told the court, "I note that the accused was not a minor according to the military order, despite the dynamics in the area of treating children under the age of eighteen as minors: the accused was sixteen."

While most would agree that sentencing Awad to life in prison was appropriate, this last particular legal dance about the letter of the military order versus the spirit and trend in which the courts had been ruling is indicative of a game that the IDF prosecution plays from time to time. At times, it will defend its policies, citing the progressive and voluntary spirit of the courts in treating minors more liberally than the written law requires. At times, it will ignore that spirit and demand the letter of the law be enforced.

Calling this a game may be insensitive to the real differences between cases that the IDF prosecution encounters. Different cases may very well require different approaches to issues where the law is not as set. Still, Neufeld could have sufficed with the arguments he had already made and with submitting binding decisions of the Israeli Supreme Court which say that a minor can be given a life sentence for murder – which he did file only a minute later.

In that light, the inclusion of this technical argument and playing with the definition of a minor is worth noting. It is also interesting that the age of minors, even in the military order Neufeld referred to and which served as formal legislation, shifted in the same month of September 2011 that Neufeld was making the argument.

Awad's lawyer Riad Aarda spoke next. He started by admitting that Awad had none of the typical legal defenses or excuses, having had full knowledge of what he did, being fully sane and not being under any specific family pressures. Instead of making a personal defense for Awad, he condemned the entire incident as an outgrowth of the occupation and the ongoing Israeli-Palestinian conflict:

If the court were to ask what were the motivations for these actions, we see that the motivations were because of the occupation. The authorities in Israel admit that Palestine is an occupied territory and also the [Israeli] Supreme Court, more than one time, has said that whoever is murdered in the territories or whoever is injured or caused damage cannot receive monetary compensation because the death or the harm are the results of combat activities.

Here, Aarda made his bold assertion that the court and the country of Israel is setting it up for future Itamars if it treats the incident merely as a point of law and order isolated from the greater context of the conflict. He cited as evidence the legal positions of several of Israel's own major organs of government, including incidents in which the families of Palestinians killed by IDF soldiers received no award based on a legal doctrine that compensation is not given for innocents killed accidentally in a combat zone, however tragic their deaths.

He continued:

In addition, regarding what my colleague the prosecutor said, that the murder of a baby is a harsh and brutal act – every act of murder is harsh. It does not matter if it is a baby, a youth, or an elderly man, and it does not matter who the murdered person is. From here, from there, it does not matter. We are all human. There is no blood that is blue and blood that is red, we are all equal.… What I claim is that the Fogel family is a victim and also the accused is a victim. Addressing the court, when you build a Jewish village in the heart of dozens of Arab villages, and you do not have sufficient security for the Jewish village, you need to expect that an incident like this will happen. I will tell the court what is happening on the other side. They are building on the land [Jews are building on Palestinian lands], there are no jobs, there are no studies, there is pressure on the people from the occupation from every direction. A child like the accused before us goes out to perform an act without knowing why he does it. He has a clean past, he has never committed any offense, he is not connected to any violent organization, the planning was only days before. I leave the punishment to the discretion of the court.

Aarda's argument presented a radically different view from how most Israelis react to an incident like the Itamar massacre. In a country where terror incidents are not infrequent, most of them, after the initial shock and horror, are quickly categorized and neatly filed into a box of "stabbing attack," "shooting attack," "bomb attack," or "rocket attack," and the country quickly moves on.

The Itamar massacre was different because the young ages of the children and the grisly photos published all over the media showing them hacked apart by hand stood out as unusually brutal, garnering national and global attention.

This was Neufeld's argument, the reason that he personally appeared at the hearing. The court itself mentioned the horrid photos and details of the murders in its decisions.

Against this backdrop, Aarda argued from a completely different point of view. His argument would not save Awad from life in prison, and Aarda did not seem to think it would. But he did want to remind the court that from the Palestinian perspective, no blood was bluer or redder than any other blood, and that however shocking the murders were, they were inevitable due to the location of the settlement and the broader conflict.

Awad himself spoke next.

He started with a general political appeal and explanation of his actions. He compared them to that of "Israeli military general Dan Halutz" who in 2002 ordered the killing of mastermind arch-terrorist Salah Shehade. He accused Halutz, then IDF chief of staff, of murdering "babies" at the same time as killing Shehade (children were among the fifteen fatalities, which Israel viewed as unavoidable collateral damage in the targeted bombing of Shehade's house, given he had been almost impossible to locate for a long period).

Awad said Halutz was asked publicly if he regretted the collateral damage to civilians and that he replied, "No, I fulfilled my orders." The airstrike on Shehade is still highly disputed because of how big a security threat he presented on one side versus the collateral civilian casualties on the other side – but both Israeli and Spanish courts (the latter being involved via universal jurisdiction, in which any foreign court can potentially prosecute war crimes against humanity even committed by foreign citizens) have said there was no justification for criminal charges.

He also cited an accusation of an incident of the killing of two Palestinians from his village a year before by Israeli security forces. In doing so, he tried to equate his actions with Israeli actions.

He named "the policy of Benjamin Netanyahu" in expanding the occupation as a reason for his actions and seemed to imply that he would live longer in jail than many Palestinians could survive under what he suggested was Israel's deadly occupation.

Awad concluded the proceeding with words that could ring across the region as a warning about the cost of not resolving the conflict as well as the monstrous ideological power of terror. He contradicted Neufeld's claim that the Fogel family's "error" was "leaving their door open." Awad said:

> The family's error was not that they left the door open, rather it was that they built a home on land that did not belong to them. With regard to the act that I committed, I am a human being like all of you. I have no mental problems. I have never had a problem or mental or physical disease; my only disease is the Israeli occupation. With regard to the court's question, I am aware of what I did, and I have no regrets.

When Hirsch addressed why he chose his job, what he found fulfilling about it, he gave one of his strongest and most emotional answers in response to this case, describing his fight against the scourge of terrorism propagated by terrorists like Awad: "Hakim Awad, it's important to remember…freely took part in the massacre and when he was convicted in court…he explained exactly what his motivations were for committing the crime. Let's just remember that we are talking about the murders of five people, including a two-month-old baby…. Can I in any way identify with slaughtering five people? Babies in their cribs? In no way, shape, or form. That's something which I think in any society would be considered to be one of the most heinous crimes, and to stand before any court of law and be proud of what you've done, express no regret… [slowing down, pausing and with rising disgust] is I think a level of demise that…that is hard to even consider and even understand in any society." He then explained that he took great pride as an immigrant to Israel in having responsibility for keeping Jews safe from terrorism and bringing terrorists who have already carried out attacks to justice.

Husam Kawasme – Mastermind of the Triple Teenager Murder

It is jarring how modest a terrorist mastermind can look in a brown or orange prison jumpsuit.

And then in the same moment that you stare at him wondering how this defeated-looking man can be behind such heinous crimes, you see how he responds to his victims and realize there is something dark beneath the surface.

In some ways, Husam Kawasme set in motion a chain reaction that led to many of the incidents reported in this book. Kawasme masterminded the June 2014 kidnappings and killings of Naftali Fraenkel, Gilad Shaer, and Eyal Yifrach. Those killings led to a massive Israeli crackdown on Hamas in the West Bank and the rearrest of the fifty-nine Schalit deal releasees discussed in detail in this book.

When he was sentenced on January 6, 2015, he was confronted by Avraham Fraenkel, father of Naftali Fraenkel. Kawasme looked at Fraenkel calmly, adjusting himself while looking slightly uncomfortable. Then he seemed to maneuver into a smirk, which concealed behind it deep, dark, and remorseless eyes. He was not alone, with ten of his own family and friends attending the hearing to support him.

The hearing started with Fraenkel addressing the court on behalf of Naftali, demanding uncompromising justice and life in prison for Kawasme. He explained that his sixteen-year-old son loved music and had many interests in and out of school, earning honors in many areas. Continuing, he said, "he helped his younger siblings and in his last years was starting to become a grown-up."

Explaining that what Kawasme had planned was "different from a criminally motivated murder," he noted that the Palestinian had buried the three bodies to erase their existence, which led to them not being found for eighteen days.

Barely looking at Kawasme, Fraenkel asked the court to give him "the full severity of the law."

Next, the IDF prosecutor spoke, also asking for a life term in prison. The prosecutor explained that the three teenagers were "not killed in a war like IDF soldiers; they received no eulogy and no prayers" when Kawasme buried them after their murders. Further, the prosecutor noted that those involved in murdering the teens had "not seen them as human…they were killed because they were Jews. When Marwan Kawasme called…he said, 'We got three Jews and killed them.'"

Kawasme had four of his own children and still did not care, the IDF prosecutor stated. He should "die old, worn out – from a cold heart – this is justice."

Kawasme's defense lawyer, Khalid al-Araj, discussed more in chapter 12, made a slight attempt at convincing the court to give him a lighter sentence. But in some ways his speech about sentencing seemed more a venting of general frustration at the Israeli-Palestinian conflict and the inability of jail sentences to bring justice or halt the cycle of violence. "Why will life in prison help? Will it help them [the murdered teens]? The 1967 situation is happening over and over again. Nothing changes except the names. Between the two peoples – why is there so much pain? Someday, maybe we will figure it all out. We will tell our leaders to bring it to an end. *Haval, haval* [what a waste, what a waste] for all the loss. He didn't kill anyone. He was an accomplice," said al-Araj.

Kawasme himself had nothing to say. Hirsch was in court only a few feet from Kawasme when he was convicted and later expressed his reading of Kawasme's reactions: "To see Husam Kawasme was definitely a traumatic thing. As part of my job, I try to the best of my ability to keep in contact with the family members of the people who have been killed. I had met with the families of the three boys. And to see their pain and to see the person behind that, who had engineered that act of terrorism, stand up in court without any type of feign of regret, say 'that's what I did' – that's something which you definitely don't see every day. On the one hand, great sorrow because of the three children who were murdered. And on the other hand, to see…a terrorist…getting his rightful punishment…he was sentenced to three life sentences for every one of the children that he murdered, a tremendous feeling also of satisfaction. And that the imminent danger that he posed also to other people was taken off the streets and forever."

Waled al-Arjeh and other Palestinian terrorist murderers such as Nedal Amar (who killed Israeli Tomer Hazan in September 2013) turned red and very uncomfortable either when confronted by family members of their victims or by the court for their actions. Asked why Kawasme had no emotional reaction and was not uncomfortable when confronted by Fraenkel's father, Hirsch explained this disparity as follows: "I think that when you consider the different backgrounds of the different people, that is where you will find the difference. Husam Kawasme is a Hamasnik, is a member of Hamas, from a family of members of Hamas, who truly identifies with the Hamas ideology, and that's what motivates the crimes."

Above all, the Kawasme case showed the side of the IDF West Bank Courts prized by Hirsch: cases that were black and white, good versus evil. Kawasme, like Itamar massacre perpetrator Awad, was a monster, and the courts existed to bring monsters like him to justice.

But not all violence and terrorism that Hirsch fought could be cleanly categorized like the Awad and Kawasme cases of murdering the Fogel family and the three Jewish teenagers.

Some Jews who were killed or injured were harmed by less obvious and blatant weapons than bombs, guns or knives. Some could be maimed or even killed by simple rocks.

Waled al-Arjeh – The Rock-Throwing Murders of Asher and Yonatan Palmer

Asher and Yonatan Palmer never stood a chance.

It was September 23, 2011, and they were driving on Route 60 to visit family for the Jewish Sabbath near Kiryat Arba along the West Bank fault-line area of Hebron.

This was a road on which many Jewish-driven vehicles had been pelted with rocks by Palestinians, but mostly they bounced off or caused only minor property damage to a side windshield. This time was different.

Asher, twenty-four, and his infant son, Yonatan, two days short of his first birthday, were killed by a rock thrown by Waled al-Arjeh from a moving taxi driven by Ali Saadeh. Arjeh's rock broke through Asher's front windshield, causing him to lose control of the car, which eventually overturned.

Asher's pregnant wife Puah would give birth to their second child five months later, a baby girl Asher would never meet.

It was several days before the security forces and the Defense Ministry recognized the incident as a terror incident, though they eventually gave it that categorization.

According to the Judea Military Court that convicted Arjeh and Saadeh, it was not a random, small roadside stone that the assailants tossed. Rather, the object was large and deadly.

Palmer family lawyer and former IDF West Bank Judge Adrian Agassi said the stone was "thrown from an oncoming vehicle that was traveling in the opposite direction…at that velocity, it was like a shooting bullet."

As Asher's father, Michael Palmer, told the court in a series of heart-rending moments leading up to the April 2013 conviction of Arjeh, when he arrived at the family's home he saw "a gurney with Asher's body wrapped in a tallit, and a little box on top; in the box was Yonatan's body."

Palmer at one point gestured toward Arjeh when talking about how difficult it was for him to speak about the tragedy while "the murderer is sitting here in court."

Arjeh for his part appeared unexpectedly calm before the hearing and when the lawyers were speaking, cracking jokes with his supporters. Yet he turned ashen-red and appeared teary-eyed and tense when Palmer was speaking about the loss of Asher.

Leading up to the court sentence, Palmer also talked about an enduring picture in his mind he has of "Asher, Asher's wife Puah, and their son Yonatan sitting together on the Shabbat [the Jewish Sabbath]" and of the "tremendous love between the father and the son." He noted that "Yonatan, like his dad, loved to smile, to be happy, and he was just starting to talk – that is when Arjeh killed him."

Palmer said that Asher and Yonatan's lives "were taken by people who did not know them, who had never even seen them, for the simple reason that they were Jews."

Puah added that her child, Orit, would never know Asher other than from pictures, and that she did not know how she would make do economically.

The attack was a powerful incident for two reasons. First, it made the case that rocks can kill, and rock-throwing incidents should be treated as security crimes. Here was a surviving grandfather, Michael Palmer, painting as awful a picture as one could imagine of the deadly effect of this form of so-called "nonviolent" protest.

Second was the battle over the economics of the sentence. The prison part was straightforward and unsurprising. The April 2013 court sentence for Arjeh was two life sentences plus fifty-eight years. But the economics of the sentence entered hugely new territory. On July 24, 2013, Asher's father, Palmer, asked the Judea Military Court for a "legal price tag" of approximately NIS 10 million in damages for wrongful death and compensation – to go along with the multiple life sentences.

Attacks by Jewish right-wing activists against Palestinians and Israeli Arabs, their property, and sometimes their places of worship in revenge for their community's acts of terror against Jews – or to deter the Israeli government from evacuating settlements – are called "price tag" attacks. That was not what Agassi and Michael Palmer were talking about in this case. Rather, they were appropriating the catchy phrase to describe heavy fines that might deter crime more than just lifetime jail sentences, which often end early due to a prisoner exchange or pardon.

Explaining the "legal price tag" idea in an interview, Agassi said, "Michael has taken on Israel, the EU, and the White House, and said, you may be legally able to release a murderer, but if so, there will be a price to pay." As with so many cases impacted by bigger political issues, Agassi was referencing the 2011 Schalit prisoner exchange as well as the release of Palestinian security prisoners with "blood on their hands" as part of the US-sponsored July 2013 to April 2014 peace talks.

Unlike "price tag" attacks, which break the law to achieve political aims, his legal price tag would use the law to achieve political aims. Such a legal consequence could not stop Israel (under pressure from the PA, the EU, and Washington, DC) from releasing murderers early in prisoner exchanges or as good faith gestures in peace talks. But they could make those exchanges harder or at least cost more for groups like Hamas.

At the time, there was constant daily attention on whether Israel would release Palestinian prisoners with blood on their hands to the Palestinian Authority, and Agassi believed he had found a new and innovative method to block such releases. According to Agassi, the monetary damages for a murder victim's family in such cases are equivalent to a special fine, which according to general legal principles must be paid off before a prisoner can be released, regardless of the length of the prison sentence.

Still, there was nothing straightforward about the request to set new precedents for higher fines. Agassi noted to the court at the July 24, 2013, hearing that Palmer could not file a regular civil lawsuit in Israeli civilian courts relating to the criminal trial, since military courts, including the IDF West Bank Courts, are generally viewed by Israeli courts as separate. In other words, said Agassi, the only way to compensate victims of terror from Palestinians living in the West Bank and convicted by the military courts was also through the military courts.

Agassi acknowledged that the argument was novel, but added that it made sense based on the legislative scheme of the military courts. It could be a stronger deterrent to Palestinians from committing crimes if they can be hit with fines that would block their release in a political deal. Further, Agassi told the court it must be "sick and tired" of sentencing terrorists "and the government releasing them again," with the Israeli Supreme Court routinely saying it was powerless to intervene.

Arjeh's defense lawyer, Khalid al-Araj, appeared to want to highlight that Palmer's damages were not concrete and were hard to quantify.

Agassi responded that the damages also related to the victims themselves, Asher and Yonatan, as well as their families.

There were also several dramatic exchanges between al-Araj and Palmer.

In one of the most dramatic moments, Palmer lashed into al-Araj when asked about what government victim payments Asher's family had received, declaring with unconcealed distain: "Yes, we received payments after your client killed my son and grandson."

Al-Araj was questioning Palmer in the context of cross-examining him about the veracity of the damages being claimed by the family.

Another significant moment was when al-Araj did not understand what Palmer said, as he was testifying in English, followed by a translation to Hebrew which the defense seemed not to fully understand. He was also not expecting Palmer to make comments other than those specifically related to monetary issues.

In the surreal exchange, the translator and the judges repeated several times to al-Araj Palmer's statement about Arjeh having "killed my son and grandson," until finally, suddenly understanding, al-Araj exasperatedly said this was not the point of cross-examination of monetary damages.

The moment did capture the dilemma of going for monetary damages in the context of a terror murder.

For a highly extended period there was no decision, in large part due to the novelty of the issue, as Israeli civilian courts in similar cases are capped from granting punitive damages beyond NIS 200,000 (less than $50,000). On December 14, 2014, the Judea Military Court panel of three judges granted massive punitive damages in the amount of NIS 3.5 million (around a million dollars) to the family of Asher and Yonatan Palmer and against Saadeh (the driver of the taxi Arjeh was riding in when he launched the lethal rocks). This was lower than the NIS 10 million that Agassi had originally requested, but was still unprecedented, and Saadeh was expected to appeal.

The NIS 3.5 million punitive award (about NIS 1 million for Yonatan, NIS 2.2 million for Asher, NIS 200,000 special damages to Asher's wife, Puah, and some other smaller amounts) was based on Agassi's expansive reading of Section 182 of the applicable Security Law, which, unlike in Israel, has no set financial limit. But until now no one had pushed the limits like Agassi, who gave sub-stantial credit to Palmer for his perseverance and for "taking on the system" since he said the IDF prosecution would not have originally pushed for such high damages.

A similar ruling, but with some nuanced differences, was reached on April 21, 2015, for the Palmers against the second defendant, Arjeh. A three-judge panel of the Judea Military Court granted massive punitive damages in the approx-imate amount of NIS 3.3 million. However, despite the unanimous ruling to grant at least some symbolic damages to the family, the judges split 2-1 over the size of the massive punitive compensatory damages award it gave. Judges Dahan and Berman voted in favor, and Judge Afik voted for a lower amount.

Following the unprecedented ruling on December 14, 2014, in which a different three-judge panel first granted a massive punitive damage award, the overall impact of this second ruling was to potentially solidify the new trend. However, Afik attacked his fellow judges for allowing the military courts – which generally stick to criminal jurisdiction – to wade into the arena of granting what were essentially large wrongful death damages meant only for civil cases in the civilian courts. The fact that one of the three judges said that the military courts had left their criminal military jurisdiction and crossed into civil law and the role of civilian courts – exactly what al-Araj had been arguing – strengthened grounds for an appeal.

Despite the split decision, the precedent-setting ruling, and the talk of an appeal, no appeal was actually filed.

This new legal price tag approach to deterring terrorism was led by the victims' family in the Asher and Yonatan Palmer case. But the IDF prosecution would open a new front in fighting the economics of terror by starting to use the approach itself in a more systematic manner as well.

The Grandma Who Raised Money for Hamas

Rasmia Baluna was not a typical terrorist. Over fifty, female, and with adult children, she did not fit the profile for being dangerous. And yet on September 18, 2014, she pled guilty to terror financing and possession of the assets of an illegal organization as part of a plea bargain. She had helped transfer around NIS 100,000 to Hamas on behalf of her son, a Hamas operative in Gaza.

She was given the fairly light sentence of twelve months in prison and an NIS 24,000 fine. But the original sentence handed down by a Samaria Court judge was not particularly unusual. The interesting part came on appeal when IDF West Bank Appeals Court judge Lt. Col. Zvi Lekach (who ruled against the IDF prosecution and in favor of Merav Khoury's client Abuhara in 2013) granted the IDF prosecution request to set a new precedent by exponentially increasing the fines.

In a landmark ruling, Lekach more than doubled the fine from NIS 24,000 to NIS 50,000.

The December 11, 2014, decision by the IDF West Bank Appeals Court judge had the potential to substantially set back Hamas's terror financing. Baluna was given a fine that was a far higher percentage of the transferred funds than any previous ruling. Until now, the fines against those convicted for terror financing had been exponentially smaller than the amounts those convicted had transferred to Hamas, with one recent case having a fine equal to just over

10 percent of what Hamas received. Hamas had received around NIS 600,000, and the fine was only around NIS 70,000.

The ruling, first reported by the *Jerusalem Post*, was aimed at opening up the floodgates in hitting every single Hamas terror financier with exponentially higher fines, particularly since it was handed down by an appeals court judge like Lekach. When an appeals court handed down a ruling, it bound future lower courts in both Judea and Samaria to the new trend.

True, the actual fine was only NIS 50,000. However, that fine was 50 percent of the value of the NIS 100,000 transferred by Baluna for Hamas, more than double the original fine handed down by the lower Judea Military Court, and around five times the relative amount of many fines routinely handed down until then.

In dramatic fashion, Judge Lekach noted the historic power of his ruling, stating that he recognized that "the fines that have been imposed until now did not reach" anywhere near "the amounts transferred" by those convicted of terror financing, "and were even substantially lower than them." But, Lekach said, "it seems to me that the time has come to set new punishment policies," since "there exists a great and significant need to fight terror financing."

Even in the late 1990s and early 2000s, Israel had recognized terror financing as a new and distinct front in fighting terror generally. The Israeli Supreme Court recognized this trend in a 2009 decision, calling for recognition of the threat of terror financing and making it a permanent part of the global agenda. It also cited the 1999 international Convention for the Suppression of the Financing of Terrorism, which Israel had ratified by 2002. Lekach wrote that Israel had been making changes with the understanding that "the struggle with terrorist organizations requires fighting also on the economic plane."

The legislative process in Israel is slow, but by 2005, it had passed a new law to better empower law enforcement to fight and criminalize those connected to terror financing. The parallel anti-terror financing legislation in the West Bank gave courts the power to sentence terror financiers with fines up to three to five times the value of the terror funds they transferred.

This would mean not just a fine of 10 percent of the amount of terror funds transferred, but potentially even far more than Lekach's 50 percent fine in the Baluna case.

In that respect, as important as the 50 percent fine was, more important was that the court left open the future possibility of raising fines to being equal to the full amount transferred for terror financing. Hirsch requested this when he took the unusual step of personally arguing the appeal.

This was Hirsch at his most proactive, and he thought, at his best: making civilians safer by coming up with new ways to slow down or bankrupt Hamas. At the same time, Lekach said that even as he gave a vastly higher fine than usual in this particular case, he still would not grant the full NIS 100,000 fine the IDF prosecution requested.

This might have made the ruling a mixed victory for Hirsch, but what made it an overwhelming victory was that Lekach added that his not granting the full fine the IDF wanted was essentially temporary. Legal precedent, he felt, dictated that major changes in punishment policies must be made somewhat incrementally.

In other words, Lekach said that once there were a few more rulings published with much higher fines, the court would become comfortable with fining Hamas terror funding accomplices shekel for shekel.

One of the unique aspects of the case, the court noted, was how "normal" and "clean" Baluna was, with no prior record. She had no direct connection to Hamas and had the perfect cover of being a harmless woman whose age put her far outside the typical terrorist demographic, as opposed to a hardcore Hamas member being the front for receiving the funds. She only got involved as being a conduit for receiving and distributing Hamas funds in the West Bank at the request of her son.

Hirsch hoped the multiplied increase in fines could hit Hamas on multiple fronts. First, the higher fines could make it harder for Hamas to recruit "normal" and less hardcore West Bank Palestinians to serve as terror finance bundlers for fear of new astronomic fines. Second, Hamas has generally paid fines for those working for it in order to send a message to future recruits that it takes care of its own. If Hamas continued to pay fines such as Baluna's as expected, the much higher fines would be a systematically higher drain on its funds away from other terror projects for which it might otherwise have used the funds.

The argument that Hirsch made to the court was a large part of what opened the major policy shift in punishments. The IDF prosecution had three major new arguments that were part of what convinced the court. First, Hirsch said that legal precedent on terror financing has always said that fines should be substantial compared to the amount transferred for terror purposes. Next, the IDF prosecutor noted that there is precedent with other financial crimes, such as tax evasion or fraud schemes, for fines imposed to be even greater than the profit gained.

Third, the IDF prosecution stated that Hamas had changed its historical pattern and was more often intentionally using innocent bystanders who don't arouse suspicion, such as an over-fifty-year-old woman like Baluna, to bring funds into the West Bank. This new strategy required a new response by the judicial apparatus to effectively deter the new tactic.

Besides the central ruling, the court also dismissed Baluna's counter appeal to reduce her twelve-month prison sentence. Palestinian lawyer Jamal Hatib had argued for leniency on the basis of her age, her clean record, and the fact that from her viewpoint, she was only assisting with a financial request from her son.

Hatib argued that she did not even know she was committing a crime, or at least not a serious crime, and that the Palestinian public viewed these kinds of fundraising initiatives as legitimate and not as taking part in violence. The court found that Baluna knew that the funds she helped transfer were earmarked for terror purposes and would be given no leniency.

This was a massive change in the IDF prosecution's approach to fighting terror financing. If in the first stage of seriously fighting terror financing in the early-mid 2000s, the IDF started to see it as just as primary as fighting terrorists themselves, now it had moved on to a far more advanced stage.

This December 2014 change did not happen in total isolation. In parallel, there were ongoing attempts in the Knesset to strengthen the Israeli prosecution within the Green Line and the IDF prosecution in fighting terror financing.

In June 2016, after many rounds of battles and amendments, these efforts led to a new major anti-terror law that addressed a range of issues, including financing. According to the law, charity groups that indirectly but substantially contribute to terror groups can be declared illegal, and many categories of those involved in such groups can be sent to prison by association. The concept was to better catch terror financing by cutting through straw-man companies that might serve dual legal and illegal purposes.

Connected to those efforts, the defense minister could now seize financial assets even pre-indictment and conviction if he found the assets relate to terrorism, much the same way he could issue administrative detention orders. Until now, assets could only be seized at the indictment and conviction stages.

Most closely connected to the Baluna case, now those funding terrorists could be fined up to twenty times the amount they were convicted of providing to terror groups. It was unclear exactly how this would be implemented in the West Bank, but it could only support the new trend of higher fines.

The radical change meant that the Knesset, on a bipartisan basis, had recognized that today's terrorists may sometimes be more deterred by losing money than by prison sentences. Israel and the IDF prosecution were starting to understand how to use socioeconomic dynamics to attack the underlying infrastructure that allowed terror financing to take place.

Forcing Hamas to choose between abandoning its bundlers and financiers by failing to pay their fines or continuing to pay ballooning fines that could quickly exhaust their resources put Hamas in a catch-22. Hirsch was aggressive in trying to fight Hamas and terror in new ways that could reset the playing field, and he undertook this with a strong sense of mission.

Attempted Assassination of Avigdor Liberman

Many terror attacks are random, killing whoever just happens to be unlucky enough to be in range. An example of this type of "by the way" terror attack is the one that killed British citizen Mary Jane Gardner. In her late fifties, Gardner was slain in March 2011 during a tourist visit to Israel. She was waiting at a bus stop across from the Jerusalem International Convention Center when she found herself in the middle of a terrorist attack that also wounded thirty-nine others. The terrorist, incidentally, was Hassin Kawasme, brother of Husam Kawasme, who masterminded the triple teenager murder.

But sometimes attacks are specifically targeted.

No story of recent years in the West Bank Courts is complete without a brief discussion of an assassination plot against then foreign minister and later defense minister Avigdor Liberman. The plot to blow him up using a rocket-propelled grenade launcher shows that terrorism and the terrorists passing through the courts are not only random "by the way" terrorism such as that which took the life of Mary Jane Gardner, but also designed to attack Israeli officials at the highest levels.

It was mid-August 2014, and the Gaza war between Israel and Hamas was in full force, having lasted over a month already. Three Palestinians, Ibrahim el-Zir, Ziad el-Zir, and Anans Bech, all from the Palestinian village of Harmala, tried to assassinate Liberman with the hope that his death would somehow end the war. In a sign of the unpredictable spread of terror during that time, the three were not connected with Hamas or another larger organization and were operating their own cell.

These last two points highlight the amorphousness of the terror threat faced by Israel. One might think of lone-wolf terrorists as dangerous only because they can grab a kitchen knife and stab a random Jewish bystander in the neighboring settlement. Yet some of the worst attacks of the in 2015–2016 Knife Intifada were perpetrated by lone wolves who managed to get their hands on weapons more deadly than a kitchen knife, still with little planning and organization. Here, an unaffiliated and therefore mostly untrackable small group of lone wolf–like Palestinians came close to pulling off the assassination of the country's foreign minister.

Also amorphous were their motivations. While obviously their broader motivation was fighting the Israeli "occupation," their immediate impetus – thinking Israel would stop fighting Hamas if its foreign minister was assassinated – shows how difficult it can be to define terrorists' ideology.

In some cases, the ideology may at least have some internal consistency. Here, however, there is no chance that Israel would have stopped fighting Hamas in Gaza because of an assassination of its foreign minister (had it succeeded) by non-Hamas-linked Palestinians in the West Bank. It would have had no impact or might have encouraged Israel to escalate its attacks as a general reprisal for terror.

Of course, part of the basis of the plot was a much more practical and logistical decision. Harmala is close to Liberman's home in Tekoa and gave the plotters many instances to observe his entourage of vehicles traveling in the area. Part of the plan also included measuring the time of traveling between Herodian and Beit Fahoo Junction.

Ibrahim, one of two brothers involved, was the leader of the cell and the one who tried to purchase an RPG to murder Liberman. The cell was arrested in mid-August 2014 by security forces when Ibrahim tried to purchase the RPG and was interrogated on an extended basis until they were indicted in November 2014.

The three were charged with conspiracy to commit murder as opposed to attempted murder (since they were arrested before they could get closer to commission of the crime) and were eventually sentenced to between two and three years in prison.

What Is the Alternative?

Recent years have shown that the terror challenge Israel faces emanating from the West Bank is every bit as real and lethal as it has ever been. Suicide bombers have sometimes been replaced by lone wolf attackers and fifty-year-old women smuggling terror funds, but there is an evident need to deal with terrorists who are caught.

None of Israel's critics have suggested an alternative to Israeli prosecution of Palestinian terrorists, and under international law, these terrorists mostly must be prosecuted by military courts. At best, defense lawyers for Palestinians and other critics have suggested that sending Palestinian terrorists to jail will not save lives from future terror attacks as long as the Israeli-Palestinian conflict continues.

But this point is inapposite. The IDF West Bank Courts may deter some terror and stop some terrorists from committing future acts, but it is obvious they cannot entirely stop terror as a phenomenon, nor can they bring peace. Regarding terror cases, they exist primarily to bring justice to terrorists' victims, also usually ignored by Israeli critics. They don't address all concerns of justice, as only other courts, not the IDF West Bank criminal courts, can address Palestinians' criminal and other claims against Israelis for violence or for perceived land grabs. (Land disputes are a civilian matter, and the military courts were never given civilian jurisdiction over anyone. It may simply be viewed as politically and diplomatically problematic to have members of the military deciding land disputes that relate to Israel's foreign relations.)

In that sense, the IDF West Bank Courts deal primarily with repairing one piece of the past, and they have little power to fix the future. But justice, even if it is only a piece of justice, is not unimportant. International criticism and the attention of would-be reformers or abolishers of the courts tends to focus exclusively on the treatment of Palestinian minors. Yet the main reason the courts were established was to deal with terrorism. Hirsch and other prosecutors will tell you that if there is ever peace with the Palestinians, and if the Palestinians could be trusted to prosecute their own terrorists, the IDF would be happy to either make bigger reforms or pack up and close the courts. As it stands, anyone looking to reform the courts must seriously contend with the question of how to handle terrorists.

Chapter 11

Administrative Detention under Scrutiny

The Context

A major issue of balancing national security versus human rights that comes into play in the IDF West Bank Courts, although it comes into play within Green Line Israel as well, is administrative detention. This is a special legal proceeding first used in Israel in the pre-state days of the British Mandate that allows indefinitely detaining a suspect without following standard criminal law rules or principles. For critics, this is the blackest stain on the IDF West Bank Courts, the greatest proof of the injustice of the courts.

The IDF says that its administrative detention policies stem from Article 78 of the Fourth Geneva Convention (1949) and international humanitarian law principles permitting special detention measures where the goal is not to punish for past crimes, but to prevent future terror crimes.

In administrative detention cases, there is no innocent until proven guilty, there is no full trial in the traditional sense, and secret intelligence can be presented. Defense lawyers can demand to see a paraphrase of the classified evidence, but they do not get to fully review it. These issues often make big headlines in the media worldwide and before UN human rights oversight bodies.

For supporters, administrative detention is a tool that saves lives in a country that faces greater and more constant national security threats from terrorists than any other democracy on the planet. Israel defends administrative detention as a last-resort procedure that is imperative for security reasons to prevent future terror acts. It says it is only used against arch-terrorists or for temporary periods against lower-grade terrorists during periods of heightened violence to maintain order. Further, Israel says the secret evidence element is necessary to protect intelligence sources.

Supporters emphasize that there is judicial review of administrative detention by special judicial panels, that judges view even the classified evidence to get a full objective picture, that detentions are often shortened by judges, and that Israel's Supreme Court can strike down detentions approved in the IDF West Bank Courts.

Most of this book is not about these issues. In fact, from 2006 to 2014, the percentage of administrative detentions to criminal indictments often fell below 5 percent and likely topped out at between 10 and 15 percent in 2014. The range has been around 150 to 700 administrative detainees at any given time, mostly averaging closer to the range of 250 to 300 detainees. The statistics show that this issue is not a part of your average case. However, to the extent that this is a major headline item that makes us grapple with some of the deepest issues in the balancing act between national security and human rights, it cannot be ignored.

Much of the world views administrative detention as a sham trial, though the United States used a variation of administrative detention at Guantanamo Bay after the September 11, 2001, attacks for hundreds of detainees and still holds dozens of detainees there in indefinite detention. Australia, France, Germany, Mexico, Malaysia, and some others have also used variations of administrative detention in smaller numbers. But any analysis of Israel's use of administrative detention in greater numbers than other democracies must keep in mind the unique security context.

Israel is a country of under nine million people in a very small area, leaving it in the 140s in ranking according to size out of over 190 countries. According to a February 2019 report by the Meir Amit Intelligence and Terrorism Center, during 2018, the volume of rocket and mortar attacks had skyrocketed to 1,119, as opposed to 31 in 2017 and 15 in 2016. From 2006 to 2016, there were 10,412 rocket attacks on Israel from Hamas in Gaza, at an average of 947 per year. It is true that "only" 15 rockets were fired in 2016 and 24 in 2015, but that was after Israel had fought its fourth war since 2006, including on different fronts.

In addition, during 2016 alone there were 142 significant violent incidents in Israel. That number fell to "only" 82 significant violent attacks in 2017 and 55 in 2018 – but there have been other years that were much worse in the last twenty years. In addition, the Shin Bet homeland intelligence security agency has said that in 2018 it had thwarted around 480 significant attempted violent attacks.

According to a February 2017 publication by the US National Consortium for the Study of Terrorism and Responses to Terrorism (START), in the United States, one of the largest countries in the world with 324 million people, there have been 109 jihadist-linked terror plots developed from 1993 to 2016, with thirteen attacks actually being carried out.

A graph put out by START showed a high of over fifteen plots in 2015, but under five plots each in 2014 and 2016, with an average of about 4.5 plots per year. Dividing up the thirteen attacks would mean only one every two years. And the United States is considered one of the more targeted democratic countries in the world.

Some Meir Amit "significant violent incidents" may be less severe than START's "jihadist plots," but then again the START data only has thirteen plots that came to fruition over twenty-three years. Israel has so many plots against it that this data was not in the report, and the number of significantly violent ones was 142 in one year. And that is only part of the threats facing Israel.

Whether this context justifies Israeli administrative detention policies and whether some wars could have been avoided or not, Israel does face unique security challenges that make threats on the US mainland pale in comparison.

Israel's Argument in More Detail

The administrative detentions desk of the IDF prosecution is divided between Ofer, near Ramallah north of Jerusalem, and Ketziot in the south, forty-five miles southwest of Beersheba. Most male administrative detainees are currently held in prisons or detention centers at Ofer, Ketziot, and Megiddo, thirty kilometers southeast of Haifa, and a small number of female administrative detainees are held in Hasharon Prison, ten kilometers north of Kfar Saba.

Each time an administrative detention order is issued, it is in effect for a maximum of six months, after which the IDF central commander who is also the top military commander for the West Bank must review it. A military court judge must also review the case and either fully extend the order, extend it but reduce the six months to a smaller number, or terminate the order.

Approaching the classified evidence issue from a completely different perspective, the IDF says that having classified evidence hearings just between the IDF prosecutor and the IDF judge, without the defense lawyer, is a positive, as it allows presenting the full case to the judge. Without this secret hearing, the IDF judge would not get to see the full classified evidence and also would not be able to deeply question the intelligence it is based on.

The presumption is that the IDF judge takes on the role of defending detainees' rights in administrative detention hearings, since the defense lawyer is not allowed to see the classified evidence. The IDF judge is assumed to be able to fairly defend a detainee's rights about as well as his defense lawyer could, even though the judge is supposed to be either neutral (not the detainee's advocate) or somewhat pro-prosecution, since he must also be concerned about maintaining public order, even if that impinges on a detainee's rights.

Yet, even if one assumes the IDF judge can maintain complete neutrality, weighing collective Israeli security versus the individual Palestinian detainee's rights totally objectively (a hotly debated assumption), the IDF prosecution gets a leg up with judges. They get to press judges on the veracity and significance of the classified intelligence without any advocate for the other side. Even the most objective judge is likely to be at least partially slanted when pressed by only one side on key aspects of the evidence.

Former Israeli Supreme Court Deputy Chief Justice and Attorney General Elyakim Rubinstein has worked extensively on the issue of administrative detention from the perspective of a judge hearing appeals on the issue. He describes the reasoning behind the procedure and proposes a suggestion for reform, as follows:

> Administrative detention is not the desired form of proceedings in the eyes of a jurist. In "normal" situations, you would like a "regular" criminal case to be conducted with the evidence being presented to the

defendant, who could cross-examine the complainant and the investigating authorities. However, while this applies to the majority of cases, real life and the crucial and critical fight against terrorism sometimes necessitate unusual approaches. Administrative detention, as a matter of prevention, is one of them. It has its origins in this country in the British Mandatory Emergency Defense Regulations of 1945. The reason for using these regulations nowadays is the fact that most, if not all, the evidence gathered against some suspects has been gathered by intelligence services, either Sigint (signal-technological) or Humint (evidence accepted from human sources). Revealing these types of evidence to the suspects or their lawyers may mean either compromising critical gathering methods (in the first case) or exposing the sources to a harsh fate, sometimes fatal (in the second case).

Administrative detention is aimed at prevention. This means that the relevant military authorities believe, based on the above-described evidence, that the suspect is about to perform terrorism acts. The detention, therefore, is preventive – but how do you make sure, as much as possible, that the authority's decision is right? Indeed the suspect and his attorney do get a paraphrase of the suspicion. But is that enough? Moreover, sometimes the initial investigation of the suspect is rather limited, for the same above reason – that you do not want to reveal critical sources.

Here comes the role of the courts. These are two, and for all practical matters three, layers of courts that are responsible for checking the evidence, two in the territories, and one in Israel per se. The three courts are the First Instance Military Courts in Judea and Samaria or the West Bank, the Military Court of Appeal of the area, and above them, petitions to the Supreme Court of Israel in its capacity as the High Court of Justice. Each of the courts searches the intelligence material in its entirety and in a way serves as "representative" of the suspects, endeavoring to see whether their rights have been properly observed. The fact that three justices of the Supreme Court sift through the intelligence evidence of each petition speaks for itself. Sometimes the court will, even without a full-fledged learned decision, recommend to the authorities to change course, and in most such cases, they will agree. Indeed, there have been suggestions to further develop the system with the interests of the suspects in mind, such as appointing a person – a former judge or the like – who would have the full clearance to review all the classified evidence on behalf of the suspects, and make recommendations to them without revealing the sources; this has yet to be fully explored. But even without that, there is a huge effort to achieve justice.

The Palestinians' Argument in More Detail

In the media, one product of the secrecy typical of administrative detention situations is an almost schizophrenic view of certain cases. In one case in June 2016, one side's charming circus clown was another side's terrorist. On June 13, 2016, Amnesty International condemned the IDF for administratively detaining a circus clown who performs for disabled children, saying the legal proceedings behind the detention were themselves a "circus act."

Muhammad Abu Saha was first administratively detained by the IDF in December 2015, and his detention was extended for another six months by a military court in Ofer in June 2016. Clowns from the United States, England, Germany, France, Italy, Spain, Brazil, and a list of other countries loudly protested the detention, getting even more attention for the case than usual. An Amnesty spokesman said that all they had been told was that Saha was accused of being a member of the Popular Front for the Liberation of Palestine, but with no details about him being dangerous or concrete evidence to back up the claim.

The spokesman added that Abu Saha was convicted of low-grade stone throwing when he was seventeen in 2009, but that the IDF presented no new evidence against him. The IDF did not publicly respond, but the *Jerusalem Post* exclusively reported that on January 5, 2016, a military court ruled, on the basis of secret evidence presented by the IDF, that Abu Saha is "currently active in the PFLP" and that his perpetrating a terror attack "was only prevented by his arrest and the arrest of others."

Further, the military court said that the security threat posed by Abu Saha was "decisive…and high level" and that his activities were "not political." In contrast, Amnesty's Hilal Alush called the detention a "political crusade to silence"

Palestinian voices opposing the occupation. With the secrecy that enshrouds administrative detention, it is impossible to know whether Abu Saha was a terrorist or just a clown.

The criticism of the secrecy side of administrative detention is only the tip of the iceberg. Critics of Israel's administrative detention such as the Addameer Palestinian prisoners support organization and the B'Tselem human rights organization say that it ignores "international standards related to the rights of detainees."[9] They cite Articles 4, 9(2), 9(1), and 14(1) of the International Covenant on Civil and Political Rights (ICCPR) that recognize the right of an individual who is arrested to "be informed, at the time of arrest, of the reasons for his arrest," demand public and transparent trials, prohibit "arbitrary arrest or detention," and prohibit administrative detention other than in the case of a national emergency.

Even as Addameer admits that "international human rights law permits some limited use of administrative detention in emergency situations,"[10] it argues that Israel does not follow the basic rules and limits on that detention. The NGO and other critics say that use of administrative detention obligates the detainers to give a fair hearing at which the detainee can challenge the reasons for his or her detention. They would say that Israel's use of classified evidence violates this obligation.

Israel would say that it has not violated anything and that all judicial systems, especially administrative detention proceedings, have a place for keeping certain classified evidence under seal for national security reasons.

For Addameer, B'Tselem, and others, the historic numbers themselves, especially during the First and Second Intifadas, prove Israel has used administrative detention in too sweeping a manner and not based on a case-by-case evaluation.

In the first years of the First Intifada, around 1988–1990, the number of administrative detainees increased to between eight and ten thousand. Hirsch has said that at the height of the Oslo peace process in the 1990s, the number

---

9   Addameer Prisoner Support and Human Rights Association, "On Administrative Detention," July 2017, http://www.addameer.org/israeli_military_judicial_system/ administrative_detention.

10   Ibid.

dropped to five detainees, and Addameer says that the number was only twelve on the eve of the Second Intifada.

Only two years later, in late 2002–early 2003, Addameer says that number had jumped back up to over a thousand Palestinians in administrative detention. Between 2005 and 2007, the average monthly number of Palestinian administrative detainees held by Israel remained stable at approximately 765. Since then, as the situation on the ground stabilized and violence tapered off, the number of administrative detainees dropped to two or three hundred. But with the onset of the knife attacks in 2015, the number reached over seven hundred again.

The IDF views international law's limit on administrative detention – that it must be for "imperative reasons of security" – as meaning it must be for saving lives, but includes in that category even smaller scale terror attacks. If permitting certain terrorists to remain free is going to lead to loss of life in the near future, the IDF would say it has the right to detain them to prevent that loss of life. This would obtain even if the evidence of their terrorism would not be persuasive in a criminal trial.

In this narrative, there is no numbers game or limit. If when violence is down, the number of detainees dropped to five, and with violence up the numbers spike into the hundreds or even thousands, that is the correct and proportionate result.

The IDF would reject allegations of politics being involved, saying that Addameer does not comprehend the vastness of the security threats Israel faces, even as Israel is the more powerful party in the Israeli-Palestinian conflict in the broader sense. The IDF would argue that the collective punishment argument falls by the wayside, as it is a simplistic understanding that critics plug in to explain Israel's motives only out of their own ignorance of the extent of the security threat.

Israel would label the suggestion of critics that they use house arrest in place of administrative detention as naive. This might be a stronger question for minors, low-grade offenses, and non-dangerous rock throwing. But most security experts would expect a genuinely dangerous detainee to flee house arrest. Further, house arrests cannot practically be enforced in the West Bank, since the IDF has no constant presence on the ground inside Palestinian cities and villages.

Israel's defining the status of the entire era since 1948 as a state of emergency may be overly dramatic and may not match every period. But there also have still been very few periods where there were no flare-ups or terror threats emanating from the West Bank for more than a few years.

Critics also attack whether an IDF judge's or Israeli Supreme Court review is serious or a rubber stamp. There are multiple levels of review. However, administrative detention orders are usually confirmed, meaning primarily the military commander gets what he wants. Also, the vast majority of appeals are rejected.

Accordingly, though it is rare, a couple of administrative detainees have even been held for around eight years.

A current issue from 2015 through 2016 included the question whether there was fair use of administrative detention against Palestinians detained for terrorism versus Jews detained for terrorism. Addameer claims only nine Israeli settlers have been held in administrative detention. Hirsch says the number of Jewish-Israelis who have been held in administrative detention is closer to dozens – most notably three Jewish Israelis detained for six to ten months in July 2015 relating to the Duma terror attack that month.

Critics say these numbers show discrimination against Palestinians. Israel usually says, as outgoing justice minister Ayelet Shaked has said concerning house demolitions, that these extreme measures are used far less with Jews because there is far less Jewish terror.

The Supreme Court, Administrative Detention and Hunger Strikes

One area where the Israeli Supreme Court's oversight has had a significant impact on the IDF West Bank Courts is the arena of administrative detention and hunger strikes.

This impact has been not only legal, but has had political consequences on the ground. The bottom line has been that the IDF has had to release some administrative detainees whom it might have held longer without Supreme Court intervention (provided that the danger they presented was limited).

In 2015–2016, administrative detainees (along with some other security detainees) led a wide hunger strike against being held in detention without trial or being held in detention after serving their time for a conviction. As late as April 2019, there were reports of a possible new hunger strike by prisoners over some related issues.

After two rounds of broad hunger strikes by detainees in 2012 and 2014 and two years of fiery parliamentary debate, the Knesset passed a forced-feeding law on July 30, 2015, which permitted hospitals to force-feed hunger-striking detainees whose health was in jeopardy.

The idea was that the Israeli government could blunt the impact of hunger striking as an instrument of public relations pressure and resistance if it showed that it would let detainees hunger strike until they got deathly ill, but would then make sure they did not die.

Without the risk of death and the potential explosive public relations and moral impact that could have on the Israeli government, the theory was that detainees would give up hunger striking as futile.

Key moments in the Palestinian hunger strike drama were on August 19, 2015, and in March 2016.

On August 19, 2015, the Israeli Supreme Court panel of Deputy Chief Justice Elyakim Rubinstein, Hanan Melcer, and Neal Hendel did something no court had ever done before. It "suspended" hunger striker Muhammad Allan's administrative detention pending him recovering in the hospital as part of a deal to end his hunger strike in exchange for a concrete release date from Israel. It had suspended the detention due to health reasons, without extending, reducing, or terminating the detention – the only actions it had ever previously taken.

At the time, it was unclear how the decision would impact future cases and whether it was merely a one-shot splash in the pan with little future impact.

That picture became clearer in February and March 2016.

On February 4, 2016, the Supreme Court once again suspended administrative detention – this time for hunger striker Muhammad al-Qiq.

Following the Supreme Court's ruling, which put pressure on the government to decide how dangerous al-Qiq really was, the Israeli government quickly cut a deal with him and released him by May 2016 in exchange for his dropping his hunger strike.

Then in March 2016, with Mahmoud al-Fasfas hunger striking against his administrative detention, Amnesty International campaigned for him with a statement that said the Israeli government's detention policy is a "balloon... popping over and over."

Amnesty argued that a number of recent instances in which Israel released detainees under the pressure of their hunger strikes had exposed "the bankruptcy of the administrative detention tactic."

It insisted that al-Fasfas be released and that in the future, Palestinians who are arrested be brought to trial under the regular criminal process without secret evidence and indefinite detention periods that come into play in administrative detention.

Amnesty cited the Israeli government's February 2016 agreement with al-Qiq as well as deals with Allan and others as a sign that the state is not willing to let hunger striking detainees die. Therefore, Amnesty said Israel should release al-Fasfas and others earlier on as opposed to just making them suffer and delaying their eventual and inevitable release.

This was the first time that opponents of administrative detention attacked Israeli policy on the issue on the basis of Israel starting to "surrender" to hunger strikers once faced with the Supreme Court being ready to suspend detentions.

One issue that had been lost in the recent agreements by Israel to release hunger striking detainees had been that it had not been using the Knesset forced-feeding law.

The *Jerusalem Post* reported exclusively based on an anonymous source that a primary reason for this was the Israeli Supreme Court's game-changing rulings of suspending administrative detention when confronted with the hunger striking detainees controversy.

Some observers viewed the Supreme Court's rulings as having little impact, since the hunger strikers ignored the temporary suspending of detention and continued hunger striking until Israel promised them a full release.

However, the *Post* reported that some Israeli officials viewed the Supreme Court rulings as having made the legal structure underpinning the forced feeding law essentially irrelevant.

According to this view, the Supreme Court's creation of suspended administrative detention removed detainees from the definition of "prisoner." The forced-feeding law was only applicable to "prisoners," meaning that suspending detention likely made the new law inapplicable.

This view would indicate that the Israeli government was deterred by the Supreme Court ruling from using administrative detention in some borderline cases.

As a side note, the Supreme Court declared the forced-feeding law constitutional on September 11, 2016. But if the forced-feeding law was outmaneuvered and unused because of the Supreme Court's innovation of suspending administrative detention, then the forced-feeding law became less important in practice.

Up Close and Personal with a Case

One way to get a better understanding of the dilemmas in administrative detention is to get up close and personal with a case, such as that of Wajia Nazal. Wajia Nazal was arrested and put in administrative detention on May 24, 2007. His administrative detention order was initially approved by the IDF West Bank Courts and extended at least until September 2008. But then something unusual happened.

On September 28, 2008, the court extended Nazal's detention only until January 20, 2009 – four months. The judge told the IDF prosecution that he would not extend the order again unless new intelligence was produced about new dangers presented by Nazal. Basically, the judge was saying that even acknowledging that past intelligence of Nazal being dangerous was accurate, he was still going to free him in four months if nothing new was produced.

Nothing new was in fact produced, and Nazal was eventually released, earlier than some others like him. Essentially the judge ruled that even if Nazal was somewhat dangerous, some of the intelligence that was provided to show that he would continue to be dangerous was not convincing. The judge also seemed to be unimpressed by some of the political calculations that the IDF prosecution may have mixed in with its more traditional security concerns.

The IDF and the Israeli government had offered Nazal an almost unprecedented compromise in exchange for freeing him from administrative detention – an offer he had rejected. In exchange for a vow not to provide any future aid to terror activities and "to not fulfill his role in the city [of Qalqilya]," he had been offered his freedom.

A vow not to provide any future aid to terror activities was standard. But what did Nazal serving or resigning as a councilman in Qalqilya have to do with his administrative detention? Was this not the very crossover of politics and law that the IDF argues does not exist in the IDF West Bank Courts system?

This was exactly what the defense lawyer argued. He said, "We are dealing with a political detention in all respects. We are not talking about a person who constitutes a danger to the area, rather a person that the security authorities do not want to serve in the post to which he was elected," said the defense lawyer.

Further, the lawyer explained that Nazal was fine with vowing never to be involved in aiding terror activities again. He just was unwilling to resign his Qalqilya council seat, which he thought was none of the IDF's and Israel's business, since he was democratically elected by the Palestinians of Qalqilya.

The lawyer said, "There is no justification and it is inconceivable that this would be decisive regarding how dangerous he is…he will commit not to exploit his [councilman] position to any activity which is directed at supporting terror. He will not commit not to serving on the city council. In my opinion, this condition is a political intervention into the internal affairs of the Palestinian Authority with intent to change the situation on the ground that, at the end of the day, will not lead to any change or consequence for the security in the area."

This case brings the hardest questions in administrative detention to the fore. Was the judicial proceeding fair? Did politics dominate the decision to detain Nazal with his being offered his freedom if he stayed out of politics? Did the court show independence with its unusual rebuke of the new intelligence and with a deadline on Nazal's detention? Or did it give the IDF prosecution too much leeway and ignore that political considerations were invading a legal process?

And how could the IDF be ready to release a man they said was a dangerous senior Hamas terrorist if he merely resigned a city council seat? Why did they care about the city council?

Maurice Hirsch explained the IDF prosecution's perspective on the bizarre Nazal case and why it viewed his city council seat as a "security" issue and not "politics." He said, "Wajia Nazal, as with many other…elected officials within the Palestinian Authority, was a member of the Hamas. The Hamas knows, understood, and clearly set as a goal taking over, as it were, by democratic means, all of the leadership infrastructure of the Palestinian Authority. Just to remind you, in 2006, in the elections that were held in Judea and Samaria and in Gaza, the Hamas won. The Hamas is the elected government, and not the PLO," he said.

"Wajia Nazal was in administrative detention not because he was an elected official...rather because he was furthering the goals of the Hamas...and using and abusing his...elected position to achieve that goal. Which is why the alternative could have been...to renounce...that you are now representing the Hamas... and forwarding the goals of [the Hamas in] Qalqilya...that could have contributed extensively to lessening the danger he posed to the area."

Next, Hirsch addressed how the IDF could offer to release Nazal merely for dropping out of politics if he was so dangerous. "I would like to say that all of the dangerous terrorists in Judea and Samaria are all in jail. That's not the case. Administrative detention requires a very, very high standard of danger posed by that person in order to warrant their administrative detention," he said. His view was that the IDF allowed many Palestinians who were dangerous to roam free since it could not detain everyone.

Overall, in Hirsch's eyes, there is no collective punishment. But the collective security situation does lead him and the Israeli security establishment to administratively detain a larger number of Palestinians.

Is Israel administratively detaining larger numbers of Palestinians because of collective security concerns or as collective punishment? That probably depends which side of the political divide you stand on regarding who is most responsible for the ongoing Israeli-Palestinian conflict.

Partial Reform of Administrative Detention

Recently there is a third side to the administrative detention debate. Some of the biggest advocates of the reform, surprisingly, are current and former IDF prosecution and judicial officials, including former IDF chief prosecutor retired Col. Liron Libman.

While such a background is possibly surprising for the job of reformer, IDF prosecutors are also uniquely positioned to advocate for reforming administrative detention proceedings. In this push, one powerful ally is IDF West Bank

Courts chief justice Col. Netanel Benishu, who wrote a journal article strongly supporting the reform. Benishu also wrote that four out of five Supreme Court justices queried about the issue in the past said they supported the idea.

For the first time ever, the reform also has more support on both the left and right ends of the political spectrum, even if still on the margins. There have always been harder-left politicians who wanted to reform or even do away with administrative detention.

But after administrative detention was used in 2015 against a group of extremist Jewish residents of Judea and Samaria after the terror attack on a Palestinian family in Duma, Bayit Yehudi MK Betzalel Smotrich started to support reform along with more centrist Likud MK and former Shin Bet director Avi Dichter.

What reforms are these former and current officials pushing for? Essentially, they hope to address the secret evidence issue, seeking to make the process more open. But how is this possible when the reason that Israel does not allow defense lawyers and detainees to see the intelligence evidence against them is usually to protect its intelligence sources?

Their answer is to appoint a special defense counsel, likely with a military judicial or other high-ranking judicial background, who will be cleared to view all classified materials and act as an intermediary arguing for the detainee based on all of the evidence.

In this case, Israel could still avoid giving the classified intelligence evidence to the detainee and the detainee's personal lawyer – persons it might not necessarily trust with the information. But at the same time, the special defense counsel could meet with the detainee to learn from him what kinds of legal issues he might be able to raise once he gets to view the classified evidence.

Libman explained in a report in the *Jerusalem Post* in July 2018 that in some places where this type of special defense counsel exists, such as in England and Canada, once the counsel "is given the classified material, he cannot be in touch with the detainee anymore."

This is the flip side of what makes this counsel "special." On one hand, the counsel can make arguments on behalf of the detainee that the personal lawyer cannot. On the other hand, the special defense counsel can never act as the detainee's personal lawyer, as a personal lawyer "cannot limit his client's access to information" in his possession.

Supporters describe multiple pluses for the defense from the creation of a special defense counsel. The counsel not only can make arguments based on viewing the full classified intelligence which the personal lawyer cannot make, he can also press the court to declassify more of the off-limits evidence. Some aspects of the counsel's arguments then would be made in the presence of the detainee and his personal lawyer, while other aspects would be solely with the court and the prosecutor present.

What about the other big problem with administrative detention – to wit, detaining a person for something he has not yet done? Libman says Israel must live with this dilemma and that there is no obvious fix. "Administrative detention is unavoidable in Israel. I have seen the intelligence material in dozens of cases. I did not see a single case that was ridiculous."

Supporters cite the same above statistics proving that the volume of administrative detentions can be directly correlated to how hot the security situation gets to prove that Israel does not abuse the practice. But they say that it is still problematic, so it is important to limit and reduce the problems by using a special counsel to make the evidentiary process less secretive.

With substantial backers from the system itself and some from the Right and the Left in politics, is the reform compromise of sorts moving forward? All signs to date are that despite the reform's strong supporters, it is currently stuck with opposition mostly from the Shin Bet and from some within the Justice Ministry, while others in the ministry support the change.

The Shin Bet has declined to respond other than to indicate that it has provided its position to the government officials handling the issue.

But it was reported in the *Jerusalem Post* in July 2018 that there are concerns that a special defense counsel would lead to fewer detentions even when necessary – creating more danger to civilian lives – and that there would also be some enhanced risk of intelligence sources being exposed.

Responding to the opposition, supporters suggest that doubts could be addressed by starting with a pilot program in select cases with Palestinians in the IDF West Bank Courts to see how it works in practice.

Beyond that, they say that the whole point of the special defense counsel being required to be someone with top-secret security clearance and likely a former IDF judge is that they are extremely trustworthy and leak-proof. Also, the counsel would only be able to view classified intelligence in specific secure areas.

Another problem the reform has is that just as there is some support for it from the Right and the Left, there is also bipartisan opposition. Ironically, many Palestinians and their defense lawyers oppose the reform as stridently as the Shin Bet, though for very different reasons. Gaby Lasky and others oppose the reform because they are only interested in eliminating administrative detention entirely. In their view, any middle-of-the-road "reform" will only serve as a fig leaf which could confuse global critics and help whitewash what would still be an illegal practice.

Also, each limitation on the counsel that that supporters praise as safeguarding leaks, Lasky and others view as turning the counsel into just another agent of the occupation under the guise of helping Palestinians. Supporters respond to this criticism contending that administrative detention is legitimate in the belligerent-occupation legal context from an international law perspective. They say it is better to get a bit more justice than there was until now, even if not all problems can be solved.

This is another issue about which compromise from either the Palestinian side or the international community could help encourage Israeli officials who are on the fence to experiment.

Chapter 12

The Defenders: Jewish and Palestinian Defense Lawyers

Wanting to put into relief the views of our four personalities, I interviewed other top defense lawyers, both Palestinians and Jewish Israelis. I would have liked to interview other prosecutors as well, and initially I received strong signs that the IDF would allow me to do so – on April 28, 2013, a spokesman even named five potential interviewees. But despite my repeated requests over the years, in the end I was never allowed to interview anyone except Maurice Hirsch.

To the extent then that the added color of views here is only from the defense lawyer side, it is solely because that was the wish of the IDF (though I understand some from the inside pushed for greater access). Why the IDF made this choice leads to some hard questions about its public relations strategy that can leave both pro- and anti-Israel activists scratching their heads.

Khalid al-Araj

Khalid al-Araj is one of the leading Palestinian lawyers who defends Palestinians, having practiced in the courts for around twenty years. His high-profile defendants include Husam Kawasme, convicted murderer of three Jewish teens in June 2014, and Waal al-Arjeh and Ali Saadeh, convicted murderers of Asher and Yonatan Palmer by rock throwing in September 2011. Both of these cases are discussed earlier, in chapter 10.

Most lawyers for Palestinians today are themselves Palestinians. While there are similarities between them and Israeli Arab lawyers such as Khoury, there are also differences, so it is important to hear their voices directly.

Al-Araj's big-picture view of the courts is not much different from that of many other defense lawyers for Palestinians, though he has more of a philosophical bent. He called the IDF West Bank Courts "very unusual, you cannot find any place in the world like them. Primarily, we are 'enemies.' The courts represent the conquerors, and we represent the conquered. We should not be able to get anywhere together."

Supporting this idea, he quoted an Arabic saying: "An enemy cannot be a friend."

Then, being a man of paradoxes, al-Araj shifted directions. He said that even though you would think enemies cannot be friends or even work together, he and IDF prosecutors and judges do work together every day. He explained that the paradox arose from his answering yes to the threshold question "Will we Palestinians recognize, work with, and make appearances in the court?"

Continuing, he said, "If not, then not, just as with the rest of the occupation, as [the courts] are just part of the occupation. But it was decided that we would work together." Al-Araj meant that if they answered no to the question, Palestinians would treat the courts the same way they treat the Israeli occupation in general – by boycotting it as much as possible. For instance, many Arabs who are Israeli citizens don't vote in Israeli elections even though they have the right to.

Asked when Palestinian lawyers as a group made this decision, he referred to a time after the First Intifada in the 1990s. Before that, he said very few Palestinian lawyers appeared in the IDF West Bank Courts. They were unfamiliar with the complex patchwork of Jordanian, British, Turkish, Israeli military, and international law that applied. At those earlier stages, they also had difficulties with legal Hebrew. However, over time, he believed Palestinian lawyers in the courts have gone from operating at a lower level to outdoing the Israeli lawyers who defend Palestinians.

His willingness to work with and appear in the courts, however, did not mean he pulled his punches when criticizing the system. Even when the courts act fairly, the "occupation" cannot be escaped. Like many critics of the IDF West

Bank Courts system, al-Araj could not accept that Jewish settlers in the West Bank are brought to trial in different courts from their Palestinian neighbors. As an example, he chose the least political scenario: "If a Jewish settler is speeding on the road or doing drugs…why can't that settler be brought to the same military court" as Palestinians?

I asked Al-Araj about former chief justice Aharon Mishnayot's principle that one cannot claim discrimination because Palestinians are foreigners and Jewish Israelis living in the West Bank are citizens of Israel – meaning their differing citizenship trumps the fact that they live in the same place. Mishnayot also pointed out that Israeli Arabs, in contrast, are tried in Israeli courts just like Israeli Jews, showing that when citizenship is the same, Arabs go to the same court and get the same treatment.

Al-Araj got visibly irritated and raised his voice, vehemently rejecting the citizen status distinction as artificial, saying, "What is the difference between them?" All that matters is "they live in the same place"; a Jew and a Palestinian "living in Hebron should be brought to the same court."

He also took issue with the courts' "selective use of Supreme Court decisions." He claimed that when Israeli Supreme Court rulings support the IDF prosecution, the IDF West Bank Courts follow Israeli Supreme Court precedent. However, when Israeli Supreme Court rulings favor Palestinians or are not convenient to the direction that the judges seem to want to go, they often ignore the rulings.

Next, he complained that it is too difficult for Palestinians to go directly to the Israeli Supreme Court for help, since they may only do so for administrative detention cases or for cases in which the IDF West Bank Appeals Court has mistakenly misinterpreted a narrow legal issue. In contrast, appeals from Israeli district courts go automatically to the Israeli Supreme Court potentially even on factual issues, though it rarely overturns findings of fact by a lower court and usually also focuses on narrow legal issues.

Al-Araj admitted that IDF prosecutors do not control IDF judges, and that judges do occasionally rule against the prosecution. Nevertheless, he argued that army prosecutors still have far more sway over the judges before whom they appear than their civilian counterparts. The initial charges that IDF prosecutors develop, even those less grounded in evidence, heavily influence the lens through which IDF judges view cases going forward.

After all of the criticism, one thing that was unusual about al-Araj was that even as he criticized the courts, he was a rare Palestinian who was willing to give limited praise to the courts, saying that many of the judges were top-notch and very professional, and that they handed down fair and unbiased rulings. In that spirit, he complimented three past and present judges: former judge Amir Dahan, former chief justice Aharon Mishnayot, and current appeals court judge Zvi Lekach, who ruled in the Ibrahim Abuhara case handled by Khoury.

He complimented Dahan for "trying to make a difference" in being fair to Palestinians and also called Mishnayot "fair." As for Zvi Lekach, Al-Araj told me two stories about his sense of fairness. In one case, a Palestinian was accused of illegal weapons possession. Lekach was hearing the issue of whether to keep him in police custody or release him. The lower court ordered that he be released. On an appeal heard by Judge Lekach, the IDF prosecution raised new charges.

Lekach held the IDF prosecution's feet to the fire, giving them only three days to come to the next hearing with a full explanation of the new charges and why they should be allowed to raise them now when they had not raised them at the lower court.

Three days later, the IDF prosecution had not showed up by 5:07 p.m. for a 4:00 p.m. hearing. Lekach ordered the Palestinian released both because the prosecution had raised new charges and because they had held up the Palestinian suspect's hearing. Al-Araj relished the story. He said that he remembered the exact time of 5:07 p.m. when the release order was stamped, since it was such an unusual event.

Al-Araj acknowledged that since the July 2009 amendment, the system had made "substantial changes to the laws, especially regarding [Palestinian] minors." That part of the story is covered earlier in chapter 2 and chapter 7. "If there was a problem with the interrogation, they [judges] may disqualify statements or give serious thought about how much weight to give statements from the interrogation," said al-Araj.

Even the IDF prosecution, before filing indictments, takes into account whether detainees, especially minors, were properly advised of their right to remain silent and to consult a lawyer. These considerations also influence the prosecution in deciding what jail sentence to pursue and whether to negotiate plea bargains, he said.

Lastly, we discussed what kinds of cases al-Araj would refuse to handle – his red lines for clients. He said the main category of defendant he would not represent was rapists. He said, "Emotionally, I cannot because many of the victims are girls who are minors. It is very difficult. I would have no explanation to myself to justify it."

With a thief, he said, it was not hard to justify. "I have an explanation, maybe it is a good one, maybe it is not a good one," but many thieves are poor and their crime does not harm people physically.

Honing in on a more controversial issue, I asked al-Araj how he felt justified in representing Husam Kawasme, convicted of masterminding the murder of the three Jewish teenagers in June 2014. He immediately launched into a narrative that was entirely different from what the court had accepted. He said Kawasme "did not want the murders, they happened incidentally, and he only wanted [his operatives] to kidnap one Jew alive to do a swap for a Palestinian prisoner." He added that the actual murderer, Marwan Kawasme, lost his cool when he and his accomplice accidentally kidnapped three teenagers, having only planned on kidnapping one, and that they had not known how to manage them.[11]

Marwan acted under pressure and killed the three of them without thinking – and without Husam being on the spot to stop him, al-Araj claimed. In other words, he was not arguing that Husam was innocent, only that the crime he was accused of was too severe.

Whether one accepts al-Araj's justification for defending Husam Kawasme and his red lines or not, understanding al-Araj's perspective on those issues can help to provide a window into how defense lawyers for Palestinians and the Palestinian side in general conceive of their actions in the IDF West Bank Courts.

---

11   In the full audio of the emergency call made by Gilad Shaer from the kidnappers' car, one hears the kidnappers declaring, "We got three" and singing. See "In Full Recording of Teen's Emergency Call, Kidnappers Heard Celebrating," Jewish Telegraphic Agency, July 2, 2014, https://www.jta.org/2014/07/02/israel/in-full-recording-of-teens-emergency-call-kidnappers-heard-celebrating. Full audio can be heard at Itay Blumental "Gil-Ad Shaer's mother: Police said the shots were blanks, we had hope," Ynet, July 2, 2014, https://www.ynetnews.com/articles/0,7340,L-4537127,00.html.

Mahmoud Hassan and Jawad Boulos

Mahmoud Hassan is legal manager at Addameer, the Palestinian Prisoner Support and Human Rights Association, and Jawad Boulous is director of the Palestinian Prisoners Society and a lead lawyer for the Palestinian Authority for many years. They are two of the most prominent Palestinian lawyers who represent a large volume of Palestinians, including high-profile cases, in the IDF West Bank Courts.

Among others, Hassan has represented Palestinian human rights activist Ayman Nasser in 2013 and Palestinian Authority parliament member Khalida Jarrar in December 2015 in their criminal proceedings in the IDF West Bank Courts.

He has criticized the IDF West Bank prosecution for what he characterized as playing games in bouncing Palestinians between criminal proceedings and administrative detention. For example, in Jarrar's case, he slammed the IDF prosecution for initially placing her in administrative detention, where she could have been detained indefinitely without standard judicial proceedings. Hassan claimed that the IDF prosecution only brought standard criminal charges against her after there was an international outcry.

At each stage of the case, he complained that the IDF delayed bringing charges against her, which hampered his defense. He criticized the IDF's use of classified evidence during her detention hearings, which he was not allowed to view.

Jawad Boulos has represented a long line of high-profile Palestinians in administrative detention, especially hunger strikers who have received international press coverage, such as Khader Adnan in June 2015, Muhammad Allan in September 2015, Mohammed al-Qiq in February 2016, and many others up to the present.

For years, Boulos has been the Palestinians' leading spokesman against Israel's force-feeding law and its administrative detention policies. He has condemned the Israeli Supreme Court for allowing such policies to stand. These criticisms are part of the classic view of most Palestinian lawyers that, due to special rules in the areas of administrative detention and otherwise, the IDF West Bank Courts are not fair to Palestinians and are an "arm of the occupation."

Leah Tsemel

Two legendary Jewish Israeli defense lawyers who cannot be skipped in getting a full picture of the IDF West Bank Courts are Leah Tsemel and Avigdor Feldman. They have generally sided with Palestinian human rights against the Israeli establishment. They are often thought of as "cause lawyers," that is, activist lawyers who use the law as a means of creating social change in addition to helping their individual clients.

Feldman, however, does more of his cause lawyering in Israeli courts, including in the Israeli Supreme Court. He has also represented many famous criminal defendants who have nothing to do with a particular cause. In contrast, Tsemel is more purely a cause lawyer. Her practice is heavily focused on defending Palestinians in the IDF West Bank Courts and defending east Jerusalem Arabs in Israeli Jerusalem courts, and she pretty much sticks to cause-lawyering.

I interviewed Tsemel about recent reforms that have occurred since 2009, including for Palestinian minors. She responded that "there have been some changes from the original system – some components of the structure have changed," but she said that it is "overall irreparable."

She said many might "go in innocent" to the courts and "dream about an acquittal," but they are almost all disappointed. She has not seen any broad-based improvement; indeed, "more and more, everything is just to get a conviction. Even if you win, the system does not care. The prosecution can appeal or else it sends the defendant to administrative detention."

She argued that "it is not an independent court because it does not live with the people it judges; it sees the Palestinians as the enemy, and the military deals with Palestinians under the guise of a legal front only in order for judges to manage them and enforce order."

The job of the courts is to "maintain the occupation. The military courts do the job of the military."

Are the courts needed in some fashion to address dangerous terrorists? She responded, "The really dangerous people get killed. The courts do not even deal with the really dangerous people. They kill people in the field instead of giving them the legal death penalty."

Though the courts have not implemented the death penalty for a long time, Tsemel said that over twenty years ago, she handled a case in which the death penalty was initially handed down by the trial court, before it was reduced to life in prison on appeal.[12]

Tsemel said that the IDF uses the issue of dangerous terrorists as a smoke-screen to "justify the existence of a big system" which "mostly deals with throwing rocks" or arresting unemployed Palestinians who illegally cross into Israel looking for work.

She remarked that "it used to be an even much bigger system," but that it has survived "like a company in bankruptcy, not as international law intended as being necessary for security."

Discussing the system's judges, she did not note significant differences in how the judges applied the law, focusing mostly on the idea that they took the jobs because they pay good salaries and allow them to advance into the Israeli civilian court system.

One exception was former IDF West Bank Courts judge Amir Dahan, who "tried more and was sometimes OK, but not in the end," since some of his liberal rulings were overruled. Other times he ruled less liberally out of concern that he would be reversed by the appeals court. Still, she said, "He stood out, he was more balanced, more humane, here and there handed down more acquittals. He was a very nice man and tried to see the other side."

She also complained about a double standard between the treatment of Palestinians and Jewish settlers, even though they live in the same area. She said "many settlers are not arrested" for crimes against Palestinians. And even if they are arrested, she noted, they are sent to Israeli civilian courts, while Palestinians are unfairly stuck in military courts. On the spectrum of defense lawyers for Palestinians, Tsemel was definitely one of the leading critics of the courts, viewing them as utterly unsalvageable.

---

12 While Israel has not enacted the death penalty since Adolf Eichmann's execution in 1962, and courts within the Israeli system do not have the option of imposing it, the IDF West Bank Courts do have the option to condemn a terrorist to death, although this has never been implemented.

Avigdor Feldman

Many would call Avigdor Feldman the dean of defense lawyers. We met him at the start of this book, when Hirsch described how this colorful personality had decisively won an appeal against the young Hirsch twelve years earlier.

Although Feldman appears in this book multiple times, he would have had an even more prominent role except that, as he himself noted, in recent years he has appeared at fewer hearings in the IDF West Bank Courts. When he does handle such cases, it is usually on appeal to the Israeli Supreme Court, where he has made history more than once. He also handles high-profile security defendants' cases in Israeli courts that sometimes engender parallel cases and issues in the IDF West Bank Courts.

For example, when Merav Khoury handled most of the Palestinians who were released in the Schalit deal, and whom Israel tried to send back to prison via the IDF West Bank Courts, Feldman, her mentor, handled those Palestinians or Israeli Arabs who for some reason were to be sent back to prison via the Israeli civilian courts. In my interview with him, Feldman said the cases "were all political; there was no connection to the law and there were no hard crimes" committed by the prisoners whom Israel and the IDF wanted to send back to prison for long sentences. He said he hoped the Israeli Supreme Court "can be free from politics, but who knows?"

Feldman also has a lot to say about interrogation tactics, being the lawyer who got the Israeli Supreme Court to declare torture illegal in 1999. Feldman also handles many high-profile administrative detention cases. He contended that the Israeli Supreme Court "can be convinced to reduce the length [of administrative detention] at most, but never outright cancels administrative detention."

Asked what Israel should do to keep its citizens safe from an arch-terrorist when the evidence against the terrorist is from intelligence sources and therefore not usable in court, he replied with his unique flair: "How should I know? I don't know. I don't have the secret evidence." As far as Feldman was concerned, his job was to worry about Palestinian defendants' rights. Others could worry about security. He certainly was not going to opine about a theoretical case in which he did not get to see the classified evidence – another dig at the system.

Feldman was also one of a kind like Alan Dershowitz in the United States in that unlike many other defense lawyers for Palestinians, he unabashedly said he had "no conscience, no red lines" for whom he would represent, and was focused on "interesting cases."

Chapter 13

Can the Courts Be Fair?
Ideas for Reform and
Views of the Future

Beyond what a broader cast of defense lawyer characters, including more Palestinians, said generally about the IDF West Bank Courts system, coming full circle also meant comparing their visions of the future.

One such vision developed and went into at least partial effect as this book was developing. The first discussions of this book dated back to December 2012 and early 2013 and by mid- to late 2014, I had performed initial interviews with a wide range of defense lawyers and received voluminous materials from both them and the IDF. But most of the book's serious writing took place between April 2016 and September 2016, and major reforms occurred in March 2015, smack in the middle of my interviews and gathering materials.

Had I finished the book at the end of 2014, the focus might well have been on looking toward the potential reforms that came into effect in March 2015. Instead, there was a larger focus on potential reforms not yet enacted, some of which have never been previously discussed. Yet the debate over the March 2015 reforms still revealed a lot about our main personalities and the system. So before getting into the latest vision for the future, we look at the reforms of the recent past whose impact is still debatable and very much in flux.

The chapter begins with a discussion with former chief justice Aharon Mishnayot, whose ideas formed the basis for the 2015 reforms. In the rest of the chapter, we explore others' reactions to the reforms and examine other ideas for reform that have been proposed.

Mishnayot's Reform Ideas

Aharon Mishnayot on His Reform Ideas

In a 2014 article, Mishnayot proposed his solution for improving the plight of Palestinians in the IDF West Bank Courts by giving them more rights when defending themselves. He felt that doing so would also improve outsiders' perception of the courts' fairness to Palestinians. He believed that the way to make the courts more fair was for Israeli civilian law to be further adopted by the West Bank Courts. These were the ideas that formed the basis of the March 2015 reforms. In an August 2015 interview, I discussed with him what his thinking was when he proposed the reforms that were eventually adopted.

He explained that even if from a "strict legal perspective there is no valid claim of discrimination" between how Palestinian and West Bank Israeli defendants are treated, "we need to honestly admit that the existing situation raises very uncomfortable feelings, and it is hard to ignore the lack of equality between different offenders who commit exactly the same crime, even if there is a legal justification. In these circumstances, it seems fitting to me to weigh the possibility of reducing the legal gap between the different populations in the area [the West Bank]," he said.

Mishnayot then discussed two options for making the criminal process for Palestinians and for Israelis living in the West Bank more similar. In his very cerebral and intensely legal way, he divided the options into "institutional" and "normative."

Really what he meant by "institutional" was moving West Bank Israelis into the IDF West Bank Courts alongside the Palestinians without changing the West Bank laws to be more like Israeli civilian laws. Even if the military law is different from Israeli civilian law, the effect would be more equal because the same military law would apply to both Palestinians and West Bank Israelis.

Really what he meant by "normative" was changing the laws in the West Bank Courts to be even more like Israeli civilian law. Even if West Bank Israelis were still tried in different courts than Palestinians, the laws that would be applied to each group in these different courts would be more similar than they are now.

With this legal flourish, Mishnayot has revealed a bit of a "dirty secret": current Israeli law does allow the possibility of trying West Bank Israelis in the IDF West Bank Courts, but for decades no government or attorney general has ever done this. Why they have made that decision Mishnayot explained a bit later. First, he explained why he preferred the option of keeping West Bank Israelis in Israeli civilian courts and making the laws of the IDF West Bank Courts for Palestinians more like Israeli laws.

Methodically explaining his thinking, he used double negatives ("no one can disagree with X…" as opposed to saying "X is a good option") to prove that where he wanted to go was the least bad option, instead of arguing for it as a good unto itself. He said that "no one would disagree" that Israeli civilian law was more advanced, liberal, and based on more updated legal thinking than the Jordanian law that applied in the West Bank dating back to 1967, some of which is still used in IDF West Bank Courts today.

Once again, under international law, an army that is in a state of belligerently occupying territory beyond its borders is obligated to continue applying the law that applied there before it occupied the area. This is supposed to guarantee that the occupying state does not implement harsher and more punitive laws for the foreign population it is managing.

Continuing to use negatives to make his arguments, Mishnayot noted that "there cannot be doubt" that the process leading to legislation in Israel is "more appropriate and carefully constructed" than IDF West Bank Courts legislation. After all, Israeli legislation was debated by a wide range of government and opposition parties in the Knesset before it passed, whereas West Bank laws are ultimately passed by the IDF central commander by fiat.

Further, even if it was morally "uncomfortable" to be judging a foreign people (the Palestinians) in military courts, he noted it was at least legally consistent and anchored under international law. He also implied there was just no other option for Palestinians – an assumption that critics could question. We will see such criticism later in this chapter.

In contrast to Palestinians in military courts, which he called only undesirable, he said trying Israeli civilians in military courts would actually be legally problematic unless there were no other choice. He derived this using the fundamental democratic rule of law principle that military courts should usually only be used to try soldiers.

International law creates an exception to that rule for trying foreign civilians in military courts. It prohibits trying a foreign people, the Palestinians, in Israeli civilian courts, in order to avoid both discrimination and any suggestion of annexation of their country or identity. That leaves military courts as the only option, he says, however non-ideal.

Yet Israeli West Bank civilians can be tried in Israeli civilian courts with no inherent problem – except for the indirect discrimination that seems to create for Palestinians. Mishnayot noted that two bodies, the Israeli Supreme Court (in its major 1983 decision known as the Moshe David decision) as well as the 1994 Meir Shamgar Commission, both found that it was preferable to keep West Bank Israeli civilians in Israeli civilian courts, and that it might be legally problematic not to.

Put differently, if international war and peace have created a freakish situation in which Palestinians are tried in Israeli military courts, that should be limited as much as possible, not expanded needlessly to include West Bank Israelis.

Commenting on the reforms that were put into effect in March 2015 and how far there is to go, Mishnayot said, "We are doing big things to fix problems, but we still need to improve. This is very important."

Addressing critics who say the reforms are superficial or fig leaves to hide problems with the occupation, Mishnayot said, "I do not always think their motivations are legal. I'm not political. I don't know what to say. I need to be very careful. I understand them – they think politically. I say the courts are not part of the occupation. But they are anti-occupation."

In April 2016, I returned to former chief justice Mishnayot to ask about similar issues and about whether he has done enough to further change. He said, "With the normalizing of West Bank law to be more like Israeli law, yes, I think I'm OK, though I know it is not equal to Israeli law."

Concluding regarding his reform ideas and reacting again to critics who want more change, he said, "I understand them. As long as there is an occupation, they will say, 'How can you make it normal?'"

Maurice Hirsch on Mishnayot's Reform Ideas

Maurice Hirsch was clearly not a fan of Aharon Mishnayot's 2014 article and the 2015 legislative changes that were made in its spirit. For many years, dating back to 2002–2003 and even to the present, there have been continuous calls by the courts to adopt Israeli penal law Amendment 39, or what became known as the March 2015 reforms, into the West Bank Courts' law.

"I famously objected to that change. Everyone knows I objected the first time. They decided to move forward with a process that would lead to adopting it when I was out of the Judea and Samaria Military Courts, serving as legal advisor to the Israeli air force and a prosecutor for deserters." According to Hirsch, it was adopted in March 2015 over his objections as current West Bank prosecutor, partially because the train had left the station at a time when he was not involved in the debate.

Why did he oppose Mishnayot's initiative?

There are multiple reasons.

First, "There are legal reasons: international law requires that you do not change the law in the area unless it is absolutely necessary. The changes in 1967 were sufficient to provide a basis for a substantial legal system until 1996. I didn't see the justification for adopting the new rules." (To arguments such as this, Mishnayot has responded that the passage of time itself is what has turned what was just borderline unfair into something intolerable.)

Second, according to Hirsch, "If you go with Aharon Mishnayot's argument, what you are doing is you are annexing Judea and Samaria." He added that as soon as the March 2015 reforms were "adopted, the immediate response of the Palestinian Prisoner Authority wasn't to commend the military commander for his step in improving the substantive law" for Palestinians. "It was exactly what I had argued – they called it another step toward annexation."

Mishnayot's article anticipated objections such as these. He gave specific examples of where the IDF West Bank Courts have already adopted Israeli laws in certain areas of evidence as well as in drug-related crimes, without anyone attacking the adoption of Israeli law as creeping annexation.

I asked Hirsch what he thought of Mishnayot's two examples. Hirsch answered, "That is a very rosy way to look at things. When you choose two specific cases like that. The rules regarding evidence from 1967 are one of many different military legislative orders given" regarding the Judea and Samaria Military Courts. "We can talk about the law of criminal procedure, the law of evidence as separate things, but let's save time. Why go through all of the individual changes? Just say let's do things like in Israel."

Hirsch added that adopting Israeli law for drug-related crimes also proved nothing, as that one unique case related to rapid changes in the different kinds of illegal substances being used and distributed.

The political class, including the PA and the PLO, does appear to have opposed the changes, but as we will see later in this chapter, defense lawyers for Palestinians have had both positive and negative reactions.

Asked how the Palestinians' defense lawyers reacted to the March 2015 reforms, he said, "Ambivalently. Many didn't understand the ramifications. The amendment in its entirety provided some benefits to defendants, such as the exemption from indictment based on withdrawal." (This refers to an exemption from indictment that was added for suspects who work on a crime, but then withdraw from committing it before there are any permanent negative results.)

He told a story from around ten years ago, when Palestinian Morad Tawalbe was planning to carry out a suicide bombing. Tawalbe got to Haifa with a suicide belt, saw the eyes of the people walking around, and decided not to carry out the bombing. He threw away the explosive device and went home.

But still, he was eventually arrested.

"What was the meaning of 'he went back'?" asked Hirsch rhetorically. "Before, you got leniency for going back at the punishment stage, but now, in order to encourage people to go back, withdrawing from the crime gets you a full exoneration."

Tawalbe got 13.5 years in prison for withdrawing from the crime, instead of life in prison, but his defense lawyer appealed. Eventually, the prosecution agreed to reduce the punishment to eleven years in prison. The IDF West Bank Appeals Court judge did not accept the new plea bargain and reduced the prison time to seven years, said Hirsch.

But after all that reduction of prison time, "It would have been even better for Tawalbe if the March 2015 reforms had already taken place." On the other hand, he explained, "Many other laws, such as what is an accomplice, are broader and expanded existing definitions, which have even stricter consequences. In many cases, this is not in the best interests" of Palestinian defendants.

In other words, the old definition of an accomplice might have only included a small number of actions for helping commit a crime, and if you were not on that short list, you could not be convicted. More modern definitions of an accomplice, including the definition adopted by the March 2015 reforms, have a longer list of actions that can make someone an accomplice, making it easier to convict people who assist other criminals in any way.

"The more you adopt Israeli law," he concluded, "the more you give ammunition to those attacking us for annexation. Aharon Mishnayot could be seen as more enlightened, but you cannot necessarily adopt Israeli law into Judea and Samaria without the danger of the argument of annexation being raised. If the Palestinian population does not appreciate that a change has been made, if they see the change is only for marginal cases, then the entire effect is very much the opposite," he said.

In other words, if the Palestinians themselves either don't understand how they benefit or believe that they only benefit in very technical and marginal ways, then they will most likely view the change as negative and see it as Israeli "creeping annexation" of the West Bank.

Khalid al-Araj on Mishnayot's Reform Ideas

When I asked Khalid al-Araj about the March 2015 reforms that defined crimes in the IDF West Bank Courts more similarly to those in Israeli civilian courts, he paradoxically did not give them a high grade.

Mishnayot has campaigned for this process of making the IDF West Bank Courts laws more similar to Israeli law, calling the Israeli law more liberal and updated in terms of modern approaches to defining crimes.

Al-Araj acknowledged that the March 2015 reforms made the law more lenient regarding Palestinians who withdraw before committing a crime, but he said that even the changed laws were not quite as liberal as the Israeli versions of the same laws.

In addition, he said that in April 2016, after Israeli law had been modified to add a minimum punishment of twelve months for certain kinds of rock throwing, the IDF West Bank Courts laws were also modified. Before this change, there had been no minimum sentence. In this case, becoming more like Israeli law made punishments more, not less, severe for Palestinian defendants.

Gaby Lasky on Mishnayot's Reform Ideas

Put differently, if international war and peace have created a freakish situation in which Palestinians are tried in Israeli military courts, it should at least be severely limited to be as minimally encroaching as necessary, not needlessly expanded to West Bank Israelis.

This position is generally accepted orthodoxy on the Israeli side – that is, except when it breaks down in individual cases. Gaby Lasky described a December 2013 case in which her firm represented a Palestinian family named Nawaja: "The Nawaja case is an interesting case since it simplifies the reasoning of the existence of that court. Palestinian locals [and] settlers [got into] a fight, some throwing stones one at each other. The Palestinians [were] brought to trial [and] indicted whereas the settlers were not at all – although they committed the same behavior toward the Palestinians. In the end, since we were able to prove that the settlers committed the same offense toward the Palestinians that the Palestinians were charged with, but that the settlers were not being brought to trial or indicted, the case also was annulled, in this case because…the discrimination was too blatant."

The IDF West Bank Courts, in annulling the indictments against the Palestinians, stated that it was because after three years, "the prosecution failed to act and also the Israeli police failed to act" against the Jewish Israeli residents of Judea and Samaria who had been involved in the fighting.

The court further accused the IDF prosecution of intentionally "folding its hands" and failing "to make the Israeli police aware of incriminating evidence" it possessed against the Jewish Israeli residents of Judea and Samaria. It even ordered that a copy of the decision lambasting the IDF prosecution and police be sent to the chief IDF prosecutor essentially as a rebuke and to ensure that the lessons of the case would be internalized throughout the law enforcement apparatus.

Basically, the court admitted that in this case, having separate systems for the Palestinians and for the Israeli residents of the West Bank led to discriminatory treatment, which forced it to annul the case against the Palestinians.

Lasky's firm has encountered a few similar cases in which the IDF West Bank Courts intervened and annulled cases against Palestinians because West Bank Israelis who were involved in the incident were not properly prosecuted.

Do these cases prove that the IDF West Bank Courts are properly ensuring that even as Palestinians and Israelis are prosecuted in separate systems, discrimination is stomped out when it rears its head – as the Israeli side would argue? Or does discrimination occur on a broader basis, and all that is unique about the Nawaja story is that it is one of a tiny number of cases in which a video or some other special circumstance flag the discrimination in a way that is too blatant to ignore?

How should this impact the question of whether Israelis could be brought to trial in the IDF West Bank Courts side by side with Palestinians? As a practical matter, even Israeli liberals see no possibility of this actually occurring in the current domestic Israeli political environment, but it is important to acknowledge this as the elephant in the room. So when I interviewed Mishnayot and Hirsch, I did not spend much time dwelling on the possibility of Israeli settlers in court with Palestinians.

Incidentally, the Nawaja case is another in which IDF West Bank chief prosecutor Hirsch disagrees with the court decision, arguing, "The decisions of the courts there were interesting decisions. The comparisons made by the court were not necessarily the right comparisons…. Without question I do not agree with the decision that was handed down. The case against the Israelis… was closed for insufficient evidence because the first group of Palestinians who claimed that they been attacked, whilst they came as witnesses for the defense, for the Nawajas, refused in any way, shape, or form to come to the police to submit a complaint…. Therefore, the case against the Israelis was lacking any evidentiary basis."

Once again, even as the IDF courts and IDF prosecution are far closer to each other on most issues than they are to the Palestinian side, the Nawaja case makes it clear that the IDF courts sometimes take the side of the Palestinians even if it means butting heads with the IDF prosecution.

Merav Khoury on Mishnayot's Reform Ideas

In June 2016, when I interviewed Merav Khoury about Mishnayot's reform ideas, she explained, "it is true that in recent years, the [IDF West Bank Courts] system has tried to become the same as the Israeli justice system with regard to various judicial doctrines, such as the 'defense for reasons of justice.'"

The defense "for reasons of justice" means that there might be enough evidence to convict a defendant, but the court might decide to acquit anyway on the grounds that rights were violated or some other unusual injustice was perpetrated that makes punishing the defendant "wrong" when looking at the big picture.

"And recently they even applied 'limitations on criminal culpability' in military courts, but I still think that the system of laws needs to be the same with regard to detaining defendants during trials. In that case, it would be possible in appropriate cases to release [defendants] on bail or with alternative detention options," she argued.

She also added that even where reforms to the West Bank Courts law have reduced detention times for defendants in some areas, Palestinians could still be detained for eighteen months during a trial, whereas Israelis could only be detained for nine months.

Khoury's Reform Idea

Khoury Reform Idea, November 26, 2014

Moving on from Mishnayot's reform ideas, which were already partially adopted in March 2015, we arrive at some more radical ideas suggested by Khoury.

I had first met and spoken to Khoury in June and July 2014 when I watched her in action during the hearings held to determine whether to return to prison the fifty-nine Palestinians who had been released in the Schalit prisoner exchange. Later, on November 26, 2014, I drove a couple hours north and met with her in her office in Nazareth. We discussed the issues described in chapter 4.

In that conversation, I asked her how things could be improved. To this question, every lawyer for Palestinians or NGO supporter of Palestinian rights I had ever spoken to had the same simple and straight answer: end the occupation and end the West Bank Courts. Khoury, too, had heavy criticism for the courts, for their unusual measures such as administrative detention, and for the Schalit prisoner exchange cases, which she called "insufferable."

Other defense lawyers had suggested fewer indictments and more acquittals. Khoury, too, felt that more acquittals would allow "people to believe more, to be ready to believe in justice. They want justice."

But none of these people had any kind of program. Their ideas were just pipe dreams, whether good or not.

But this time, after hearing the condemnations that I had expected, something shocking happened in a world in which I was rarely shocked. Khoury said, "The problem is the judging of another nation. The judicial panels should have someone, a judge, from the Palestinian side."

This was still not ideal. But if Khoury and the Palestinians were stuck with the courts anyway, she was saying that possibly a historic compromise could improve them by having some panels with a combination of Israeli and Palestinian judges.

What was fascinating about this idea was that the Israeli government itself had endorsed having foreign observers on a quasi-governmental committee, the Turkel Commission. That body (named for its chairman, former Israeli Supreme Court justice Jacob Turkel) investigated both the May 2010 *Mavi Marmara* flotilla incident and whether Israel's apparatus for self-investigating its security forces for alleged crimes complied with international law.

It included two international observers who received all the classified briefings from top government and military officials and the top-secret documents that voting Israeli commission members received. The committee's reports on the two issues were published in January 2011 and in February 2013, and they included far-reaching policy findings and recommendations for the country's law enforcement apparatus.

I asked Khoury if aside from Palestinian judges, she thought a compromise of continuing IDF courts but adding in foreign judges and foreign observers might be able to improve the situation, and she said she thought they might. My question arose both out of the government commission model and out of my knowledge that as objectionable as the IDF would find any non-IDF judges, theoretically they might object less to US or NATO judges or observers as opposed to Palestinian ones.

Khoury Reform Idea, June 2016

Going forward, Khoury and I were in touch from time to time, but mostly on narrow issues such as developments in the Schalit cases.

Then, nearing the end of the process of writing this book, I returned to Khoury in June 2016 with the same question about potential reforms. Restating her initial assessment from November 26, 2014, she said, "The best solution is obviously to end the occupation and to completely eliminate this entire disgraceful system which is called the military judicial system."

But once again she was more practical and less ideological than your typical defense lawyer who represents Palestinians. Under the assumption that the West Bank Courts are not going anywhere soon, she offered a new idea. "If there is no choice, I think that the time has come to have an oversight body above the military prosecution that one can turn to regarding arbitrary or careless treatment of specific cases," said Khoury.

She continued, "Lately, I am hearing more about cases the military prosecution lost in the 'criminal' proceeding that it filed with the military courts, but then immediately pulls out a request for administrative detention for the same poor person. This is a procedure in which the accused's opportunity to defend himself is nearly zero because of the secrecy in which the classified evidence submitted to the judge is enwrapped," she explained.

Although Khoury dreamed of no occupation and no IDF West Bank Courts, she was ready to entertain ways to improve them as long as they existed. She also did not repudiate her November 26, 2014, suggestion of Palestinian or foreign judges or observers sitting on panels with IDF judges.

Over the next few years, I discussed the very unusual idea – of Palestinian or foreign judges or observers sitting on panels with IDF judges – with several people, including some of this book's main personalities. By the time I had checked back with Khoury and she mentioned the additional idea of a public comptroller type of figure over the IDF West Bank Courts, I had already wrapped up my interviews and was not able to discuss that idea with the other major personalities.

But they had quite a lot to say about a Palestinian or other foreign judge or observer sitting on IDF West Bank Courts panels.

Hirsch on Khoury's Idea: Completely Impractical

Discussing Khoury's idea of bringing in Palestinian or international observers to the IDF West Bank Courts' panels, Hirsch fell back on the requirements of Articles 64 and 66 of the Geneva Convention – the prior laws which applied must continue to apply, and military courts must be established for bringing occupied persons to trial. He felt that these requirements disqualified the idea. He also called it "completely impractical. We need properly constituted non-political judges who are part of a hierarchy."

I asked Hirsch why the arrangement would not be good enough for the West Bank Courts if it was good enough for the Turkel Commission.

Hirsch said, "That was a public commission, where you can have outside observers. In a criminal court, that is not the case."

Next, Hirsch referred to the Rodney King case, in which an African American taxi driver was beaten by four white policemen in the Los Angeles police department following a high-speed car chase. A video of the beating was aired around the world and drew attention to police brutality against minorities. The policemen were indicted, and the United States was riven by racial tension over the trial. The initial verdict that exonerated all four policemen is generally considered to have triggered the 1992 Los Angeles riots in which fifty-three people were killed and two thousand injured.

"It would be the same as arguing in the Rodney King case that there should be external black observers for the jury to make sure the white Los Angeles policemen" would not get off because of racial prejudice. "Would such an argument ever be justified or be given any kind of validity?"

Speaking practically, Hirsch said that the idea would also not be accepted by the Palestinians because the military judges would still be there. On one hand, Hirsch said that Israeli military judges were required by international law, but on the other hand any judicial body including those military judges would be a non-starter for Palestinians.

He also asked, "Who are these advisers? Will they be Palestinians? If so, then they will be labeled as collaborators. If they are external [meaning neither Israeli nor Palestinian], then critics will say they must be pro-Israel if they agree with any of the courts' decisions – never mind the weight of the evidence."

Mishnayot on Khoury's Idea: Interesting but Not Realistic

I discussed Khoury's ideas with Mishnayot at two different points. He had a similar response, though the first time, in August 2015, he was surprised and expressed some curiosity about the idea even if he mainly tended to think that it was impractical. He said: "First of all, the idea is very interesting. I never heard it until now. Very interesting. I think it is not realistic. I will tell you why it is not realistic. Because the Palestinian population always relates to the courts as an arm of the occupation. No matter how fair we are, and consider human rights, and ensure a fair trial, and appoint defense lawyers to those who need, we will always be seen as an arm of the occupation.

"And I don't think it is realistic to expect between Israelis and Palestinians, or a foreigner to agree to be part of an apparatus which is viewed as an arm of the occupation. So it is just not realistic. Isolated from the real world it sounds nice.

"It does not seem reasonably likely to me that this move will increase faith, not the personal-individual faith which I think does exist today, but the group and political faith in the system which will always be perceived as an arm of the occupation. Therefore, this solution is not realistic, this idea is not realistic. It is interesting. It is not realistic in my eyes.

"What could be? I think that the Palestinian population does have faith in the Israeli legal system. Far more than a few Palestinians file petitions with the Supreme Court on many issues. The military courts are a body which is overseen by many. Critics petition against us many times to the Supreme Court, mostly in the field of administrative detention, but not just there."

After Mishnayot staked his answer in August 2015 on the suggestion being impractical, I challenged him with the question "What if there were Palestinian volunteers – would you support it?"

"This idea is interesting. I need to think about it. I'm surprised by it. Maybe it's an idea that could be thought about in one way or another. But I think that it is not realistic. Totally not realistic," he replied.

In April 2016, we discussed the issue again. not long before he was appointed as a Beersheba district judge, limiting his ability to continue to speak to the media.

This time he enumerated a range of objections.

Regarding having observers similar to the Turkel Commission, he said, "There is a giant difference between a committee of inquiry and a court. The law decides who is on a panel. Anyway, many observers from the EU come to the courts, and they are transparent."

Then Mishnayot tried to pivot back to his focus on making the IDF West Bank Courts law regarding punishments more similar to Israeli law. "The court is not part of the occupation. They think the court is part of the occupation, that it cannot be improved or fixed. They won't do any work on it to improve it, for greater cooperation."

He said he understood that people are concerned about the sovereignty of Palestinians, but that bringing Palestinian or international observers onto IDF West Bank Courts panels was "not practical or realistic" – expressing something close to revulsion and rejecting the idea in an uncharacteristically emotional way.

Comparing his answers from the two sessions and having discussed his own solution more with others, it occurred to me that maybe Mishnayot opposed the idea so strongly because this would admit a point that cannot be admitted about the occupation. It would admit that the courts and their legal rulings, because of the factual mosaic of Israeli-Palestinian conflicts they interact with, cross into politics.

There was then significant crossover between Hirsch and Mishnayot about the reasons to oppose Khoury's idea. They both emphasized that Khoury's idea was (1) impractical; (2) problematic from the perspective of the functions and rules of how courts operate, and that the Turkel Commission as a public inquiry commission was different; and (3) unacceptable to the Palestinians because of their view of the courts as occupation courts, for which Palestinians and foreigners would not volunteer.

Hirsch and Mishnayot had differences, though.

Hirsch did not emphasize that the courts are already transparent and have frequent EU observers, probably being less concerned about that as an issue.

Mishnayot did not emphasize that the argument about a lack of fairness was ridiculous (Hirsch had used the Rodney King case as an illustration) or that the change would violate the Geneva Conventions. Perhaps he did not get into these issues because he personally was uncomfortable with the courts being perceived as unfair.

He seemed willing to risk critics saying he was violating the Geneva Conventions as long as his motives were pure and the change would improve Palestinians' experience in the courts. This was probably also why he showed some initial curiosity about the issue (even as he eventually dismissed it as impractical).

Saeb Erekat on Khoury's Idea: An Inherently Invalid Legal System

On May 18, 2016, I attended a conference for the *Palestine-Israel Journal* in Jerusalem on the "Dual Legal System in the West Bank."

I spoke to PLO Secretary General Saeb Erekat, a top aide to the late Palestinian leader Yasser Arafat and to Mahmoud Abbas, the current PA president. I told him about Khoury's idea, not mentioning her name, but noting the idea was proposed by a defense lawyer for Palestinians.

He rejected the compromise idea as a solution for resolving disputes about the IDF's West Bank Courts and about alleged dual unequal legal systems for Jews and Palestinians living in the West Bank. Erekat called it "playing around with" an inherently invalid legal system, instead of trying to take apart that system, which is what should be done.

He responded to the compromise idea, saying, "It's not about…the Geneva Conventions or international law. There was a law invented [by Israel]: the law of getting away with it. Everyone hears and sees what Israel is doing to the Palestinians over fifty years," he continued, and repeated that "the real law" was getting away with violating Palestinian rights.

The PLO secretary general then recounted his personal experience with the IDF West Bank Courts when he was arrested and brought to an IDF court in

Nablus in 1987. He said that his lawyers were fined NIS 1,500 for asking the court a question about his case, and said, "The courts are the tools of apartheid."

Putting on a more positive spin, he added, "In the long run, Palestinians and Israelis are destined to live together in peace and security."

We had come full circle. The gulf between Israeli and Palestinian views had seemed too great. Then a possible creative compromise had been suggested. But neither the official Israeli nor Palestinian sides were interested in this "compromise."

For Israel, first it was impractical, and the Palestinians would never agree (which seemed to be a correct prediction). Second, it would be betraying Israel's sovereignty, meddling with judicial hierarchies that are key to the rule of law, and incorrectly implying that its system was unfit.

For Palestinians, it would give the IDF West Bank Courts and the occupation a fig leaf of legitimacy when they were more interested in drawing attention to their illegitimacy.

Charles Shamas on Khoury's Idea: Nobody Imagined Such a Thing

One more interesting perspective on Khoury's idea came from scholar and activist Charles Shamas of the MATTIN Group in Ramallah. Though Lebanese himself, Shamas married a Palestinian and has spent much of his adult life working for various Palestinian causes. In 1979, he was one of the founders of al-Haq, the first Palestinian rights NGO focusing on the IDF West Bank Courts. Shamas is viewed globally as a senior human rights expert and activist.

He also has been a regular invitee and speaker at Hebrew University Law School conferences hosting renowned experts in international law from around the world – not typical for scholars from the Palestinian side.

In May 2016, Shamas attended the same *Palestine-Israel Journal* conference described above at which I met Saeb Erekat and responded to the reform idea after Erekat had finished. Shamas said that the idea was not entirely new and had been experimented with even decades ago, but that it was considered impractical. Also, few Palestinians believed that Europeans would want to "get their hands dirty" with the IDF West Bank Courts.

Later, in August 2016, Shamas and I spoke again. I asked him to clarify what discussions about reform had occurred in the past. Without mentioning an exact date, he explained that the discussions were informal and had occurred over the years among Palestinian activists in the 1980s and 1990s, starting with activists connected to al-Haq, and eventually including some of those involved in newer organizations such as B'Tselem.

He said the discussions arose out of "a sense of non-correspondence between...the people in the military justice system and how they understood applying general norms and rules...with the prevailing external consensus" among Palestinians, Europeans, and international organizations.

The idea was "some kind of peer engagement and review, to basically engender an approximation among the judiciary to apply the law to what is externally [including among Palestinians] considered desirable and proper."

He said the discussions were an organic outgrowth of writing reports on the IDF West Bank Courts system for foreign countries to assess and criticize it and press for change. "If you write a report, you have to ask what is the purpose of the report.... You try to connect your informational strategy with a corrective scenario," said Shamas.

However, as we delved deeper into the ideas that Shamas and his colleagues had discussed in the 1980s and 1990s, it turned out that no one had been audacious enough to suggest what Khoury was suggesting.

"The Israeli side was more concerned with reflecting on reform strategies. The Palestinian side did not feel particularly empowered about that.... Nobody imagined [what Khoury suggested] would be possible. Observers meant a fact-finding mission, sitting in on court hearings," not a Turkel Commission-style judge or having someone play the role of an involved observer.

Shamas and his colleagues' ideas were certainly out of the box for their time, but it took a second conversation for us to realize that what Khoury had suggested was even more audacious. It simply was so far beyond the normal discourse that when I had asked about it at the conference, the very sophisticated Shamas had assumed I meant the idea of having more passive observers.

In any event, Shamas also did not find the idea realistic.

The Practicality of Various Reform Ideas

Khoury's External Observer/Participant – Possible?

The episode with Charles Shamas sheds some light on one of the problems with any suggested reform to the IDF West Bank Courts.

Ultimately, both sides at the official levels seem most comfortable viewing the courts as a front for conflict. They stake out their positions, then sometimes engage in limited cooperation where it is perceived as necessary. When confronted with completely new ideas, both sides immediately lapse into painting the other side as noncooperative and a lost cause unless their ultimate broader aims in the conflict between the two peoples are achieved through the new ideas. Since the other side would often view this as capitulation, little progress is made.

This is not to say whether Khoury's idea could practically be implemented or not if there were slightly more openness on both sides. It is to say that there are major limits on how much the system can be improved and how much Israelis and Palestinians can reduce conflict over the courts. The initial instincts of both groups are still strongly defensive, and each group tends to immediately criticize the other one.

In a world where the sides might be less defensive, perhaps Khoury's idea could be implemented in the narrowest and least radical fashion as a pilot program and then be evaluated. A respected US or European judge could be co-selected by both Israel and the Palestinian Authority. Or perhaps Israeli and Palestinian lawyers could sit as nonvoting observers on one panel for one case with IDF judges. The observer judge could ask questions of participants, take part in private judicial deliberations, and have access to all of the evidence.

At the end of the case, the observer could offer a public report (with some limits for judicial confidentiality and national security considerations) about the conduct of the proceedings, and the IDF and the Palestinians could decide what to do from there.

There are probably myriad other narrower or alternative versions of ways to involve outsiders more deeply in the proceedings, which would force both sides to take the results and the other side more seriously.

Replacing Night Arrests with a Summons – Possible?

One crazy idea that would never have been believed not long ago is actually partially happening. Initiated in 2014 after extensive negotiations with UNICEF, which involved itself on behalf of Palestinian interests, the pilot summons program called Palestinian minor suspects to Israeli West Bank police stations via summons.

This was intended to replace, or partially replace, the usual practice of night arrests of Palestinian minors. The program has continued between the IDF and individual suspects, but cooperation fell apart between Lasky-Ramati and Hirsch, who had originally discussed working together on the program. Each side accused the other of "using" them and acting in bad faith. Actually, the IDF had never intended to completely eliminate night arrests. As things stand, a vast majority of suspects are still arrested at night.

But in the first half of 2016, thirty summonses were sent to Palestinian minors. Ten of these minors appeared in court voluntarily without the need for night arrests. This was an improvement over the attendance rate in 2015. The point here is that the IDF is trying an idea that it completely opposed as an ultra-red line for years. This is a program that no longer features any organized cooperation between the IDF prosecution and the defense lawyers, as originally intended. Rather, now there is only ad-hoc coordination between the IDF and individual defendants.

There was a point when the IDF and UNICEF were working together. But that cooperation broke down when IDF reforms fell short of what UNICEF expected, and UNICEF refused to support the IDF on night arrests if a good faith effort failed to convince Palestinians to come to court voluntarily.

How much more committed to the program might the IDF be if more defense lawyers, PA officials, UNICEF, and even foreign diplomats were working cooperatively with the IDF? We will never know until more of them try.

Maybe it does not work out and Palestinians' "fig leaf" fears materialize – but the absence of the fig leaf is not exactly going to lead to the whole IDF West Bank Courts system disappearing tomorrow. If the Palestinian side and international diplomats ever offer more cooperation, the IDF also might consider greater flexibility in implementing new programs. It might even move its notoriously slow bureaucracy faster so as not to see the good faith it gained with the Palestinians or international community squashed by the simple frustration of continuous and unending delays erasing hope for the future.

Each side could strategically consider offering or agreeing to new ideas. If you assume the other side will refuse no matter what you offer, what do you have to lose? You just gain the ability to blame them for being close-minded.

All of this may be fantasy. But maybe if both sides were more open to talking about pie in the sky ideas, even if they were only implemented as part of a project for a trial period, an idea might surprise both sides and actually succeed.

Improved Arabic Services – Possible?

After all of these dreamy ideas on which there is no agreement, there was uniform agreement about one issue. Hirsch, the defense lawyers, and Mishnayot all agreed that sometimes the translation from Arabic to Hebrew and vice versa is subpar.

In Israeli civil courts, a nineteen-year-old translator with only a short training course would never be providing translation services. In the IDF, due to budget considerations, that is what most translators are. There is no legal obligation for the translators to be of a certain age or competence level. Most of the time all sides say that the translators muddle their way through hearings well enough that Palestinians on trial understand what is being said and their testimonies are properly recorded.

However, all sides also agreed that at times, the nineteen-year-olds are not fully up to the job. In some high-profile cases, older officers in their mid-twenties provide Arabic translation to ensure a certain level of accuracy.

In that light, it is unclear, other than budgetary considerations, why all or a larger number of translators could not be older and better trained. If the IDF is concerned about legitimacy, from a policy perspective, this would send a much stronger signal about the IDF's commitment to the courts. In contrast, having nineteen-year-olds provide translation services gives fuel to the criticism of many that the IDF is "going through the motions," appearing to care about justice for Palestinians, but not really caring.

This can be seen from comments even by Hirsch and Mishnayot. Though Mishnayot was more disturbed by the issue than Hirsch, it is interesting to hear both their comments.

Hirsch on Translation Issues

Hirsch explained that translation is a problem for both the prosecution and the defense. He also said that the running translation into Arabic, while done for the benefit of Palestinian defendants, disrupts the rhythm of the line of questioning for both sides.

Hirsch noted that all of the translators are dual native Arabic and Hebrew speakers. He said their level of Arabic is high, and that they are sent to an intense almost six-week-long course to learn legal terminology in both languages.

He admitted that their legal terminology was "not so extensive" and that there were "occasionally some words which they only know in Hebrew."

Hirsch said there had never been a discussion about requiring all translators to be older and more experienced.

Mishnayot on Translation Issues

Mishnayot has been quoted in the IDF's news magazine, *Bamachaneh*, saying that one of his few regrets from his time as chief justice of the West Bank Courts was "*Haval* [It's too bad] that I did not learn Arabic." This raises a whole new front on the issue.

In light of claims by defense lawyers that translators are weak and his own quote, I asked Mishnayot an even more radical question: Should all West Bank Court judges and prosecutors have to learn Arabic and hold the proceedings in Arabic?

Looking frustrated, as if he were dealing with a tiresome question from a child who did not understand the rules of the game, he responded, "The reality is that Arabic is not the mother tongue of most people who serve in the IDF. What can we do? The judges who serve there are military judges. If in advance you set a restrictive threshold for serving in judicial positions in the area to only Arabic-speakers, you substantially reduce the group from which you can choose.

This position of being a judge in the area is very complex. More complex than to be a judge in the military courts in Israel," he said.

I press on, asking: What if the IDF offered to pay for language and other studies, or offered a higher salary?

Interrupting in an uncharacteristically impatient way, he explained, "This doesn't matter.... This is not connected to money. They offered a course to the judges…a course in Arabic for our judges. We started to learn, also myself. It does not go to an advanced enough level. I can hear, I can understand a small number of words here and there. I cannot manage a hearing in Arabic. What can we do? In an instance like this, the best way to bridge the gap is to obtain good translator services, and I am not sure that the human resources that are invested in this are the optimal ones who can give the best translation services," he admitted.

But he said that the judges "do the best we can within the framework in which we find ourselves to also deal with this problem. Sometimes, for example, the defense lawyers claim that the translation is not accurate, and this does happen.... So there have been times that I have asked to have a more senior translator brought in. But I agree that this is a weak point. This is a point that needs improvement. But this is the existing situation," he added.

If Mishnayot and Hirsch think the translation can be improved, and the defense lawyers complain about it regularly, why not improve it? And even if having all judges and prosecutors speak Arabic is unrealistic, why couldn't the courts try to push for more of them to learn Arabic?

Once again, this is not a question of fixing a violation of international law. It is a question of policy: How can Israel best represent to the Palestinian people and to the world that wherever it can invest in respecting Palestinian rights, and can be seen as respecting them, it does so, and does not just go through the motions?

Where security sacrifices might be involved, the balancing act is harder. But here, where it seems to be just a budgetary question, it is hard to see why the IDF is not taking more seriously the quality and availability of Arabic in the courts, whether that means offering proficient translation, or more radically, having Arabic-speaking prosecutors and judges.

On a positive note, in September 2016, the *Jerusalem Post* exclusively reported that Hirsch would be replaced in the coming months by IDF Lt. Col.

Asem Hamed, the first Druze Israeli to fill the job. Hamed is also believed to be the first Druze Israeli to rise to the rank of lieutenant colonel within the IDF legal division.

Doubtless, Hamed's appointment is part of an attempt to improve the West Bank prosecution's image. Unfortunately, no public announcement was made or planned in the months following the appointment, even though it was official and final. Surprisingly, this pattern of the IDF underplaying Hamed's Druze background and native Arabic language skills has continued throughout his term. In a February 2019 profile in the *Jerusalem Post*, Hamed would not even speak off the record; at most, sources close to him made a few short comments focusing on his high level of professionalism and downplaying the significance of his Druze background. Defense lawyers such as Khoury, al-Araj, and Tsemel all spoke about his Druze background as a mixed bag: they found him easier to work with than Hirsch on a personal level, but they also felt he was sometimes forced to take a tough line representing the system to prove his loyalty to the IDF. Lasky declined to address his unique background, mostly criticizing the system's continued alleged mistreatment of minors, though she agreed with the other defense lawyers that he was professional and calmer to work with than Hirsch.

It has been announced that Hamed is slated for promotion and to become the IDF's chief legal adviser for Judea and Samaria toward the end of 2019. It may be in the end that the IDF sought only to calm issues with the defense lawyers – which Hamed appears to have succeeded at – but without grander ambitions for employing him to make the system more Arabic-friendly both in terms of language and culture. One other change for defense lawyers during his term has been a new Muslim prayer space for defense lawyers, paralleling a long-existing Jewish prayer space. But it is unclear how involved Hamed, as opposed to the office of the courts, was in this change. Still, more moves like this could make a difference.

Whether the reform regarding administrative detention discussed in chapter 11, or the above reforms regarding observers, summons replacing night arrests, heavily increasing the use of Arabic, or other ideas, there are ideas out there that Israel, the Palestinians, and foreign diplomats who are routinely involved could pursue if there were a readiness to meet halfway.

Chapter 14

Parting Shots

The Main Personalities Discuss Each Other

We have learned about who Maurice Hirsch, Merav Khoury, Aharon Mishnayot, and Gaby Lasky are and what makes them tick. We have seen them compete or intersect on some cases. We have seen how they play a part in the general interaction between the IDF prosecution and courts on the one hand and defense lawyers for Palestinians on the other. We have heard their views of the future.

But what do they think personally of each other? Hirsch, Khoury, and Lasky each made some careful comments about the others. Mishnayot made none.

Lasky on Hirsch/the IDF Prosecution

Gaby Lasky disliked a number of issues related to the prosecution. While trying to remain professionally respectful, Lasky's dispute with some prosecutors such as Hirsch was not only substantive, like between Khoury and Hirsch, but personal.

For one, in 2013–2014, Hirsch and Lasky had tried to work together, along with UNICEF, on a West Bank Courts pilot project to summon Palestinian suspects, especially Palestinian minors, to Israeli West Bank police stations instead of arresting them at night. Though the pilot program still technically continued, the cooperation had fallen apart in acrimony.

Hirsch had believed that Lasky dropped out once she realized that even as the initiative might be good for Palestinian minors, it might also provide positive press for the West Bank Courts – something she did not want the courts to get.

Lasky had believed that Hirsch or the courts were trying to use her as a fig leaf for a fledgling program that they were not really committed to in order to put on a show about being open to reform.

Keeping that history in mind, I showed a video to Lasky of part of my interview with Hirsch – the clip of Hirsch speaking about how he preferred peace and was a "baby of the Thatcher years." In the clip, he explained that if the world were different, he would have wanted to focus on the value of economic growth, in the style of British prime minister Margaret Thatcher (1979–1990), a role model for him as he was growing up, instead of dedicating his life to prosecuting Palestinians.

Momentarily laughing, she eventually returned to her serious mode and commented, "He was a baby during the Thatcher years. What can I say? If someone really wishes that…he wouldn't have to prosecute Palestinian minors, then he has to wish and work for the end of occupation. And even then once you have to do it [prosecute Palestinian minors], you have to be more lenient in taking into consideration the effects of bringing a child to court and bringing him to jail – what does it do to him and for your fight against terrorism and crime?"

Asked specifically about Hirsch's character, she demurred. "I don't want to talk about Maurice [Hirsch] as a specific person. I know he talks about me, but I don't want to talk about him, as it should be. I think the prosecution as a whole is very political, and it shouldn't be," she said.

Responding to another clip of Hirsch talking about how Palestinian minors do not fully know what they are doing when they commit crimes, and how he has made efforts to balance their special needs as minors. Lasky responded, "Some kids don't know what they're doing. They live under occupation. If such is the nature of their wrongdoing, then why would the prosecution want to… send them to jail for different periods of time? These are the things that have to be taken into consideration before you ruin the life of a thirteen-year-old."

She added, "When I find the prosecution fighting as hard as they can in order to keep a minor in detention until the end of the trial or in remand hearings, then I think these things [minors' special needs] aren't being taken into consideration."

Finally, responding to a clip of Hirsch saying that Palestinians have a right to legitimate nonviolent protest, as long as they do not cross the fine line into committing crimes, Lasky said, "In the legislation of the occupied territories, there is no fine line that allows the Palestinians to present frustration against the occupation. If even the mere fact that you organize a demonstration becomes a criminal offense...I don't believe that there is a possibility...of allowing Palestinians actually to get their voices...[heard] that they are against the occupation. The thin line between freedom of speech and freedom of demonstration against occupation and the fact that the occupier does not allow you to fight nonviolently against it is...part of occupation. It is not only frustration that you want to show, it is the fact that you want to end the occupation," she said.

Concluding, she said, "So without putting the political argument [on the table], you cannot really be saying you are allowing people to show their frustration.... The prosecution will always bring to trial people who are fighting occupation nonviolently because they want to perpetuate occupation, unless the people of Israel and the government of Israel decide that it's about time to end the occupation."

Hirsch on Defense Lawyers

According to Hirsch, the fact that Lasky and Ramati consider the courts to be occupation courts means "[they] never allow its decisions to be justifiable. You can explain away any conviction, and it's irrelevant to the weight of evidence that stood before the courts because the courts' a priori disposition is to convict Palestinians. Their idea is the courts in and of themselves are illegitimate because they 'serve the occupation.' Any measure in which you can attack the occupation, including the courts, is justified, to the point that no decision ever given by the courts, no matter how legally based it is, will ever be acceptable," he said.

Asked about IDF judges Amir Dahan, Zvi Lekach, Aharon Mishnayot, and others who have established a reputation of ruling against the prosecution at least on occasion and more often than some others, Hirsch said, "Some judges play along with their narrative. They find more favor in their eyes. Lasky and Ramati don't say all the courts' decisions were unjustified – only those in their favor are justified – whether legally correct or not."

Regarding his personal relations with Lasky and Ramati, he said they did not actually meet very often to negotiate plea bargains or debate points of their cases. "They never get to me. Their cases were not big enough [in terms of the maximum potential jail sentences they could receive]. I usually only get personally involved with security detainee cases, and most of their cases involve stone throwing." The latter cases may be politically significant and high profile, but do not carry heavy jail sentences that tend to draw in the chief prosecutor.

Hirsch on Khoury

Hirsch related to Merav Khoury differently. He called her "much more of a lawyer – she uses more legal arguments" as opposed to emotional and political attacks on the court's jurisdiction – so her "level of success is much greater."

She "takes heavier cases and is coming from a different starting point." He explained that even though Khoury had emphasized her ideological bent in that she had red lines for the kinds of clients she would not take on, Hirsch felt that she was less ideological than Lasky and Ramati when it came to client selection.

He noted that she chose not only high-profile cases, but like a typical defense lawyer, also sought cases that generate sizable fees. In contrast, he said Lasky and Ramati's ideology heavily impacts their client choice. They may pursue high-profile cases against minor stone throwers, which do not necessarily generate as high fees.

Hirsch also felt that Khoury had a greater ability to see the strengths and weaknesses of a file without letting emotions cloud her judgment. None of this was Hirsch saying he respected lawyers more for going for high-fee cases than for being ideological. He merely was commenting on who took a more dispassionate approach to the law, which translated into being more formidable for him as an adversary in court.

He also said he had a good rapport with Khoury, and that while he "tries not to talk politics at work" with defense lawyers and others, they do "talk about their children and family."

Hirsch in his mind seemed to divide lawyers into two groups. He considered those like Avigdor Feldman and Merav Khoury to be "more legal-minded," and those like Lasky and Leah Tsemel as solid lawyers, but "more ideological."

Khoury on Hirsch

Responding to Hirsch's comments about her, Khoury said, "It is nice to hear that Maurice respects me and has a high regard for my professionalism. To be honest, even though I think he does his work also out of ideological motivations, the issue does not bother me in our interpersonal relations, as I know how to get work done with all human beings. At the end of the day this is my worldview and it is not in my power to change it," she added.

Continuing to describe her interactions with Hirsch, Khoury said, "It is true that we sometimes speak about personal matters and one time a personal problem even came up with me about which he did not hesitate to support me and to assist me when I requested. Since the work we do is ongoing, I think that all of the issue of difference [Arab versus Jew] is less relevant, since it is less expected that a Jew would represent a Palestinian than an Arab," she added.

Al-Araj on Hirsch

Interestingly, top Palestinian lawyer Khalid al-Araj had positive things to say about Mishnayot both to me and in a 2013 interview in the IDF's *Bamachaneh* magazine. Hirsch also regarded him as one of the top Palestinian lawyers whom he said he respected. But when it came to Hirsch, al-Araj did not seem to reciprocate the positive feelings expressed by Hirsch toward him.

Though he said that his relations with Hirsch had been better at an earlier point in his term, by the time we spoke about Hirsch in September 2016, al-Araj called him "attacking, hyper-aggressive, ready to fight about everything, and unclear about what he wants."

In contrast, al-Araj said that Hirsch's predecessor, Robert Neufeld, if not more ideologically sympathetic, was at least "calmer and more ready to listen" to his clients' side of the story. Despite an earlier relationship, al-Araj said that as of September 2016, he and Hirsch "do not even say good morning and cannot talk" and that he was postponing many cases until Hirsch stepped down.

Reflecting on Their Own Work

We began this journey by exploring questions about what values our four main personalities view themselves as fighting for: whether they defend security, justice, or human rights; how they struggle with moral dilemmas; and how their perspectives evolve.

We later focused on Khoury and Mishnayot's ideas for reform. We conclude by revisiting Hirsch's and Lasky's views on balancing the IDF West Bank Courts' human dilemmas. We first explore what they are most proud of, and then move on to how they cope with dilemmas in gray areas.

Lasky Reflects on Her Career

Leading defense lawyer for high-profile Palestinian minors' cases Gaby Lasky felt she was doing something valuable when defending Palestinian rights as part of her broader commitment to defending all human rights.

Describing the connection between defending all human rights and Palestinian human rights, she said, "As a human rights lawyer, I…act against the infringement of the rights of any person. It does not matter what color they are, or nationality, or religion, or gender." She pointed out that there are people who identify themselves as human rights lawyers yet would never get involved in trying to rectify the infringement of Palestinians' rights. For Lasky, the idea of limiting whose rights you defend on any side of the political spectrum contradicts the principles of being a human rights lawyer.

Explaining why she felt it important to specifically defend Palestinian human rights, she stated that even as "justice is blind," since "I do believe that as a state we have responsibility over what the occupation is doing to a people – then we have the responsibility to try to stop the violation of those rights."

Continuing, she said, "There are many infringements of rights that are individual, but here the infringement of rights of the Palestinian people is a collective infringement of rights. And it is being done systematically, because Israel has an agenda that is not being discussed regarding the occupied territories and the occupation. And so in that sense, all of us that are human rights lawyers, advocates, we have to say loud and clear that we have to put an end to occupation."

But as long as it lasts, "We have…to do everything within our capabilities to stop the infringement of rights, mostly when we are talking about minors – that they are not part of the conflict, that they are not part of the essence. And in that sense, as a nation, I will say as an Israeli, as a democrat, even as a Jew, I have the responsibility to do everything in my power to stop the infringement of the rights of minors in the occupied territories."

She summed up her views on the Israeli side's portrayal of the IDF West Bank Courts as dealing in gray, saying, "Occupation is not gray. It is a question of black and white. Whether there is occupation, whether there is no occupation. And the courts, using different shades of gray, cannot erase occupation."

Lasky was at least as sure of her position defending Palestinian rights as Hirsch was of defending Israeli security. But her answers regarding truth in the Islam Ayoub case, both what she said and what she did not say, revealed her struggle with the dilemma of defending those she might believe to be guilty according to the letter of the law. At Ayoub's trial, the court had slammed the police's conduct in interrogating Islam in the case about as hard as it could, but ruled that his confession was still admissible in court.

The court said that it happened to be that the police had illegally questioned Islam, but that what he had said was still the truth. Did he tell the truth, and what did Lasky believe about whether Ayoub's confession was true?

Lasky responded, "First of all, there are ways, legal ways to annul a confession. One of them is that the confession was taken under duress, torture, that is one thing, and then you need to look into the truth of the confession.

"Then there is another way to annul a confession. It's like 'fruit of the poisonous tree.' …It says that even if the confession, every word is true, since it was obtained illegally, you cannot use it. So this is what we were arguing in this case: it doesn't matter if what Islam said has a degree of truth.… So the matter or the degree of truthfulness in what Islam said is of no relevance regarding the question of annulling his confession," she added.

Then there was a final short exchange between myself and Lasky about whether the confession was true. I could not resist asking Lasky what she herself thought.

Me: Do you think Islam's confession was true or not, since you spent time with him?

Lasky: It's not relevant.

Me: You don't want to answer?

Lasky: No. It's not relevant. When a lawyer represents a client, we are not detectives – it's not relevant.

The "second way" of annulling confessions regarding the "fruit of the poisonous tree" was Lasky's view. It appears that she may very well have believed that Ayoub's whole confession or at least elements were true.

But she vehemently opposed on principle the idea of abusing the right of a young minor like Islam Ayoub for a low-key crime involving a protest that was not really dangerous (distinguishing Ayoub's non-dangerous rock-throwing from throwing rocks at moving vehicles or other dangerous rock throwers). Even if the IDF considered Bassam Tamimi, their real target in Islam's case, to be an inciter to violence, Lasky did not, and she did not think helping to prosecute a nonviolent activist justified abusing Islam Ayoub's rights.

She believed this so strongly that she said this case was evidence that Israel has "gone at some points…in the wrong direction. Infringement of human rights of civil liberties, of democratic rights should not be done by a democratic state. And if I want it to be otherwise to change it, it's because I love Israel, because I want it to be better…. It is for those reasons that I do what I do."

This for her was the essence of choosing "free life" and "moral life" over "living by the sword" and was far more "relevant" than whether the confession was true.

Hirsch Reflects on His Career

IDF West Bank chief prosecutor Lt. Col. Maurice Hirsch felt he was doing something valuable and worthwhile when he put terrorists in jail to try to save Israeli civilian lives: "As you can quite clearly understand from my English and my accent, I am not a native-born Israeli. I immigrated to Israel in 1996 at the age of twenty-three. As a Zionist, as someone who truly sees the value of a country for Jews where they can feel safe…, a place where Israel can have its homeland…to see myself having the privilege of heading a prosecution [whose] job at the end of the day is to ensure that terrorists are sent to jail and to ensure that the law is enforced in Judea and Samaria – I would never have dreamed that I would get to this position. Being a lawyer, being a Zionist, moving to Israel, being an officer in the army –without question, there is no other job that I want.… I defend the State of Israel, I defend the citizens of the State of Israel. And at the same time, I realize my professional goals as well. That is something which cannot be replaced by anything.… In the thousands of cases that I have dealt with through the course of my service in the prosecution, there are definitely cases that will always stand out, for all types of reasons. Children that are murdered. Shalhevet Pass, a baby sitting in a stroller in Hebron who was shot by a sniper. The case of the three kids who were abducted and murdered. The Itamar trial… But there are certain cases [that stand out even among the standouts]: arch-terrorists, Abdullah Barghouti, someone who was sentenced to sixty-seven life sentences. Sixty-seven lives that he took. Ibrahim Hamid, fifty-four life sentences, whole worlds that were destroyed by these people. Irrelevant. They don't care who they kill."

Next, Hirsch mentioned the murder of British citizen Mary Jane Gardner, who was killed at a bus stop in a random terror attack in Israel in March 2011. Hirsch said that Gardner was a tourist who had nothing to do with the conflict and was simply "murdered 'by the way.' That's terrorism. Terrorism doesn't distinguish who it's attacking, who its victim is going to be. Terrorism has one goal. Kill as many people as possible, irrespective of who the victim is. And if I can say that I am part of the process which in any way fights that type of violence? Then, yes, I am proud to do it and I will do it full-heartedly."

Hirsch had struggled, though, with the moral dilemmas of prosecuting Palestinians: "There really is a very gray side to the prosecution here. Obviously the ultimate goal would be there would never be any type of criminal offenses, there would never be any idea of occupation, that terrorism would never exist.… I'm a baby of the Thatcher years in England. Understanding capitalism and Thatcherism to its end. Let everyone enjoy their lives, make their money and look out for their family. I think that any prosecutor would wish…that crime did not exist. Specifically in the context of my work, definitely when it comes to prosecuting children, I think that age does play a tremendous factor…and it's impossible to be immune to the human feeling that in some instances, these kids simply don't understand what they are doing."

He thought his outlook on the courts had basically stayed the same, but specifically in regard to cracking down on mostly benign Palestinians illegally crossing the border, he had become somewhat more liberal. "My attitude toward [certain offenses such as] illegally crossing the border into Israel has developed. Now I see that people really are just trying to go to work."

This lowest level of crime, which even some IDF prosecutors view as almost analogous to a traffic violation, does, however, have a security dimension, he said. "Many terror attacks are carried out by illegal border crossers, so we have a general necessity to crack down on them."[13]

Sometimes it is challenging for Palestinians to meet the terms and requirements for getting a permit through no fault of their own. Also, Hirsch points out that the "cost for employers of getting them a permit is very substantial and takes time."

Hirsch described the broader and more difficult question of whether enforcement should focus on those illegally crossing the borders or on the employers who pay them even when they know their workers are crossing the border without permits. He said he is now "more sympathetic" to Palestinians who might be illegally crossing the border but who are doing it to "legitimately earn a living." In that light, there are Palestinian offenders whom he does not indict and others for whom he seeks shorter jail sentences.

He said he still might not be lenient with Palestinians who cross the border illegally if they are committing multiple related crimes, such as forging fake permit approvals or identity card documents.

However, Hirsch has become more hardline in some areas. Regarding stone throwing, he said, "When you have seen enough cases and many different prosecutions, you already, now more than ever, see a correlation between stone throwing and more serious offenses. The willingness to throw stones, no matter what the circumstances are, indicates more of a willingness to break the law in

---

13　A prominent recent example was the terror attack at the Damascus Gate outside the Old City of Jerusalem on February 3, 2016, in which nineteen-year-old border police officer Hadar Cohen was killed.

a relatively violent fashion and [is often correlated with] future more serious offenses," he said. He noted this trend in light of many recent violent terrorist attackers having had prior records as stone throwers, and pointed out that Israeli law within the Green Line is also cracking down harder on stone throwers for the same reason.

Simply put, Hirsch said that "the initial step into violence makes them less afraid of doing more violent things." He also added that stone throwers who get worse are not necessarily those who were convicted of stone throwing and sat in jail. It could also be that "someone let them off and they went further," which explains why Hirsch said he was more aggressive about indicting stone throwers now.

"At the end of the day, I only have myself to look at in the mirror. And [I have] to ensure that what I have done during the day justifies my position and really satisfies my conscience," stated Hirsch.

Hirsch understood the human tragedy caused by sending Palestinian minors through his criminal justice system very well. He even spoke of viewing Palestinian minors' crimes as not that different from the phenomenon of an Israeli Jewish "*tipesh-esrei*" (foolish teenager). Hirsch said such teenagers are not particularly ideological, but just get into trouble because of teenage angst, a lack of structure, or lack of an outlet for channeling their energy.

He even said he recognized the right to protest, but believed the Palestinian situation often combines protest with violence. "I think it would be unreasonable to argue that you can never see in any way, shape, or form some kind of protest coming up. Without question, in certain circumstances, there is no alternative as a way of expressing your frustration.... But I think there has to be a very, very distinct line drawn between legitimate expression of frustration and protest and committing crimes," Hirsch explained.

He did not enjoy sending such people to prison, but saw no alternative if security issues were at stake.

To sum up, those who characterized Hirsch as a security hawk because of right-wing political ideology misunderstood him. He was a security hawk and also may have had a right-wing personal political viewpoint. But his being a hawk related more to his being a detail-obsessed manager who wanted to address every possible security detail in the most comprehensive and uncompromising manner.

In terms of Palestinian human rights, he did not deny them, and in the case of those illegally crossing the border, he even seemed to have become more liberal on a pragmatic basis. He was also ready, for pragmatic reasons, to try summoning Palestinian minors to court in lieu of nighttime house arrests.

But it is true that if a conflict developed between Israeli security and Palestinian human rights, his weighing of the competing priorities leaned very hard toward security, possibly even harder than some other Israeli officials.

The Gray Zone – A Look Back

Finding objectivity in its purest sense is elusive in the heart of a court system that occupies an otherworldly gray or twilight zone and which sits on one of the great fault lines of the Israeli-Palestinian conflict. But from 2008 to the present, the story of the decades-long Israeli-Palestinian saga took some important new directions in the IDF West Bank Courts. Even in the middle of wars that cut off all dialogue between the sides everywhere else, IDF prosecutors and Palestinian defense lawyers continued to work together or at least in parallel.[14]

The unique and spellbinding story of our main four personalities in this Wild West as well as a few of the guest stars shows a narrative of human beings searching for truth, justice, security, democracy, and fairness – sometimes with those all-important values coming into conflict.

We have also explored some new ideas that might improve the situation going forward or at least engender some new dialogue and thinking.

Will Israelis, Palestinians, and their advocates chart some better paths forward, or will both sides stick to the part of their narrative that makes them feel most secure and be unwilling to take risks? The answer will doubtless have a significant impact in shaping relations between the peoples as a whole.

---

14 On May 20, 2019, well-known Palestinian lawyer Tareq Barghout was shockingly indicted on attempted terror shooting charges – which he even more shockingly confessed to. Though there was a two-day strike by Palestinian defense lawyers after Barghout and his wife were arrested, the strike ended once his wife was released.